THEATRE BUILDERS

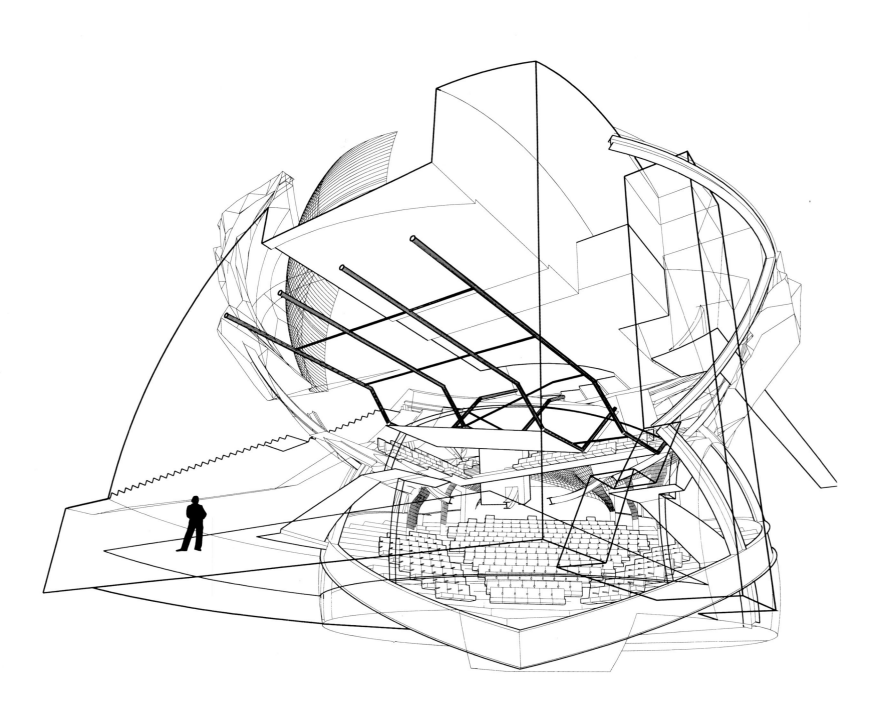

THEATRE BUILDERS

JAMES STEELE

A.D. ACADEMY EDITIONS

Acknowledgements:
I would like to thank Sharlene Silverman, Nancy Hamilton, Richard Hough and Richard Cowell of Arups, Los Angeles, and Patrick Morreau of Arups, London, for their significant contribution to the technical aspects of this book. I would also like to thank all the architects and members of their staff who have made contributions, especially Claire Endicott of Michael Hopkins Partners, Yoshio Amiga at Arata Isozaki, Kisho Kurokawa, Kazuhiro Ishii, Russell Bevington at Michael Wilford Partners, Neil Graham at Percy Thomas Partnership, James O'Conner at MRY, Barton Myers and Ben Caffe, Paul Hoet, Fumihiko Maki, Eric Moss and Janet Strong at IM Pei for all they have done to assist me.

I would like to thank Iain MacKintosh of the Theatre Projects for his direction, Anna Holden for her help in the early stages of this project, and Penny Padovani for her help. I also wish to thank my publishers, Academy Editions of London (VCH, Germany), particularly John Stoddart (Managing Director), Maggie Toy (Managing Editor), Andrea Bettella (Art Director), Stephen James Watt (Production Editor) and Sonia Brooks Fisher (Designer).
James Steele

Photo credits:
All photographs are courtesy of the architects unless stated otherwise
Andrew Holmes *p11*; Florian Beigael *p17*; Peter Mackniven *p30*; Mitsuo Matsuoka *pp32, 34*; Pino Musi *p36 (above)*; Joshua White *pp44, 46-47*; Timothy Hursley *pp54, 56–57, 116, 118-120, 172, 174, 180, 182, 184, 186*; Durston Saylor *pp58, 60*; Martin Charles *p62*; Dennis Gilbert *p66*; *Japan Architect pp80, 84*; Katsuaki Furudate *pp85, 90, 92*; Yoshio Takase *p88*; Yasuhiro Ishimoto *pp94, 96-97*; Tomio Ohashi *pp98, 100, 102, 104*; Toshiharu Kitajima *pp106-107, 108, 110, 112*; Paul H Groh *pp126, 130, 135, 138, 140-141, 146*; Todd Conversano *p142*; Philippe Ruault *pp164, 166*; Richard Payne *p168 (above)*; Nathaniel Lieberman *p168 (below)*; Paul Warchol *p170-171*; Ken Champlin *p176 (above)*; K Krolak *p176 (below)*; Richard Bryant/Arcaid *pp202, 206*; Peter Walser *p218*.

Cover: Barton Myers, Portland Center for the Performing Arts, Portland, Oregon
Page two: Eric Owen Moss, Ince Theater, Culver City, California

First published in Great Britain in 1996 by
ACADEMY EDITIONS
an imprint of

ACADEMY GROUP LTD
42 Leinster Gardens, London W2 3AN
Member of the VCH Publishing Group

ISBN: 1 85490 450 7

Distributed to the trade in the United States of America by
NATIONAL BOOK NETWORK, INC
4720 Boston Way, Lanham, Maryland 20706

Printed and bound in The United Kingdom

CONTENTS

THEATRE DESIGN: A COLLABORATIVE ART

James Steele

■ A theatre presents one of the most difficult design tasks for an architect because it combines the need for a technically perfect space with the necessity of allowing fantasy and dreams to happen. The elusive theatrical experience at its best is a tenuous combination of a good production and surroundings that do not overwhelm it; a void that is limited enough in scope to allow the willing suspension of disbelief to occur. In the admittedly subjective selection that follows, which is far from comprehensive, this delicate balance has been addressed in various ingenious ways, and in addition to that general overarching concern, five distinct sub-themes are represented in this sampling.

First among these is acoustic performance, which has come to preoccupy theatre designers more than ever before, mainly because of the predominance of computer modelling in analysing the various aspects of sound. Raul Barreneche has described this significant shift that has taken place in acoustic science as follows:

> Ten to fifteen years ago, the main acoustic consideration for theatre designers was reverberation – the length of time required for sound to decay in a room. Reverberation is dependent on a room's volume and shape, as well as on material finishes. Now, practitioners are paying attention to building geometries and other acoustic concepts such as loudness, clarity, intimacy and envelopment, which contribute to the overall sound of a theatre.[1]

The result of this shift has been a marked preference for the rectangular 'shoe box' hall which reflects sound laterally, shallower balconies that prevent sound from becoming trapped, and harder sound reflective surfaces that promote liveness. Lateral sound has added richness and fullness, adding to the impression of envelopment that Barreneche refers to, which is deemed so desirable today.

The most direct application of these changes is the Disney Concert Hall in which the restrictions imposed by the shoe box configuration prompted Frank Gehry to compensate by applying free flowing curves to mask it. Strips of paper added in collage-like fashion to the scale model of the hall, designed by the acoustician, allowed the architect to redress the aesthetic balance, and the final translation of that collage into physical form has been the cause of a representational revolution that is brilliant and problematic at the same time. The ground gained here by the Gehry office is a result of the exercise of the architect's prerogative, an endangered quantity in the extensive collaboration now required by increased technological sophistication.

The second of the sub-themes discernable here relates to this fine balance, the architect as the final creative impetus, entering by necessity into a collaborative relationship, and yet retaining some degree of autonomy. Many of the larger examples presented here – such as Glyndebourne, Nara, Escondido, Cerritos, the Morton H Myerson Symphony Hall and Birmingham – show the extent of the success of this exigency, a new role for architects, although obviously not an uncomfortable one for professionals now increasingly accustomed to working as part of a team.

In a recent overview of the revival of Broadway, Herbert Muschamp has offered the important insight that modernism and the theatre have always been uncomfortable together, since modernism is 'a product of the industrial culture' and the stage is 'a platform for artifice'. It is a place where even the most realistic situations must be recreated nightly out of 'smoke and mirrors'[2]. The paradox he notes, is that we now understand that 'the essence of theatre is literally make believe, that artifice can be a means of grasping truth.' It is hardly coincidental that Walter Gropius proposed an experimental theatre with several different positions for a circular stage, and subsequent seating arrangements for the audience. As one of the most consistent historical typologies existing at the beginning of the modern movement, the theatre was a logical target for reformation, and there was always a suspicion that, in spite of admirable technical achievement, contemporary theatres – that have seats ceilings and walls moving on air cushions and computerized hinges into various configurations – fall into this category of getting priorities wrong by placing the emphasis on mechanics rather than the artifice that Muschamp describes. In today's financial climate, such transformations are justified as providing good value for money, five theatres for the price of one with economical payback over time, and are promoted as the first and best, on the cutting edge of technology, which is an attraction in societies that place a high value on these attributes. This is a trend that will undoubtedly continue to accelerate, along with the formal exploration that Gropius helped to initiate.

Foremost among such explorers, Eric Moss is even more uncomfortable with durable typologies than Gropius was, his destruction of traditional notions of shelter in the Petal and Lawson-Westen houses providing convincing examples of his surprising capacity for deliberate reinterpretation of human institutions we take for granted. His Ince Theatre, to be built in the derelict east end of Culver City is another recent case in point. It is a four-hundred-and-fifty seat 'theatre in the park'

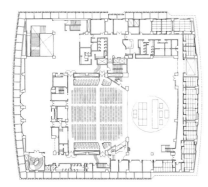

Kisho Kurokawa, National Bunraku Theater, Japan

that is intended to be a 'sociological and aesthetic hypodermic' in an area at the intersection of Washington, Culver, Venice and Robertson Boulevards, that is otherwise intended to undergo a conventional urban face-lift.

A twenties flat-iron building, revived as a hotel, adjoins the proposed city park, which will have shops, restaurants and a restored historic cinema; whilst the Sony corporation plans a substantial remodelling of its sound studios and office space used for TV production. Across the street, developers Frederick and Laurie Smith have refurbished four office buildings over the past eight years. These surround a car park at the east end of the new commercial district, which the developers plan to replace with a park, a destination for the new development to the west, and to build an underground car park. The new theatre is located in the park, across the street from the Sony office project.

The theatre will provide live performance and cinema. On the roof a projection screen, imported from a soon to be demolished theatre, will be installed so that films can be seen from an outdoor amphitheatre on the roof, surrounding offices, the park, and will be visible from the new shopping district. A pedestrian bridge connects the new Sony project to the theatre roof. The theatre is accessible down a ramp from the surrounding park, or a stair from the adjoining street.

The theatre's form is generated from the conjunction of three spheres. Irregular surfaces insulate the exterior cinemas acoustically, deforming the roof sphere. Another series of acoustic panels conforms to the internal geometry of two spheres below. The theatre has space for a small orchestra, a proscenium and a below stage space for props and dressing. An oversized lobby may finally include theatre related offices.

The theatre has many means of access, making it possible to climb all over it as if it were a giant sculpture. In a city that revolves around artifice, and the idea that daily life itself is theatrical, the notion of an architectural object that symbolizes this fact seems perfectly acceptable, even normal. Perhaps it is because this theatre celebrates artifice, rather than formal invention for its own sake, that it seems to fall in the same register as the most productive innovations of the genre in the past; such as perspective scenery devised in the seventeenth century, and subsequent auditorium variations, including horseshoe shaped seating, that evolved to improve acoustics, sight lines and most importantly, the ability of spectators to see each other.

In addition to the significantly different structural changes ventured by Moss and Hadid, others are attempting to alter the familiar profile with its predictably high box-like fly-towers and flaring auditorium walls. These departures from form follows function modernism involve experimentation with external profile and envelope, in an attempt to define new relationships between the elements of traditional configurations, illustrated in Kisho Kurokawa's National Bunraku Theater, designed during the late eighties. In the same vein as the San Diego Theatre by Holt Hinshaw, or Pelli's Blumenthal, this represents an original approach toward subverting the standard semiotics of inescapably necessary parts and of finding a new way to combine them.

The third sub-theme represents the opposite approach, which involves recognizing the value of the past and going to extraordinary lengths to restore much loved landmarks in ways that reflect the competitiveness of the current economic climate. The Portland Complex by Barton Myers is one example of how this has been achieved, but there are many others, at various scales, taking place today. Holt Hinshaw, in addition to the San Diego Theatre, is now also in the early stages of a feasibility study for the renovation of the Fox Theater in Oakland, California. This 1928, three-thousand-five-hundred seat cinema is to be redesigned for use as a state of the art live musical venue, bolstered by a number of other entertainment orientated users in the same complex.

Here, the architects are currently acting as project developers and designers, and have invited three Bay Area entertainment operators – Conspiracy Entertainment, Black Filmmakers Hall of Fame and The Great American Music Hall – to join in the formation of an *ad-hoc* consortium for the purposes of pursuing this opportunity with the city of Oakland. The Fox will be resurrected as a hub of a wider downtown entertainment, retail and dining district. The proposed plan will allow all three facilities to be booked together as a corporate meeting, conference and convention venue offering five auditoriums ranging in size from thirty to two-thousand-eight-hundred-and-fifty seats, together with exhibition spaces, bars, dining areas and party spaces, including the Music Café, main auditorium stage, theatre lounges, and the 'Buddha' VIP lofts (located within the proscenium walls). Given the proposed brief and the Fox's dilapidated condition, the only economically feasible approach will combine selected areas of faithful historic restoration and aggressive, adaptive reuse with substantial new construction. By saving, as well as making, cultural history in this way, the Fox will become a revitalized landmark that is also an exciting new destination; one that will satisfy preservationists, contemporary audiences and operators alike.

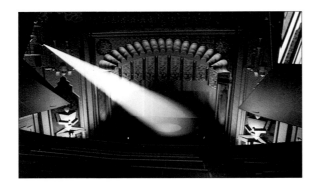

With the exception of the long demolished lobby, the entrance tower exterior and auditorium are the architecturally significant and visually magnificent parts. This landmark tower and its historic sign will continue to mark the entrance to the main auditorium – with its two-thousand-eight-hundred-and-fifty seats – and the major events of Fox Oakland Presents, which will occupy the entirety of the original theatre structure including the stage, seating, fly-tower, lobbies, basement and projection room. The commercial wings provide the Black Film-makers Hall of Fame and The Great American Music Café corner entries and street frontage.

The original theatre entrance, lobby, circulation, concession and service spaces were either relatively insignificant in architectural terms or have been ravaged by periodic modification or neglect. Modern building codes and operational requirements for exiting, fire separation, handicap access, toilet capacity, concession and bar operation, entertainment media, seismic strengthening and toxic materials abatement, also suggest that these important functional areas must be redesigned. The creative, adaptive reuse strategy for these areas calls for relocating the few remaining historic features and demolishing all non-structural partitions and ceilings, to allow clear access to currently enclosed structural spaces, facilitating toxic remediation and seismic strengthening, as well as the installation of interesting, affordable, efficient and far more durable new construction.

The rebirth of the Old Vic is equally inspiring. Originally opened in 1818, the theatre was subsidized by Prince Leopold of Saxe-Coburg and his wife Charlotte, Princess of Wales, and located near Waterloo Bridge Road, Lambeth. A major attraction, devised by Rudolphe Cabanel the architect, was the looking-glass instead of a drop curtain, 36 feet high, 32 feet wide, with sixty three compartments filled with glass panels. In 1843 the Theatres Act abolished a legal division between major and minor theatres, and as a result the gallery of the Old Vic was frequently crammed to its one-thousand-five-hundred seat capacity as the public rushed to the cheap seats to see the melodramas that became the mainstay of the house. The murder of Nancy in *Oliver Twist* was typical of the scenes they favoured most, cruelty by a villain exaggerated in the best vaudeville tradition. In 1897, Lilian Baylis took over as manager and embarked on a more 'elevated', if unwieldy, programme of Shakespearean plays and opera, which brought a new, extremely loyal audience to the theatre. Following alterations in 1928, the Shakespearean productions continued, with many famous players such as John Gielgud, Alec Guinness, Laurence Olivier, Edith Evans and Michael Redgrave making a successful start there. Bomb damage in 1941 forced closure until 1950, but audiences steadily declined and it was put up for sale in 1979. Following a bidding war, involving Andrew Lloyd Webber, it was sold to Edward Mirvish of Toronto for five-hundred-and-fifty-thousand pounds in 1982. Nearly two million more has now been spent on restoring the theatre. The architects, Renton Howard Wood Levin Partners, with Ove Arup as consultants, were confronted by a building with Georgian exterior walls, a mid-Victorian auditorium, a backstage converted from Morley College in 1890 and a hotchpotch of a foyer adapted over many years. The first priority was to adopt an effective design strategy for each area, and yet to unify the theatre into an effective whole. After agreeing on a new façade, which took some time since the 1928 composition was felt to be too austere and a recreation of the Victorian façade was dismissed since little of the original fabric remained, attention turned to the replanning of the foyers and simplification of the circulation. The past segregation of the audience between pit, dress circle and gallery has been changed. Administrative requirements were reduced to free up the mezzanine for public use, and to give direct access to the front of the gallery, reducing vertical circulation. The difficulty that the architects and consultants encountered may perhaps be best appreciated in this excerpt from the *Arup Journal*:

Before this refurbishment project began, the staircase system created a labyrinth for the audience to negotiate. The upper circle, for example, was reached up a winding staircase from the side-street.

To overcome the problems of segregated access a single main staircase was built that rises from the Pit Bar in the basement through four floors, opening onto three bars and the entrances to the stalls, dress circle and gallery (now to be called the Lilian Baylis Circle).

The new staircase has an open well, protected with cast iron balusters to an 1830 design and also a continuous mahogany handrail.

To support this and other loadings, massive box-frames, fabricated from large steel beams, were installed at each floor level. These beams were manhandled into position in cramped conditions and the structure bolted together once the pieces were in position. These box-frames were designed by Ove Arup & Partners and supervised by Kyle Stewart's Temporary Works Division.

The entrance foyer was gutted and completely refurbished with fibrous plaster columns, included to recreate the space and feeling of Emma Cons' 1880s coffee tavern. Two of these are original cast iron columns which were found encased in brickwork. These have been retained and decorated in fibrous plaster as well.

The foyer decorations have been kept simple with purpose designed lighting, while the Pit Bar exhibits scenes from Victorian life in Lambeth.

Upon entering the building, the audience will have seen themselves reflected in a 1.8 metre square mirror etched with the original design of Cabanel's auditorium. The original print from which it is taken is in fact an etching of the auditorium reflected in a sixty-three piece mirror house curtain which existed for a short period in the 1880s.

The auditorium, which now has an increased seating capacity of one thousand and seventy seven, is entered through new lobbies leading from the foyer in gangways down each side of the auditorium. The Lilian Baylis Circle is accessible through new vomitory entrances, bringing the audience in at the front of the circle rather than at the very back of the auditorium. The vomitories were made possible by modifying the existing timber structure and forming new corridors within the triangular void below the stepped seatways and above the ceiling of the dress circle.

The result of such care has been the return of a much loved part of theatre history to the public realm.

Another restoration, the Bam Majestic in New York, completed by Hardy Holzman Pfeiffer Associates in 1987, is a graphic reminder that many theatres in the past were not designed by architects and consultants in response to sophisticated and highly technical briefs, but by professional theatre designers, such as JB MacElfatrick who built hundreds of theatres throughout the United States. The Bam was built in 1903, primarily for musical reviews, but had fallen into neglect during the late sixties. The theatre reopened to stage Peter Brook's *Mahabharata*, and the architects designed the interior to reflect the *Bouffes du Nord*, which Brook had saved from the wreaker's ball. Rather than costly restoration, the unconventional interior, wrapped around new seating and stage, is a set of its own, reiterating the power of fantasy in comparison to costly technical solutions. Seating capacity was reduced from one thousand seven hundred to nine hundred to increase the intimacy between audience and performers, and the lower balcony has also been extended by six rows to bring it to the level of the raised stage.

These heroic efforts to return past landmarks to lively, contemporary use leads into the fourth prevalent sub-theme determined by many of the theatres presented here which have been planned as urban resuscitators. Interestingly, the theatre has been the one civic institution which is considered to be singularly capable of providing focus and generating new growth. With the electronic age well underway, the theatre's traditional role as the testing ground for social myth has altered to that of cultural symbol, with patronage less a quest for discovery than identification with a historically verified mark of refinement. The theatre, as seen in Birmingham, Newark and other major cities, has been commercialized and grouped with conference centres, restaurants and shops, and frequently located as an 'anchor' in a covered mall, to ease public access to it and to satisfy a seemingly insatiable need to associate with culture in an age when it is rapidly disintegrating.

This rampant commercialization, which may of course be argued to have also existed in many other forms in the theatre in the past, makes the fifth sub-theme, of a return to origins, even more poignant. Having begun as a sacred celebration of the forces of nature, the theatre has now emerged from its distillation as a manifestly urban institution, *à la* Opera House in Lyon, into a natural precinct once again, especially in Japan; Ishii's Bunraku, Isozaki's Togamura and Fumihiko Maki's Kirishima Hall for instance. It is appropriate that this return, should happen in a nation so sensitive to its parameters and qualities, and ironic that this should occur in a country that has adopted this institution relatively recently and is one of the most rapidly urbanizing regions of the world. The diametric circumstances in which the theatre continues to thrive today, regardless of the intentions of its use, point to its continuing vitality and remarkable ability to adapt to new circumstances, and there is every indication that it will continue to do so in the future, perhaps because of, rather than in spite of, the electronic revolution.

Notes

1 Raul Barreneche, 'Acoustic Performance', *Architecture*, December 1994, p91.

2 Herbert Muschamp, 'Broadway's Real Hits: Its Antique Theatres', *The New York Times*, Sunday, 30th July 1995.

HISTORY OF THE OVE ARUP PARTNERSHIP'S INVOLVEMENT IN THE THEATRE

Patrick Morreau

■ Since its foundation in 1946, the Ove Arup Partnership – which includes not only the consulting engineers Ove Arup & Partners, but also the integrated architectural/engineering practice Arup Associates and the acoustic consultancy Arup Acoustics – has grown to be one of the world's largest and most successful design firms, with more than four thousand staff in offices in forty countries. Its activities now include every kind of engineering – civil, structural, industrial – and a host of specialisms from economics and planning, to information technology and product development. How has this growth and diversification been achieved?

One factor, and arguably the most important, is the lasting influence of their founder, Ove Arup. Anyone seeking to understand the nature of the firm should turn to a talk Arup gave in 1970, a talk that has since become known as the 'Key Speech'. In it he set out the main aims of the firm: quality of work; total architecture; humane organization; straight and honourable dealings; social usefulness, and the reasonable prosperity of its members. These continue to be the aims of the Partnership. One part of the speech is particularly pertinent to a book subtitled 'A Collaborative Art':

> We must strive for quality in what we do, and never be satisfied with the second-rate. There are many kinds of quality. In our work as structural engineers we have to satisfy the criteria for a sound, lasting and economical structure. We add to that the claim that it should be pleasing aesthetically, for without that quality it doesn't really give satisfaction to us or to others. And then we come up against the fact that a structure is generally a part of a larger unit, and we are frustrated because to strive for quality in only a part is almost useless if the whole is undistinguished, unless the structure is large enough to make an impact on its own. We are led to seek overall quality, fitness for purpose, as well as satisfying or significant forms and economy of construction. To this must be added harmony with the surroundings and the overall plan. We are then led to the ideal of 'Total Architecture', in collaboration with other like-minded firms.

'Collaboration with other like-minded firms' has been one of the essential elements in the partnership's success. Indeed, one of Arup's great contributions to engineering and architecture was to raise the engineer from being a competent but subservient technician, to being co-designer; bringing to the design process both specialist knowledge and a general understanding of the overall goals. Another has been described as the 'cultivation of enquiring minds', willing to allow, or even encourage – their engineers to look beyond the technical problems to the relationship of the engineering contribution to projects as a whole. As one of their directors puts it ' . . . engineering should not be seen as a limiting art, but rather as one that supports and liberates, as a catalyst for good architecture.'

The steady growth of the partnership in numbers, skills and extent, is reflected in its work in theatres, concert halls and opera houses. In the early days of the practice, Britain was rebuilding after the war and the needs were basic – housing, schools, hospitals. So it was not until the sixties that Ove Arup & Partners completed its first concert hall commission, as structural engineer for the Queen Elizabeth Hall and Purcell Room in London's South Bank Arts Centre, fine auditoria in an unloved Brutalist complex.

The South Bank may have been the first concert hall commission completed, but it was not the first undertaken. In 1957, Jørn Utzon won the Sydney Opera House competition and Ove Arup & Partners was appointed structural engineer for a project that brought it world-wide fame, and a fair measure of controversy. The evolution of the Sydney Opera House roof exemplifies successful collaboration between engineer and architect, reconciling the conflict between the free form of the competition entry and the disciplines of structural feasibility, construction, economics and modular cladding. Thirteen structural schemes were developed from Utzon's original concept of concrete shells deriving strength from their shape, through various combinations of steel and concrete shells, arches and space frames, before eventually reaching the pre-cast post-tensioned concrete arch and rib solution which was built. The final form, segments of a spherical surface, gives a simple and consistent geometrical relationship between all components of structure and cladding.

During the seventies and eighties, the partnership worked on some sixty theatres, concert halls and opera houses in the United Kingdom and elsewhere. The same period saw the scope of the commissions extend from structural engineering to include mechanical, electrical and, through Arup Associates, full architectural design. Specialist consultancies also developed and Arup's skills in acoustics and fire safety engineering were increasingly employed.

The Industrial Revolution brought prosperity to many of Britain's towns and, with their new found wealth, they built theatres, some of great elegance and architectural interest. Restorations of these historic buildings has formed an important, and particularly challenging, part of Arup's work. The fact that several of the buildings are 'listed' meant that every detail of the restoration had to be agreed with the Historic Buildings Commission (and its successors), adding to the complexity of the challenge. One of the first restorations was the Theatre Royal in Glasgow; among others have been the Theatre Royal, Nottingham, the Buxton Opera House and the London Old Vic. Some projects have involved converting derelict spaces into theatres. The Royal Exchange in Manchester is an example in which a seven-hundred seat theatre in-the-round is suspended to avoid overloading the floor of the old Cotton Exchange. It is also the first project on which Arup's fire safety engineering was used to justify an exposed steel structure.

The scale of Arup's theatre projects has ranged from a small experimental space such as the four-hundred seat Half Moon Theatre on London's Mile End Road, to the two-thousand-seven-hundred seat New Jersey Performing Arts Center. The nature and complexity of the engineering also covers a wide range. The Sydney Opera House is probably still the structural *tour de force*, although the construction of the Barbican Arts Centre, London, in excavations abutting forty-three-storey towers, streets and railway lines, was a work of unprecedented civil engineering skill.

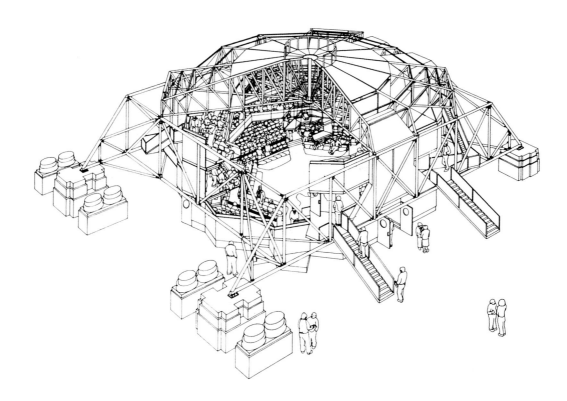

Royal Exchange Theatre, Manchester

ARUP ACOUSTICS
Richard Cowell

■ Theatre is itself a collaborative art and our sense of sound is an essential part of it. From the moment we approach a theatre, the opportunity to use sound to influence our mood is there. We know that our designs must serve the performance at least, but, more than that, they need to offer opportunities for performers to stretch their medium and enhance the quality of the event. The acoustic design depends on collaboration, and the most important collaboration occurs when mutual support is given between professional disciplines so that acoustic designs enhance the architecture and vice versa.

The client
At the crucial early stages, although we need to understand what our client believes is wanted, we also need to inform and persuade them of the full potential of the sound in and around the theatre. Conflicts of building use, usually arising from commercial pressures, normally require the provision of flexibility. The acoustic design then becomes problem solving at the expense of creativity. Agreement on a first use which is served by real excellence is the result of collaborative art.

There are examples of excellence being achieved for conflicting uses, but usually only through substantial expenditure. Renzo Piano's conversion of a courtyard in Fiat's Lingotto, Turin, is one. Here, following acoustic tests, a design emerged which permitted a change to the ceiling geometry, altering the volume and producing an excellent acoustic environment for concerts and for conference.

The size of auditoria needs an early discussion with all parties. Simple limitation by distance, the perception of facial expressions, tends to control size, as the loss of direct sound with distance can be mitigated to some degree by powerful early reflections to support the human voice. Techniques of amplification allow much larger theatres.

Controlling the aural environment
Integration of acoustic design into the building grows better as the acoustician grows strong enough to challenge the design professionals of different disciplines. This is particularly true where the acoustician is working to protect the performing environment by noise control. We are familiar with the need for mass and stiffness in structures – to exclude noise – which very often conflicts with the structural engineer's concept of an elegant structure, but there are more extreme examples. For the protection of a theatre from railway vibration, the Symphony Hall, Birmingham, for instance, not only is a rapport with the structural engineer essential, but also an understanding

of the isolation of the building services, railway engineering and the impact of building isolation on the architecture. All involved are also learning fast about the fundamentals of physics, and its impact on the buildings. This experience is invaluable on the subsequent occasions it arises. The consequence of repeated collaboration usually results in a significant technical and procedural advance.

Basic form
The basic form of a theatre calls for close discussion between architect, acoustician and theatre consultant. Although heavily influenced by size, the integration of architectural acoustical and theatrical concepts is the seed of excellence.

Background sound
In the area of building services, there is an interesting balance to be struck in establishing background sound targets for theatres. The pregnant pause can gain drama in effective 'silence'. Equally distracting noise will punctuate this 'silence' more easily. Background sound should be adjustable, just as the temperature and lighting is controlled. In the future we may expect that ambient sound in theatres will be much better controlled than it is today.

Focal points in acoustic design
From an examination of acoustics within concert halls, it soon becomes clear that theatre itself is essentially a product of a fundamental collaboration, between the performer and audience. By arrangement, this collaboration has already spread to many other formats, with the acoustician finding focal points for collaboration. The seating in theatres usually offers the largest single area of sound absorption and so needs careful assessment and acoustic testing. The increasing use of air supply below, or from within seats, to serve economic air displacement systems requires a close collaboration with the building services engineer to balance air-flow and noise control. These days research in this and related areas leaves no excuse for disturbance by noise from air conditioning.

Balconies, boxes and their fronts are another crucial area of theatre design. Apart from an obvious need to control excessive overhangs – even allowing for virtually undetectable acoustic enhancement systems – the orientation of trays of people to assist sound distribution is fundamental. The construction, solidity, transparency, decoration and shaping of balcony and box fronts bring acoustics and the character of the space face to face.

Intergrated design

Perhaps the most potent yet modest display of the acoustician's collaborative art is the absence of obviously acoustic components. There has been far too much acoustic 'junk' applied to theatre interiors, usually representing a failure to make the design work efficiently, bringing an integrated performance from the construction. If the architect wants to shout 'this is acoustic' so be it, but usually this is not so. Theatres are littered with trials of strength between architects and acousticians. Sadly, there are few beautifully integrated designs.

Multi-purpose use

A feature of multi-purpose use is often the need for variable absorption. After decades of 'hanging out the washing' and moving parts which are never moved, as nobody knows how to use them properly, this is an area which needs a great deal more focus. It may be naive to suggest that construction of single purpose theatres could be justified by the catalogue of architectural failure associated with variable absorption alone, but at the same time, with many other reasons for failures in multi-purpose theatres, it adds a powerful argument. Three buildings for the price of one is impossible if the variable absorption is so bad that no format delivers a good result.

The future

The future for sound in the theatre is exciting; offering expanding opportunities to transform human emotions with sound and light in ways which we have only begun to develop in this century. This may well transform theatre beyond all recognition. A new collaboration is in view. The impact of audio-visual systems on theatre design is in its infancy, and in the age of choice and unparalleled available controls, the participant in theatre may experience much more interaction The electro-acoustician will develop designs with communication specialists. Performers will use new media to produce new forums of collaboration.

Perhaps the most interesting acoustics question to arise now, about the future, is the extent to which high quality sound will be desired. Society of the nineties is not well educated to listen, by this I mean really 'listen' rather than just hear. A fundamental respect for high quality of sound depends on education now. How many clients and theatre architects are clear even about how quiet a theatre should be and able to explain their reasoning? Reliance on acousticians is not good enough. They need to collaborate in debates aimed at higher quality. There are such exciting opportunities awaiting theatre designs which use our aural senses to the full.

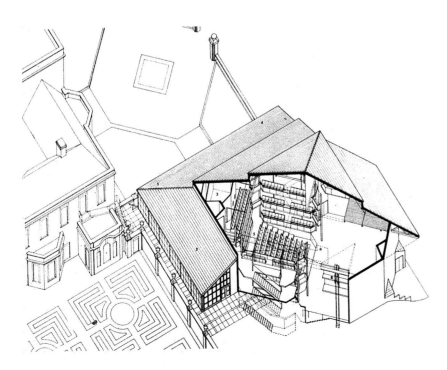

Wilde Theatre, Bracknell

WORKING WITH ARCHITECTS
Richard Hough

■ For architects and engineers, few building types are as technically challenging as theatres. Laboratories may have more complex engineering systems, but each one can be given its own spatial zone and tolerances, allowing specialist consultants to work on their own portion in relative isolation. Not so with theatres. The importance of achieving a compact, intimate auditorium with short sight lines and a sense of shared experience, puts enormous pressure on the co-ordination and integration of the parts. No geometric slack can be tolerated. It is not uncommon for an architect to engage over a dozen consultants, and they must all pile in together and argue their patch in the division of space. No system can be optimized unilaterally, and the architect becomes the artistic director of a company of specialist players. The practice of architecture may have no more consummate challenge.

Multi-disciplinary engineering of the kind practised by Ove Arup & Partners has the advantage of simplifying much of the co-ordination, clarifying choices at the multitude of technical interfaces, and shortening the settling-in period for big new consultant teams. Closer in-house communications often create the space, time and atmosphere for novel engineering solutions to emerge. The architect also has the comfort that much of the technical co-ordination is taking place automatically. In particular, the two biggest consumers of space, the structural and mechanical systems, evolve and then converge much faster if the respective engineers share a commitment to finding the best integrated solution. If the acoustics consultant is also truly bound into that process, then the three major technical influences on planning and geometry will be pulling in the same direction.

Sometimes, engineering will be an important part of the visual architectural language, whether in the form of an acoustically isolated mechanical services tower, an enveloping structural idea, or a smaller scale expression of a ventilation, lighting or structural element in the public spaces. Certainly there are demountable mobile theatres, or low-budget conversions, where a simple expression of engineering, lighting or acoustics devices can be used effectively to support a particular image and experience. In those cases, engineers who are already motivated by the expressive use of engineering in architecture have a big head start.

More commonly however, the intended repertoire and performance type are wide-ranging and do not rely on visible engineering. Indeed in North America's most versatile and highly engineered theatre at Cerritos in California, the architect chose to subsume the engineering in a much softer image. In most cases, the technical challenge is to achieve more with less, and preferably to shrink the engineering to half size. The need to minimize height between tiers, to minimize sight line lengths, to keep the room intimate and the stage close, all emphasize dimensional control and co-ordination. Intense design effort goes into cantilever balconies for example. Where, to squeeze out the last centimetre, they often end up as doubly-curved surfaces, both for floor and ceiling. In between these ever decreasing structural depths, and the need to meet comfort criteria for floor vibration, are located numerous other functions: tight mechanical zones for ventilation ducts need to meet maximum air velocity criteria for acoustic control; ceiling lighting design needs space to achieve its atmosphere, whilst the type, shape and thickness of surface materials all affect acoustic results. The articulated wing of a large jet aircraft may not require more design co-ordination.

In other building types, the structural grid is often the first thing established, to provide an anchor for the geometric generation of other systems, including cladding and finishes. For theatres it works the other way around; the interior surfaces are established to optimize the finished volumes, and the location of structure and other technical systems is then back-figured. Since surface geometry depends on pre-knowledge of the size of the technical components to be contained, there are many interactive loops of co-ordination, so that a fast and efficient feedback process must be established within the design team. Timing becomes critical because the order in which the contractor needs information from which to build, puts structure first, even if it is often the last element that can be confirmed in the design loop.

Like a stage performance, the process needs much personal energy, dedication, teamwork and focus. It is usually easier the second time around, but then the new brief can bring completely new challenges for the design team.

Structural engineering
In some countries, construction in steel is more expensive than in concrete. That is convenient for theatre design, because typical modern acoustic standards applied to city sites, point to two layers of massive construction for walls and roof; 'box-in-box' construction. Concrete walls – or concrete frames infilled with masonry – can provide both structure and one layer of the two-layer acoustic system simultaneously. Provided they do not need integrating with the horizontal air distribution system, carefully designed concrete balconies can also be thinner and less vibration sensitive than steel, although

soffit-panelling is typically still required for acoustics. Concrete roof structures are less common because of the large auditorium span, so steel trussing is typically used for primary structure, often with concrete surfaces at the top and bottom chord levels to provide acoustic mass to the loft space.

In countries where steel is more commonly used, it may be adopted for the primary frame of a theatre for reasons of cost and speed, and also because detailed column layout can be freed from the final choice of geometry for the massive acoustic walls, allowing design of the perimeter structure to progress earlier. Cantilever balcony beams occur as steel beam ribs, offering intermediate spaces for air supply plenums, or for acoustic modelling of ceilings. Integration of engineering systems in tight areas can be eased by the provision of closely spaced columns to minimize number and depth of floor beams. For most configurations of balcony tiers, vibration analysis requires full three-dimensional computer modelling of the theatre frame, because of the close interconnectivity of structural elements.

Fly-tower walls typically offer generous structural depth for spanning across major openings like the proscenium and scenery dock. Apart from supporting the roof, the wall structure also carries the gridiron with scenery and counterweights, the lighting system, and any retractable concert ceilings and other near-field variable acoustic devices. The main issue for the fly-tower structure is often limiting the thickness and cost of the vertical elements that stabilize the walls against horizontal forces. In seismic or typhoon zones, where horizontal forces increase substantially, vertical spanning of side walls around the auditorium can also become an issue; unless the horizontal diaphragm action of wraparound seating tiers can transfer horizontal forces between the rear wall and the proscenium, where a large braced stability frame can be created.

Design for acoustic criteria affects structural design in many ways. Most fundamentally, acoustic isolation joints are needed to separate blocks of structure; mainly the auditorium from mechanical plant and adjacent performance spaces, as well as public spaces such as the lobby. Sometimes the joints need to carry on down through the foundations. Properly tuned bearings can often be tolerated between structural members on each side of the joint in the superstructure however, so expensive and deep free cantilever floor zones can often be avoided. Double layer cavity construction needed for acoustic reasons, provides a zone for the structural depth of vertical or horizontal spanning elements, although the structure must usually not bridge the acoustic cavity completely. This is

feasible for wall posts, but difficult to achieve in the roof if upper and lower concrete surfaces are attached to an interstitial truss, although bearings can assist. Also, the additional weight of a suspended ceiling is available, and the roof may not be as critical as the walls from an insulative point of view.

Where a separate ceiling is used over the auditorium, its design is another particular challenge, as its shape, mass and surface need to be acoustically controlled, it is also a major visual element, and often a major device for the mounting and control of theatrical lighting. The structural challenge is to take the acoustic weight, maximize lighting crew access, integrate the air supply system, support the artistic intent of this crowning enclosure, and remain inexpensive and buildable. It is another all encompassing example of the importance of design co-ordination.

Mechanical engineering

Careful design and integration of a theatre's ventilation system is crucial, as the experience of theatre-going is distinctly diminished by cold drafts, stuffy balconies or the noise of mechanical ventilation at work.

Early choice of the noise criterion for the auditorium is the single biggest step in fixing the precautions that need to be built into the ventilation system. These include how physically remote and acoustically isolated the mechanical plant rooms will need to be, how low the supply air velocities will need to be and hence how large the ducts, and whether acoustic plenums will be needed as well. Certainly all noise-producing equipment like waste pipes, rainwater pipes, elevators and escalators, needs to be mounted outside of the auditorium shell.

Deciding where it is best to introduce air into and return it out of, the auditorium, is often the subject of some study. For ease of accommodating ductwork, a high-level supply, downward through the ceiling or lighting grid, is often attractive. Unfortunately, its drawback is that the air must first be cooled to lower temperatures for its passage through the zone of hot lights, and must be delivered at higher velocities for the same reason, with the attendant risk of greater noise.

Throwing horizontally from the side walls produces a different air movement pattern, and may be suitable if the ceiling design does not lend itself to overhead supply. Then the design of the diffuser unit becomes critical, ensuring a good throw with limited velocity, the avoidance of concentrated down draughts and stagnant spaces under balconies.

The logical place to supply the air, of course, is amongst the audience itself, where it is needed. Several theatres have now been completed using underfloor air supply, which comes close to this ideal. Here air can be supplied at a higher temperature because it does not have to penetrate the heat gains at higher levels in the auditorium. This makes the system more energy efficient, and provides better temperature control at occupant level. Low supply velocities, and careful design of diffusers, are important to minimize potential noise, given that the system is so close to the occupants. For any of these scenarios, computer analysis of air movement patterns by computational fluid dynamics methods is useful to check likely maximum and minimum velocities, and temperature distributions. Effects at the auditorium/stage interface can also be checked, in terms of comfort for performers.

Entrance lobbies are often highly glazed, with large populations for short periods. These parameters are challenging for the design of economic but effective air conditioning, and computational fluid dynamics studies are again useful in predicting comfort conditions under a range of scenarios. Servicing of bars and food in public spaces also needs early design consideration to establish satisfactory routes.

Electrical engineering

Of the specialists making up the project design team, none has a more challenging role than the electrical engineer. Electricity is needed to power the mechanical and HVAC equipment, the elevators and plumbing, the house lighting, theatrical lighting and work lighting, the rigging equipment, sound system, acoustic devices, security, telephone and data systems. So for the electrical engineer to make his contribution, the theatrical consultant, acoustician, lighting designer, sound consultant and telecommunications engineer, must all first integrate their components into the architecture. Given the potential complexity, and artistic impact, of these components, fixing them to everyone's satisfaction is no small task. If there is any time left over, that is when the engineer must rationalize the location and layout of electrical rooms and cable layouts.

His criteria will include the minimization of conduit crossovers with major ductwork runs, separation of power circuits from sound circuits to reduce noise interference, and the location of dimmer rooms, amplifier rooms and so on, to minimize the wiring served by those rooms. Apart from interaction with a multitude of other design consultants and specialists, there are also interfaces with contractors whose responsibilities will vary. For instance, rigging contractors will supply equipment for stage curtain, fire curtain and stage rigging, and there will be many small motors for variable acoustic curtains and above-stage reflectors. Each contract needs co-ordination concerning electrical power supply, and location of motors, disconnection switches, control circuits and so on.

Lighting falls into many categories, including production, house, work and exterior lighting, typically with specialist consultants involved. Production lights may be located in catwalks, gridirons, balconies and ceiling grids, and are wired back, along with house lights, to the dimmer room. For the sound system, the amplifier room is located near the loudspeaker clusters to reduce wiring lengths. Testing and commissioning of such a complexity of electrical systems as the opening night approaches, can be a performance in itself.

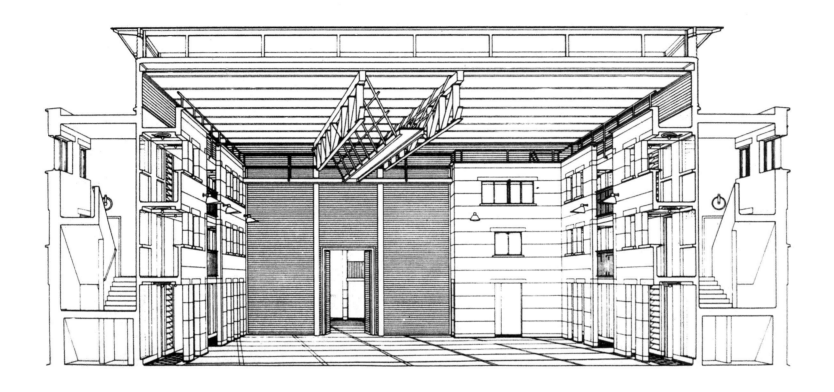

Half Moon Theatre, Mile End, London

CERRITOS PERFORMING ARTS CENTER
Cerritos, California

The Arts Center is the principal component in the one-hundred-and-twenty-acre master planned development at Cerritos city centre. Completed at the end of 1992, it provides a wide variety of performance areas, community meeting rooms and ancillary spaces.

Cerritos, a forward-thinking Southern California city with a population of sixty thousand, could neither afford nor support three separate theatres and an exhibition area. An early study by Theatre Projects Consultants had identified a need for three different spaces, suitable for music, drama and trade shows. This study showed how, using Northampton's Derngate Centre as a model, the city could afford to construct a multi-purpose hall that would satisfy its cultural ambitions. Cerritos now has a facility that is unique in North America. Its technical innovations make it one of the most sophisticated theatre spaces on the continent.

As is common in the United States, the design period was split into three distinct phases, with formal presentations to the client at the end of each. Before a job goes out to tender, it is subjected to a formal review process known as the 'plan check'. The Building and Safety Division of Los Angeles County Engineer-Facilities carried out this work on behalf of Cerritos, carefully reviewing the design drawings and specifications for code compliance.

Schematic design	March to November 1987
Design development	December 1987 to March 1988
Construction documents	March 1988 to January 1989
Plan check Phase 1	Completed June 1989
Plan check Phase 2	Completed January 1990
Bid	May 1989
Construction began	September 1989
Fly-tower topped out	January 1991
Auditorium topping out ceremony	May 1991

As well as the Arts Center, the site will eventually contain an office park, a hotel and a seventy-five-acre regional shopping centre.

An urban context was missing, apart from some undifferentiated office blocks and an ocean of car parking. This was in contrast to architect Barton Myers' previous and highly successful theatre in Portland, Oregon, which occupied a very dense city centre site, sandwiched between two buildings listed on the National Register of Historical Buildings. Thus, the first challenge to the architects was to create a sense of place. This they did by arranging the Arts Center as a series of pavilions with gardens and courtyards. The benign climate allows designers this freedom, and the forms, materials and details used are rooted in the traditions of Southern Californian regionalism. Barton Myers had several images in mind as the massing studies progressed – the clustering of buildings in a Mediterranean village, Bertram Goodhue's flamboyant designs for the 1915 Panama-California Exposition in San Diego, now known as Balboa Park; and the spirited shapes, volumes, roofs and shadows of Los Angeles' château buildings.

A particular problem was how to deal architecturally, in a parking lot, with the large mass of the fly-tower. The solution was to cascade the buildings' roofs and towers down to garden walls, thus mediating to a pedestrian scale; these also insulate pedestrians from cars. The courtyards thus formed are well-suited for outdoor receptions. Each major building component has pyramid-shaped roofs and many also support tall flagpoles. There is much rooftop lighting and the centre, which is visible from the nearby freeway, is a beacon.

The architects believe very strongly that place itself is an important part of theatre-going, and have deliberately strived for a cheerful, welcoming, carnival-like building. To this end, much attention has been given to the external cladding. As well as a creamy white stucco, there is much banded stone-work – polished red granite and French limestone – in some ways reminiscent of James Stirling's Staatsgalerie in Stuttgart. The roofs are clad in highly coloured and patterned ceramic tiles, computer-designed specially for the project by April Greiman.

The six major buildings are the auditorium and sidestage, the actors' block, the lobby and box office tower, the large meeting room, the office block and small meeting room, and the mechanical tower. The heart of the project is the auditorium. It offers unparalleled flexibility, with five basic configurations transforming the auditorium's seating arrangement, sight lines and acoustics by the use of moveable seating towers, lifts, two proscenium lines (and two fire curtains), a flown acoustical concert ceiling above the stage, and a device known as the flipper. The arena and concert configurations allow for centripetal viewing of a central stage. The lyric format is designed for opera and large-scale musical productions. The drama format is similar to the lyric, but uses the forward proscenium, a forestage (the orchestra lift), and closes the top balcony. The flat floor configuration houses community events, banquets, and trade shows.

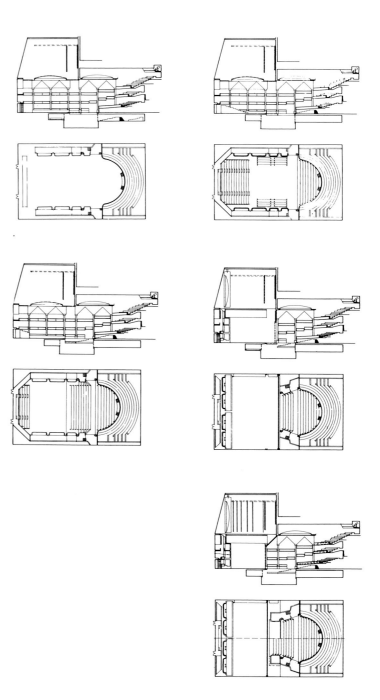

Seating configurations (plan and section). FROM ABOVE: Cabaret; in-the-round; concert; drama; lyric

Architecturally, Barton Myers had a choice when designing the interior of the auditorium, to celebrate the technology of the moving parts or to make each configuration look permanent. He chose the latter.

At its largest, in concert configuration, the shoe box shape brings to mind the Musikvereinsaal in Vienna. The seating towers form traditional boxes from which one can see and be seen. The box fronts help define the volume of the room, which is richly finished in light ash, a darker stained ash, cherry and olive green painted steel. The seating towers are constructed of tubular steel frames and lightweight concrete on metal deck floors.

A challenge to the architects lay in the contrast between the proscenium configurations (drama and lyric) and the audience-in-the-round or flat floor configurations (concert, arena and banquet). In the former there are two distinct volumes, the auditorium and the stagehouse, or fly-tower. In the arena and banquet configurations, the occupants should feel that they are in one room. This is achieved in two ways. The first is by stepping the seating tower boxes. This follows closely the rake of the two balconies so that there is no abrupt transition in the side seating as the audience wraps around from the edges of the balconies to the sides of the stage.

The ceiling treatment is the second device used to give the feeling of one room. Suspended within the fly-tower is a flown concert ceiling made of three large steel and laminated timber honeycomb panels. When not needed they are rotated to lie in vertical planes and hoisted electrically to the underside of the gridiron, an open steel platform high above the stage. For the concert, arena and banquet configurations, the panels are lowered into place, rotated and locked together at the same level as the lighting bridges and ceiling in the auditorium. In addition to its visual effect, the ceiling closes off the absorptive soft goods in the stage house, maximizing reverberation shows. The flipper, an unusual and maybe unique item of theatrical hardware, is an integral part of the fire separation between stage and auditorium. It is attached to the front proscenium and rotates on pivots to three positions: downwards (drama mode) creates a proscenium arch, angled (lyric mode) forms a second proscenium arch further upstage, while horizontal (banquet, arena and concert modes) links the concert ceiling to the auditorium ceiling. The flipper weighs approximately 27,000 lbs and is moved to its three preset working positions by an electric motor – horizontal to vertical in about two minutes. Tracking side panels suspended from the flying system adjust the proscenium width between lyric (45 ft wide) and drama (35 ft wide) formats.

Four lifts are used to reconfigure the floor, forming, as needed, a forestage (drama mode), an orchestra pit or an extension to the orchestra level seating area. The lifts also support seating wagons which may be lowered to a storage area beneath the stage. A fifth lift at the rear of the orchestra level is used to exchange seating for an in-house sound mixing location.

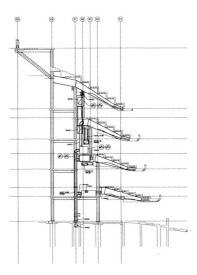

FROM ABOVE: Interior view concert configuration – the side and proscenium tower are back against the walls, the side stage towers align with them and the rear tower in the forward position completes the ring of box seating. The flipper is horizontal, aligning with the lighting bridges, and the concert ceiling is in place over the stage; mechanical balcony sections; seating tower – the vertical green tubes defining each side of the wood column are actually the structure of the tower. The red draperies are acoustic curtains that are in place when absorption is required, and retracted when absorption is not needed, allowing the room acoustics to be tuned

The seating wagons move on air-powered castors, as do the four clusters of seating towers, the auditorium side towers, the side stage towers, the proscenium towers and the rear stage tower. Microprocessors co-ordinate the movements of lifts and seating towers so that, for example, the side stage towers do not tumble into the orchestra pit.

The auditorium side towers are used in two positions, parallel with the auditorium walls in concert mode and rotated 15° inwards in lyric or drama mode. Movement is by electric winches. Hydraulic rams, with steel pipe arms located between the backs of the towers and the side walls of the auditorium, provide seismic restraint. The architectural transition is achieved by folding capitals. When the auditorium seating towers (150,000 lbs each) are rotated away from the side walls, hinged walkways known as jet ways link audience access doors to the rear of the seating towers. Raising, lowering and tracking of the jet ways is electrically powered, with an interlock system to prevent deployment at undesirable times.

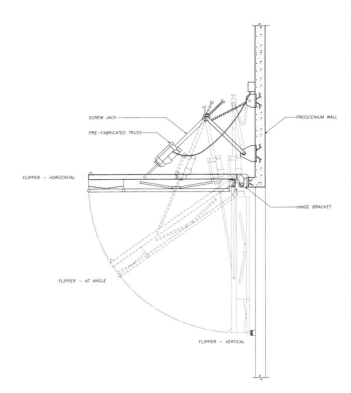

The proscenium (43,000 lbs) and side stage (140,000 lbs) seating towers are moved manually, or by electric tow tractor, on air castors between floor lock down positions (two for the side stage towers and four for the proscenium towers) which provide seismic restraint. The rear stage seating tower (225,000 lbs) is much shallower front to back than the other towers, and requires stabilization even when in transit. It is moved by an electric winch that hauls cables running beneath the stage floor. From each tower base, eight T-bar guides travel in floor slots and lock into position when stationary. Power, lighting and sound are delivered by cables supported by a cantilever arm pivoting from the rear wall.

Acoustically, the auditorium is transformed by moving parts that change its volume and the reflectivity of its surfaces. The moveable concert ceiling has already been mentioned; a freestanding orchestra shell may also be used to reflect sound towards the audience. Provided within the auditorium are acoustic banners and curtains which are intended to adjust the reverberation to accommodate a variety of uses and occupancies. Electrically operated from a control panel in the sound room, the banners retract vertically into pockets beneath the ceiling line. One set of curtains retracts horizontally into pockets within the roof void, while curtains at the rear of each box withdraw into the columns between boxes.

Curved concave surfaces such as balcony fronts are broken down to a finer scale whose convex curvature and hard wooden surfaces help scatter sound and, thus, avoid unwanted focusing.

The boxes have three principal planes: the front, which visually defines the volume of the auditorium; the back, a perforated metal screen acoustically transparent in the upper boxes but reflective near the stage to support the musicians, and the rear of the tower, which is similarly treated. Low frequency sound passes through the screens, bounces off the side walls of the auditorium, and re-enters the room. High frequency sound is reflected and scattered by the wooden panels on the box fronts. To preserve low

FROM ABOVE: Flipper adjustment mechanism for proscenium stage opening; flipper – top view of the flipper mechanism, in a horizontal configuration. The flipper is the key element at the proscenium that allows for two fire curtain lines plus finished ceiling in multiple positions. The top of the flipper is covered with a material for fire separation

frequency energy, the walls and roof of the auditorium and fly-tower are massive and reflective, either reinforced concrete or reinforced solid-grouted masonry. This posed major structural challenges both for design and construction.

All public bathrooms are in their own seismically and acoustically separated box – a floating slab on a sandbed – at ground level, adjacent to the curved rear wall of the auditorium. All associated pipe and ductwork is vibration isolated. All major plant is separately housed in the mechanical tower, seismically and vibration separated from the auditorium structure.

The auditorium contains sophisticated sound and lighting systems: theatre sound, technical intercom, paging and show relay, video, a master antenna television system, control units containing communications facilities for stage management and technical usage, a hard of hearing system and a portable sound system. The theatre is one of only two in California designed to be used for major recording sessions. Stringent criteria were applied to the design and detailing of the air distribution system. More than seven hundred and fifty dimmers are used to control the lighting.

Deliberately set off-axis, the lobby is much more than a place of assembly and dispersal. Its three upper floors overlook an internal courtyard which can be used as a performance space. Leading up to the circulation spaces behind the auditorium balconies is a monumental staircase – cast *in-situ* concrete – the set piece of the lobby, whose roof is just a little lower than that of the auditorium. Attached to one corner of the lobby is the 60 ft tall steel and glass box office tower. Cost cutting reduced the lobby space, but it is still generous when compared with those of, for example, New York's Broadway Theaters. The mild Southern California climate allows the gardens and courtyards to be used as extensions of the lobby. From outside it can be approached in opposite directions: by car or by foot via a walled entry court from the parking lot. The small, two-storey building for the centre's administrative staff opens onto a walled garden which it shares with the large meeting room.

A tall, single-storey, column-free area, the meeting block can accommodate up to four hundred for banquets. A grid of tracks for operable partitions allows it to be divided into as many as five individual, sound-isolated meeting rooms. The room is theatrically equipped with lighting and sound systems, rigging trusses, self-climbing chain hoists, draperies, a portable stage platform and a portable dance floor. A telescopic seating unit provides seats for one hundred and sixty. The room can be used as a rehearsal space while the main auditorium is being used, as well as accommodating small theatre groups or musical ensembles. Its proximity to the hotel, allows it to serve as an extra conference facility. A two-storey wing houses a kitchen and bathrooms.

The mechanical tower is a five-storey square building, housing chillers, boilers, fans, cooling towers and air-handlers. The concept of a completely separate mechanically dedicated structure springs from the need for acoustical isolation and the architectural desire to avoid a single

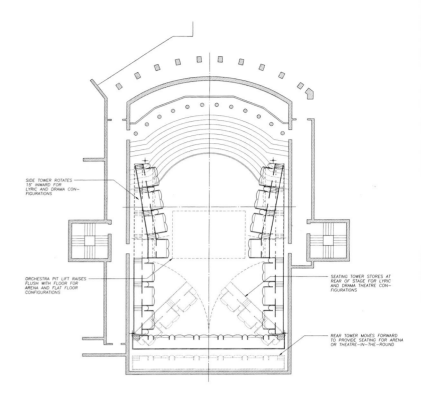

SIDE TOWER ROTATES 15° INWARD FOR LYRIC AND DRAMA CONFIGURATIONS

ORCHESTRA PIT LIFT RAISES FLUSH WITH FLOOR FOR ARENA AND FLAT FLOOR CONFIGURATIONS

SEATING TOWER STORES AT REAR OF STAGE FOR LYRIC AND DRAMA THEATRE CONFIGURATIONS

REAR TOWER MOVES FORWARD TO PROVIDE SEATING FOR ARENA OR THEATRE-IN-THE-ROUND

Seating tower movement patterns

monolith. Problems of air intake, exhaust access to equipment and acoustical separation are all solved by the presence of the mechanical tower. Its mass, taller than everything except the auditorium and fly-tower, and topped by four small pyramid roofs and a flagpole, is an essential part of the cascade of roofs, towers and shadows that help so large a theatre to sit comfortably in its surroundings.

In California, matters are arranged a little differently from the United Kingdom. First, most of southern California is in Seismic Zone 4, as defined by the Uniform Building Code; that specifies substantial lateral forces for which buildings are to be designed. Second, the investigation and the selection of the type and capacity of the foundations are the responsibility of independent geotechnical engineers.

The soil investigation by Moore and Taber, geotechnical engineers, revealed silts, clays and sands, with a design ground water level only 4 ft below the orchestra slab on grade. The recommended foundations for all buildings were driven pre-stressed, pre-cast concrete piles 14 in^2, varying from 20 ft to 60 ft in length. The geotechnical engineer designed a permanent pumped de-watering system for the site, but nevertheless the piles beneath the deep orchestra pits were designed to cope with full hydrostatic uplift minus the weight of the pits, in case the de-watering pumps failed.

The centre is arranged as a series of five seismically separated structures. As a result, each building apart from the auditorium, has a regular layout for its lateral system and could, therefore, be designed using the static lateral force procedures of the Uniform Building Code. The separations also enabled each building to have a lateral system compatible with its function. For example, the mechanical tower uses a steel ductile moment frame which allows airflow through the exterior screen wall to the air-handling units and permits easy installation or removal of large equipment, while the auditorium shear walls provide lateral strength and stiffness at the same time as acoustical mass.

Prior to the 1980 Uniform Building Code, the requirement for dynamic analysis was determined by the building official who had jurisdiction. For this project it was agreed during the schematic design phase that, due to the building's box-like nature, it could be designed using equivalent static lateral force procedures and the most stringent K-factor, 1.33. The building could then be designed for an assumed distribution of mass.

When the building was submitted for plan check a year later, the 1988 Uniform Building Code had just been issued, and under its provision a dynamic analysis was required for the auditorium building. The owner authorized Arups to carry out this requirement to verify the adequacy of the original static analysis design. The analysis showed that once the dynamic base shear was scaled to meet the static base shear, as required by code, the stress levels and behaviour of the structure closely matched those predicted by the static analysis. The dynamic analysis also showed some localized excitation of the fly-tower columns, in excess of that anticipated from the static analysis. As a result, two columns and

FROM ABOVE: The model in plan shows how the complex was split into five different buildings: the auditorium on the left, the mechanical tower directly adjacent the main lobby, the office block, and the meeting room on the right; structure of a seating tower in construction – the tube steel moment frame of the tower becomes architecturally exposed in the final room. At the base of the tower, the grillage of steel provides the support interface with the air castors below

some details were revised.

Our dynamic model was constructed and its response spectrum analysed using SAP90, a commercially available software package. The model had eight-hundred-and-eighty nodes, seven-hundred-and-fifty-one shell elements, three-hundred-and-eighty-seven frame elements and four-thousand-two-hundred-and-sixty-one degrees of freedom; forty vibrational modes were combined to achieve at least ninety percent mass participation. The building weighs approximately 16,400 kips and the design base shear from the maximum probable earthquake is 3825 kips.

The transverse shear walls are full height, 12 in thick reinforced concrete, varying in strength from 3000-5000 lbs/in². Ove Arup designed the temporary props for these walls, and in fact for the whole auditorium structure, under an appointment by the general contractor. The proscenium wall is 95 ft tall with an opening 42 ft high and 94 ft wide. The curved lobby wall contains substantial reinforced concrete pilasters to support the balcony cantilevers. Steel pilaster columns provide out-of-plane support for the stage wall.

The longitudinal auditorium walls began life as reinforced concrete with steel pilasters, but were cost-driven to reinforced masonry with embedded steel pilasters for out-of-plane support of the wall and gravity support of the main steel roof trusses.

The three warped and curved balconies are supported by deep radial, sloping, tapering, curved beams that cantilever from the rear wall pilasters. The balconies are cast as dished slabs onto which steps are later cast, in order to achieve the best control of final balcony elevations for the sight lines.

The auditorium and fly-tower roofs are supported by steel N-trusses. The flat fly-tower roof, of hardrock concrete on metal deck, has 6 ft deep trusses, spanning from proscenium to rear stage wall. Suspended from these trusses are the gridiron, three levels of catwalks and the loft blocks. The headsteel spans 72 ft, supporting 191 kips horizontally and 231 kips vertically. Most of its load comes from the pulleys over which the scenery counterweight cables run.

The vaulted auditorium roof, of lightweight concrete on metal deck, is carried by 12 ft deep trusses, spanning from side wall column to side wall column. Their bottom chords support 4 in thick pre-cast dense concrete ceiling panels. These trusses also support the lighting bridges and architectural ceiling, whose shape followed both acoustical and lighting considerations. Steel pipes and angles and wooden panels are used in both bridges and ceiling panels.

The lobby is a steel-framed structure, at its lower levels engaging the auditorium, office building and large meeting room. Above, it is approximately 80 ft². Its perimeter moment frame is designed as a back up to the monumental concrete stair which acts as a very stiff cantilevering shear wall – thus attracting most of the lateral load in an earthquake. A two-way steel truss carries the roof. The moment-framed 60 ft x 10 ft x 10 ft structure of the box office tower was fabricated in one piece off-site. It has a specially detailed sliding connection that permits earthquake induced movement independent of

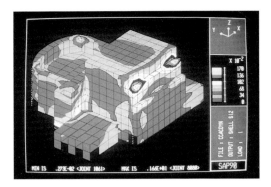

FROM ABOVE: Dynamic analysis for seismic loads – the hall was analysed structurally with a finite element analysis. The analysis showed the highest regions of stress (yellow & red) where the rear folded-plate wall steps down, and low stress levels at the CMU walls (purple); auditorium roof framing – the auditorium area is framed with 100ft long steel trusses. To achieve a double layer of acoustic isolation, the vaulted roof was poured with regular weight concrete on deck, and the attic used pre-cast panels that set into the bottom chord of the trusses. The lighting bridges hang from the trusses; balcony forming – the balconies are warped, being highest at the middle and sloping to either side. To achieve the form and to control vibrations, cast-in-place concrete was used for a series of radial beams that taper to 6 in at the front edge. The beams were skim-coated with plaster to create the finished ceiling

the lobby in one direction while linking them perpendicularly.

The 80 ft steel roof trusses of the large meeting room are supported by perimeter sheer walls of reinforced masonry. The office block, like the large meeting room, has reinforced masonry sheer walls. Its suspended floor and roof are steel-framed with lightweight concrete on metal deck. The 28 ft² by 72 ft tall mechanical tower has lightweight concrete on metal deck floors supported by a steel frame. The lateral system is a perimeter ductile moment frame. It is clad with a screen wall of reinforced masonry panels made of square blocks with openings in them.

The special features are:
- The stringent acoustical design criteria
- The flexible ductwork for the moveable seating towers
- The purpose-built supply plenum diffusers in the auditorium, stage and large meeting room
- Compliance with California's strict Title 24 energy requirements
- The seismic anchorage and restraint needed to deal with Seismic Zone 4
- The structurally separated mechanical tower
- The stage sprinklers

The acoustical performance criteria were specified by Kirkegaard Associates in terms of room criteria (RC) and preferred noise criteria (PNC) and are listed in Table One. Both RC and PNC are sets of curves on graphs of sound pressure level versus octave band.

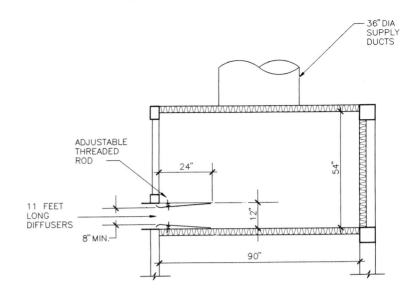

Table One

Performance space	Acoustical criterion
Audience and stage areas	PNC-15
Control rooms audio	PNC-20
Control room lighting and projection	RC-25
Orchestra pit	PNC-15
Underseat storage areas	PNC-20
Dressing rooms	RC-30
Lobby areas	RC-25
Meeting room	PNC-20
Kitchen	RC-30
Administrative areas	RC-35
Spaces opening on stage/in house	PNC-20

Kirkegaard recommended, for acoustically sensitive spaces, low velocity, low pressure air-distribution from remotely-located air handling equipment. Constant volume systems were preferred over variable volume. Ducts are lined and provided with silencers.

The lowest level of the mechanical tower houses two centrifugal chillers, each with a cooling capacity of 273 tons, specially modified to use ASHRAE Standard R-123 refrigerant. This is a chlorofluorocarbon, but with a hydrogen atom replacing one of the fluorine or chlorine atoms in its structure to make it less stable, so it will break down in the lower atmosphere and not get to the stratosphere. Chilled water is supplied at 44°F and returns at 56°F. The chillers are served by two centrifugal counterflow cooling towers at the top of

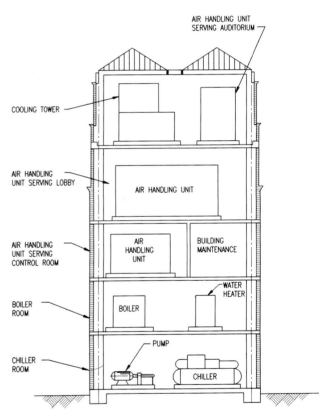

FROM ABOVE: Vertical section through auditorium seating tower, plenum and diffuser; mechanical tower

the mechanical tower. Water enters at 95°F and leaves at 85°F. Hot water is supplied by two natural gas-fired boilers. Supply temperature is 185°F and return temperature 165°F.

The auditorium is served by a constant volume, single-zone system with supply and return fans. Air is at high level from specially designed side wall plena diffusers and extracted low down the auditorium sides and beneath the balconies. Large supply and return ducts link the air handlers in the mechanical tower with the roof space above the auditorium ceiling, where ductwork is carefully integrated with roof trusses.

Each group of supply and extract terminations is fed from the main air-handling units via a separate, self-balancing, ductwork system with no dampers. All auditorium air termination devices are specially designed to provide the required air distribution with minimum generated noise. The lobby also uses a constant volume, single-zone system with supply and return fans. The meeting rooms use a multi-zone, constant volume system with supply and return fans. The office building uses a variable volume system.

Title 24 of The California Administrative Code contains limits on the energy consumption of buildings and rules for calculations. This was not written with theatres in mind, and so interpretation is a matter of negotiation between the designers and the plan checkers. It sets minimum standards for wall and roof insulation, for window insulation and shading coefficients, and for equipment efficiencies. Arups calculated the annual energy consumption of the buildings, using industry-developed energy simulation software approved by the California Energy Commission.

To deal with possible earthquakes, all mechanical equipment is seismically anchored. Some can simply be bolted down. Other equipment, supported on vibration isolation platforms, is restrained by devices that limit its travel when the ground shakes. Seismic anchorage of pipes and ducts is largely but not entirely covered by guidelines published by the Sheet Metal and Air Conditioning Contractors National Association, the design of which is generally the responsibility of the mechanical subcontractor. At the seismic separations between buildings, special connections are provided to allow substantial relative movement caused by earthquakes.

In California, detailed design of sprinklers is carried out by specially licensed contractors working to the designers' performance specification. Fire suppression and smoke extraction within the stagehouse received a lot of attention from the City Fire Marshal. The agreed scheme has gridiron level deluge sprinklers, low level high velocity horizontal

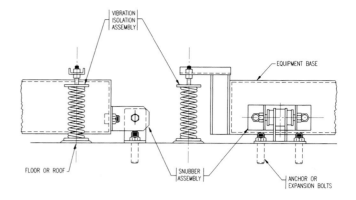

Vibration-isolated equipment restrained by snubbers

throw sprinklers on opposite sides of the stage, smoke extract vents in the fly-tower roof, and forced smoke extraction via low level ductwork when the concert ceiling is in place.

The Arts Centre receives a 4000A, 277/480V three-phase, four-wire service from the Southern California Edison Company. The main electrical room is at the lowest level of the mechanical tower, acoustically isolated from the auditorium. From the main switchboard, power is distributed via transformers to two distribution switchboards at 120/208V. The first switchboard is in the main electrical room, the second on an isolated slab in the dimmer room of the theatre. The main circuit breakers are rated at 1600A and 3000A respectively. Flexible connections limit noise transmission from the transformers. Panel board locations were carefully chosen to meet the differing needs of the architect and electrical engineer.

As with the mechanical systems, it was necessary for the electrical design to show compliance with the energy conservation requirements of Title 24. Based on work by the Illumination Engineering Society, Title 24 relates allowable power consumption to functional categories and is very task-oriented. Theatrical lighting exists as much for art as for the carrying out of tasks, and Title 24 thus is difficult to apply to theatres, with interpretation again negotiated by designers and plan checkers.

Power, sound and lighting for the moveable seating towers are supplied either via flexible conduits or by unplugging, moving the towers, and plugging in again. Some theatrical productions generate smoke on stage, and to prevent that from activating the smoke detectors at high level over the stage there is a bypass switch operated by the stage manager, which shuts down the detectors for four hours. Emergency power is provided by a 400kW generator.

Theatre Projects and Barton Myers developed the lighting concepts for the main public spaces, while Arups incorporated the lighting within the total electrical design of the Arts Centre. Many of the public areas incorporate timers as part of their lighting controls. In the theatre, lighting falls into four categories: house, concert, stage and work lighting; all controlled via seven-hundred-and-sixty-six dimmer channels, all with full memory, from the main console at the rear and from local panels around the stage and auditorium. The large meeting room has sixty control channels for one-hundred-and-ninety-two dimmers.

As this project was designed in US units, these have been retained here.

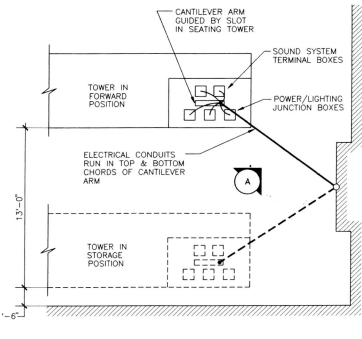

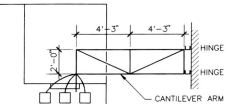

Flexible service connections to seating towers

THE INTERNATIONAL CONVENTION CENTRE
BIRMINGHAM, ENGLAND

This concert hall will seat two thousand two hundred and will be used for concerts, popular music, convention events and other entertainment. The acoustic criteria for this hall is the most stringent of all halls at the International Convention Centre, and has been the major factor in determining its location within the complex in order to ensure that noise and vibration from a nearby railway tunnel will be inaudible within the hall itself. A British Rail main line tunnel runs diagonally from the north-west corner of the site to the middle of the east side of the site, and trains passing through the tunnel generate ground borne vibrations which can be transmitted through a building structure and heard unless special precautions are taken. The noise levels associated with these vibrations reduce with distance from the tunnel.

Early measurements of vibrations originating from the railway line demonstrated that they would be extremely difficult to dampen sufficiently to prevent the symphony hall being affected by passing trains. Therefore, a graduated set of aims was agreed whereby those buildings, such as the exhibition/banqueting space, for which vibration noise was not so critical, could be situated directly above the railway tunnel, whereas those that were extremely sensitive, such as the symphony hall, were located as far from the railway as possible. Artec established the following design targets for sound pressure levels in the 63 Hz octave band, due to the passage of trains through the tunnel.

Hall	Peak Lp	63 Hz Octave Band
2	30	Trains inaudible
1 & 5	40	Trains just audible
6,7,8,9,10 &11	45	Trains more audible
3 & 4	65	Trains audible

In order to design for the above targets it was necessary to provide single structural isolation for many of the halls. However, through the careful disposition of hall one – an approximate minimum distance of 15 m from the tunnel – and the symphony hall – an approximate minimum distance of 35 m from the tunnel – it was possible to avoid extremely complex and costly double isolation.

A series of vibration dampening measures was devised which, as the location planning of the halls proceeded, were developed for each building in relation to the degree of suppression required. Unfortunately, these measures alone were unlikely to be sufficient to meet the noise level targets. Double isolation at foundation level was considered, but was rejected on the grounds of complexity, cost and uncertainty about the result.

Discussions were held with British Rail Midland Region about anti-vibration measures at track level. However, the location of the tracks near the base of a Victorian brick arch, together with the intensive use of the line, excluded the possibility of major isolation measures through a new track foundation system. Fortunately, British Rail was planning to re-lay the rails through the tunnel over a two-year period (1989-91) and agreed to place composite elastomer pads between the sleepers and the ballast during track re-laying. This measure would not only benefit the concert hall, but also all of the others, including the nearby repertory theatre which had suffered from railway noise since its construction in the early seventies. With the adoption of this additional measure, it was considered that with very careful workmanship the noise level targets could be achieved.

Consequently, the hall is located at the southern edge of the site adjacent to Broad Street and on the axis of the Civic Square. The building, which rises to some 28 m above pavement, will provide an effective closure to the western end of the square. At the same time the building's size required careful handling, stepping down in order to achieve a scale appropriate to the buildings in Broad Street.

Four main foyers service the hall at stalls, first, second and third tier levels and these will accommodate bars, toilets and lifts and also provide access to the lettable offices and ancillary spaces planned adjacent to the hall. These foyers overlook the mall and the Civic Square and will provide a dynamic, glittering spectacle at night. Access to the symphony hall for the public is directly from the mall, but the design will allow for a separation of concert goers and convention delegates if required.

In the symphony hall Artec have adopted a rectangular form in order to obtain the strong lateral sound that gives listeners the impression of envelopment in the music. As this could not be built of heavy reinforced concrete with dense quality finishes in plaster and stone, achieving the acoustic performance parameters, the structural elements have been carefully detailed using isolation techniques.

Building materials and the concert room
The halls recognized as the world's best concert halls were generally completed prior to 1905. These older halls have walls that are of solid load bearing construction more than one metre thick. The ceilings and soffits are typically of

heavy plaster construction. These materials in tall narrow rectangular rooms are conducive to a live acoustical environment. The hardness and heaviness of the building materials makes them highly reflective to all audible sound, effectively conserving the sound of musical instruments. This produces an excellent foundation for the symphony acoustics, but the acoustic of other users must also be considered; for instance using a sound system in a live acoustical environment leads to a muddled boomy sound.

Variable acoustics

The staging requirements for different users are relatively easily accommodated, whilst the acoustic requirements of the different events however are not, and many design ideas have been tried in the search for a successful solution to this problem. In some schemes the acoustical designer has sought a middle ground between the requirements for amplified speech and those for music. Yet, such rooms are invariably too dead for music and too live for amplified speech.

The design approach adopted for the symphony hall is instantly variable natural room acoustics, allowing concert music to be performed in a live acoustical environment and the sound system to be used in a dead environment. This design utilizes three principal devices to vary the room's acoustical environment; they are the reverberation chamber, acoustic curtains and the acoustic canopy.

The reverberation chamber is a larger volume of space located immediately behind the platform, rising full height in the hall, to link with additional chambers which run along the sides of the hall at high level. This permits substantial variation of the acoustics by increasing the 'liveness' of the room, which is controlled by a series of opening 'doors'. This allows a symphony orchestra to achieve both clarity and reverberance which is a rare combination of acoustical qualities. Works from the classical repertoire require a moderately 'live' environment which will be provided by the main room with the reverberation chamber doors closed.

The acoustic curtains take the form of sliding screens containing absorbent material, drawn from concealed locations on the majority of wall surfaces. These can be adjusted to achieve a tailoring of the audible 'tail', chiefly for speech events or for use in conjunction with sound systems. These curtains are specially motorized, and fabricated from several layers of heavy close knit fabrics. When extended the high resistance to the flow of air, in conjunction with the air space between it and the wall, cushions the sound as it impinges on the curtain and absorbs a portion of its acoustical energy. With the curtains extended the liveness of the room is reduced, as the sound decays more quickly to inaudibility, and the muddling of sound systems is virtually eliminated.

As the third principal device to vary the aural environment, the canopy is a large heavy acoustical reflector positioned above the orchestra and front part of the stalls. The height of the canopy is easily adjustable and may be set at any level up to 24 m above the stage. It aids in matching the scale of the performance, both visual and acoustic, to the scale of the room, and facilitates communication between musicians on the concert platforms.

The height of the canopy will be set according to the scale of the performance. Small-scale performances, which would otherwise be dwarfed by the scale of the sending end of the room will use a lower canopy height to set a smaller visual scale. For large-scale performances, the canopy will be set near its highest setting and the aural impression will be one of a large acoustic space. The requirement for an imperforate surface above the concert platform means that many technical systems must be accommodated in the canopy; including the loudspeaker array, rigging system, concert lighting, and other performance and house lighting. Thus the canopy takes on many important roles in addition to its primary acoustical function.

Critical listeners often observe that rectangular, shoe box rooms have better acoustics for music than fan-shaped rooms of similar size. Those halls, generally accepted as the world's greatest concert halls – the Musikvereinsaal in Vienna, the Concertgebouw in Amsterdam and Symphony Hall in Boston – are all basically rectangular in plan and section and would seat audiences of less than two thousand by present-day standards.

In the past, the acoustical success of these old halls has been attributed to their reverberation time, criteria that have been shown to be unreliable indicators of acoustical quality. Instead, objective acoustical characteristics, that relate more reliably to listener preference, have been established by recent investigations and some of these are strongly influenced by room shape. Much of the recent research into auditorium acoustics relates to lateral sound; the sound reflected by the surfaces in a room and arriving at the listener from the sides. Studies have shown that strong lateral sound can mean the difference between the perception of a flat monophonic sound and an enveloping stereophonic sound. Other positive attributes relating to lateral sound

include warmth and richness of tone, enhanced loudness
and intimacy.

Auditoria technical systems

The technical systems for the symphony hall are configured
to support the variety of convention events, concerts, meetings and entertainment envisaged.

Production lighting positions will be located in the front of
house ceiling, on the canopy and in the side stage areas. A
computer-based control system will memorize the levels
required for each circuit and assist in the orderly play back of
cues. Controls for auditorium and utility work lights will also
be provided, as well as projectors for 35 mm and 16 mm film.
When film projection is required a rolled screen can be
hoisted from a storage position within the stage surface. For
this type of hoisting, and other stage rigging, a series of
moveable point-hoist winches can be set at various locations
to suit the particular need.

For symphonic music, the orchestra sits on a number of
stepped terraces known as the riser, which allows them to
have clear sight lines to the conductor and also the audience
on the main floor who look at the platform almost horizontally,
and vice versa. This is vital to the acoustic design, firstly it
plays an important part in the achievement of clarity, definition and loudness of the orchestra, and secondly it improves
the hearing conditions of the musicians on the platform and
thus the ensemble. Great halls – including the Vienna
Musikvereinsaal, the Amsterdam Concertgebouw and the
Zurich Tonhallesaal – have permanent fixed riser units. The
solid construction of these units contributes to the acoustical
characteristics that give them their good reputations.

Orchestras in North America have experimented extensively with various ways of arranging the musicians on flat
stages, principally because many of the orchestras have to
perform in multi-purpose venues. However, none has found a
satisfactory solution, and many are forced to accept fewer
risers than they require because of the labour costs of
manually installing and taking down multiple rostra units;
unfortunately these tend to appear temporary due to wear
and tear, and the need to keep them light enough to handle.
Acoustically their reduced mass means that the low frequency response of the cello and basses is inferior to that

experienced in good halls.

The solution developed in the design of the symphony hall is a wagon that is powered and moves on and off the platform. The surface and structural part of the wagon are constructed from wood with a special damping design to act as a sounding board. This will enhance the mechanical coupling with the instruments that rest on the floor, and thus efficiently radiate low frequency sound. A much more solid structure is employed in the floor areas beneath the other instruments. This wagon will be used for symphony performances, but can, with a small stage crew, be moved off the stage for non-symphony uses.

The seats on the side and rear of the platform double as chorus seating for choral concerts. Similarly, the front ten rows can be retracted from the stage to provide a larger concert platform, or be removed altogether to provide clear access all around the platform for 'open stage' events.

Additional considerations

The auditorium is fully air-conditioned, and the design will incorporate very low velocity air input arrangements, through a combination of balcony level outlets to the main space and an under seat system at the rear. Extract will mainly be at high level. Extremely low velocities are necessary to ensure a noiseless system consistent with the required criteria. The balcony tiers also contain all the electrical and sound system services, lighting points and air conditioning ducts. Percy Thomas and Ove Arup worked together to integrate these systems into the smallest achievable structure and to perfect their performance. This special low velocity air system is unique to this hall, with air entering at a very low velocity through slots in the balcony edges and gently wafting over the audience. The air delivery slots and curved edge detail were developed to allow the air to move smoothly over the edge profile. The design and concealment of all ducts and wiring services required for the hall itself took many months of work to carefully integrate, whilst avoiding any intrusion on the classical simplicity of the surfaces of the room. The curved edge detail was used throughout the edges of all projecting soffits and bulkheads and became a powerful design image in itself, in 'tune' with the general curved geometry.

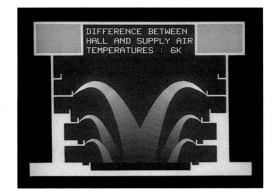

Air movement within auditorium

TADAO ANDO
KARA-ZA THEATER

Tokyo, Japan

For those only generally familiar with his work, the name of Tadao Ando suggests severely minimal, modernist buildings usually made of concrete, which are so carefully crafted that even the tie-holes are perfectly formed. In his sparse interiors, typically intended as durable receptacles of natural light, the traditional Japanese desire to connect architecture with nature is raised to a higher non-literal level and a delicate balance between east and west is struck. Light was the sacred substance of the Modern Movement, transmitting a healthier future, and encouraging use of glass and concrete or the steel frame. Louis Kahn elevated it to mystical proportions, as the shaper of space and form, his last hope for bringing social change. There are many other parallels between Ando's work and Kahn's, men from entirely different backgrounds and cultures determined to find a message in light. The most striking, revealed by this theatre is the increasing depth of an exceptional talent and a more literal expression of his culture.

The Kara-za, which takes its name from the avant-garde group led by Kara Joko, is a moveable six-hundred-seat theatre. The project began with the idea to build a permanent play house in Asakura, Tokyo, and a tall wooden structure much like a watch tower was the first design that Ando produced. The client then changed the brief and asked that the building should not be permanent, so the structure was changed to the pipes used as scaffolding on construction sites in Japan. Comparisons with Aldo Rossi's Teatro del Mondo immediately come to mind, with the difference saying much about the variety possible within a rational agenda and world view. Wishing to make his *Teatro* portable, Rossi built it on a barge, which was extremely appropriate for Venice and adjusted its scale to fit in anywhere in the city, an interchangeable typology that seems inevitable everywhere it is anchored. Ando, on the other hand, avoided the transportation problem entirely, choosing materials that are available throughout the world, so that with a set of his drawings, the building can be reconstructed in about two weeks. The drawings, of course, can also be electronically transmitted.

The plan of the theatre is a dodecagon, 27 m wide and the building is 27 m high. The exterior walls are black siding boards and the roof is a red tent. The approach, by arched bridge, symbolises the passage from reality to the world of illusion, from this world into the world to come. A Buddhist term *hican*, meaning the world after death, was the image that Ando was seeking and the black play house is surrounded by a traditional fence of woven bamboo, known as *takeyarai*, to emphasize the otherworldly nature of the theatrical space. Ando has described the project thus:

I kept in mind the memory of Kanamaruza in Shikoku, one of the oldest remaining Japanese theatres that has greatly impressed me. Within the simple wooden shelter actors and audience were close together and this established a highly intense relationship. It was there that I learned the true nature of dramatic art. I have rarely experienced similar sensations in modern theatres, where everything is mechanized. After the experience of Kanamaruza, I wished to create a theatre that would ring to the sound of a human voice.

Due to an initial lack of funds, the theatre had to be used as a temporary pavilion at the Tokoku exhibition, but was finally reconstructed in Asakura near Sumida Park, opening in April 1988. A vertical truss, constructed from tubular scaffolding with threaded rods for cross-tie chords, is used to support the external walls, whilst the roof trusses that hold up the red tent – symbolizing the one that Kara Joko used to set up when on tour – are supported by a king post in the centre of the dodecagon. Stability is provided by cross bars tied to fixing plates, and all stage equipment can be hung or clamped to stanchions or cables connected to the walls.

Ando praises the tenacity of the troupe leader and his creativity as an encouragement for the architect to do more with less. The result is one of his most evocative and least permanent buildings and, perhaps, the closest yet to his own rich heritage.

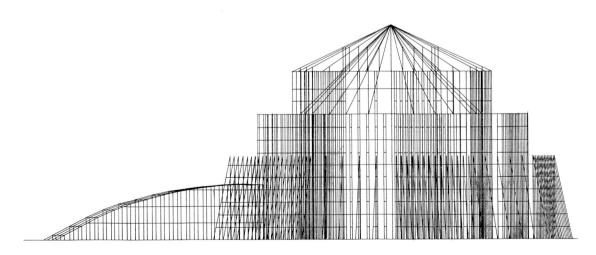

Exposed structural elevation

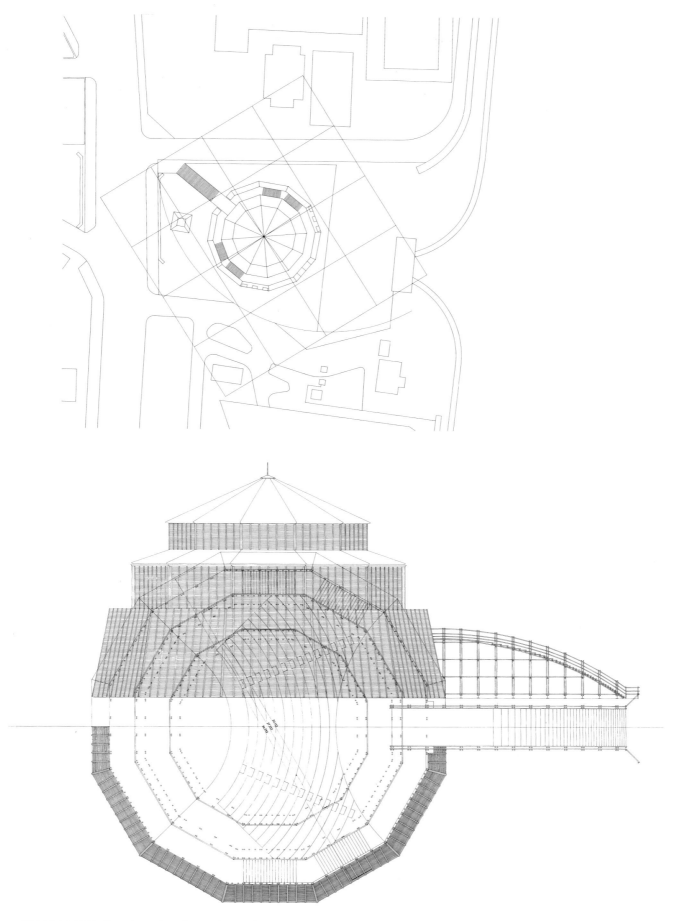

FROM ABOVE: Site plan; elevation and part plan

MARIO BOTTA
ANDRE MALRAUX CULTURAL CENTRE
Chambéry, France

After an open competition in which three finalists were chosen, Mario Botta has succeeded in receiving the commission for this cultural complex because of his recognition of the need to incorporate an existing gendarmerie into his plan. The 19th-century barracks, once used as a police posting in this small town in the foothills of the French Alps, has been restored in the process, and the east wing has been adapted for use as the theatre lobby, as well as housing an art gallery, offices and rehearsal rooms. Jean Patrick Fortier has restored the gendarmerie.

There had been hopes that this cultural centre would be the focal point of a new residential development by Henri Ciriani, but a lack of funds has stalled those plans, and the plaza in front of the theatre, which was expected to have been so full of life, is still rather barren and wind-swept. Unfortunately the theatre was intended by Botta to form a linchpin between this proposed residential zone and the barrack's quandrangle.

The main entrance to the theatre is located at the juncture with the Napoleonic barracks. From here the audience pass under the raked floor of the semicircular main auditorium, the outer perimeter of which is a high, narrow clerestoried space, providing access to their seats. Botta also utilizes the rake of the seating to conceal the volume of the cinema, located on the ground floor.

The fly-tower and its associated appendages form the second major volume of Botta's geometric puzzle, its rectilinear stability offsetting the sweep of the theatrical hemicycle which it is carefully articulated against. In contrast to the bicycle spoke trusses that make up the theatre roof, the tower is more conventionally structured, with concrete beams above. This volume also contains the stage highlighting the paradox common to most theatres: the creativity of the stage is contained within the most rigid form, whilst the passivity of the audience is contained within the most flamboyant form.

The perimeter, or public face of the cultural centre, is one of Botta's most eloquent urban statements to date, even though the reciprocal city has not yet surrounded it. The historical sources – include fortresses and Romanesque churches – emerge here in the massive outer walls which face the plaza, sliced or jointed only where necessary to let light into an office, or allow the expansion of the thick striated limestone cladding to occur. Theatre as castle, or church, with the dependencies around it becoming residential in scale to meet the square, the metaphors are not hard to find, as one would expect with an architect who makes no secret of seeking such typologies. The

effect here however, in this primal natural and urban landscape seems more than just passingly appropriate, the simple grandeur of the theatre perfectly in tune with its surroundings.

The simple, almost severe exterior, on which the only sign of capriciousness is the emergency exit stair and the geode-soft glass interior exposed by the eroded outer shell, is a stark contrast to the elegant auditorium inside. The nine-hundred-and-fifty seat theatre has the plushest seats of any of the halls included here, the final reward for an unremittingly hard exterior shell, a long vertical climb along a barren brick wall, and the cold comfort of crisp detailing. The exterior emphasis on stone is continued here as well, in the curving inner auditorium wall with alternating smooth and jagged bands reminiscent of much of Botta's seemingly endless inventiveness with materials that others consider to be mundane. The result is one of the finest interiors of any of those to be found today: one which is not slavishly formed and fitted out according to acoustic considerations. Instead it is balanced, serene, comfortable, easy to get in and out of, and most importantly able to serve as a backdrop for the ineffable transfer of energy between actor and audience. Botta has not ignored the most important of all dictums in theatre design; he has kept it simple.

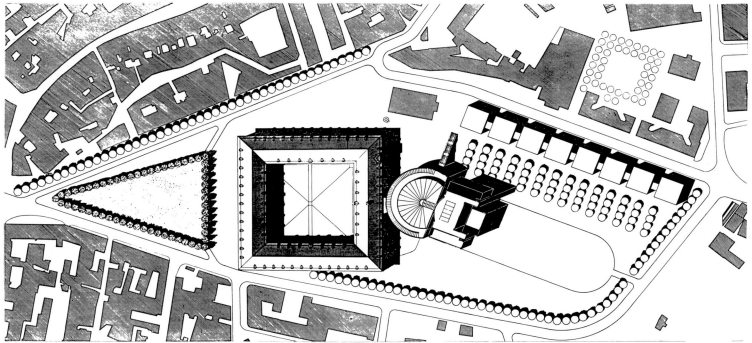

Site plan

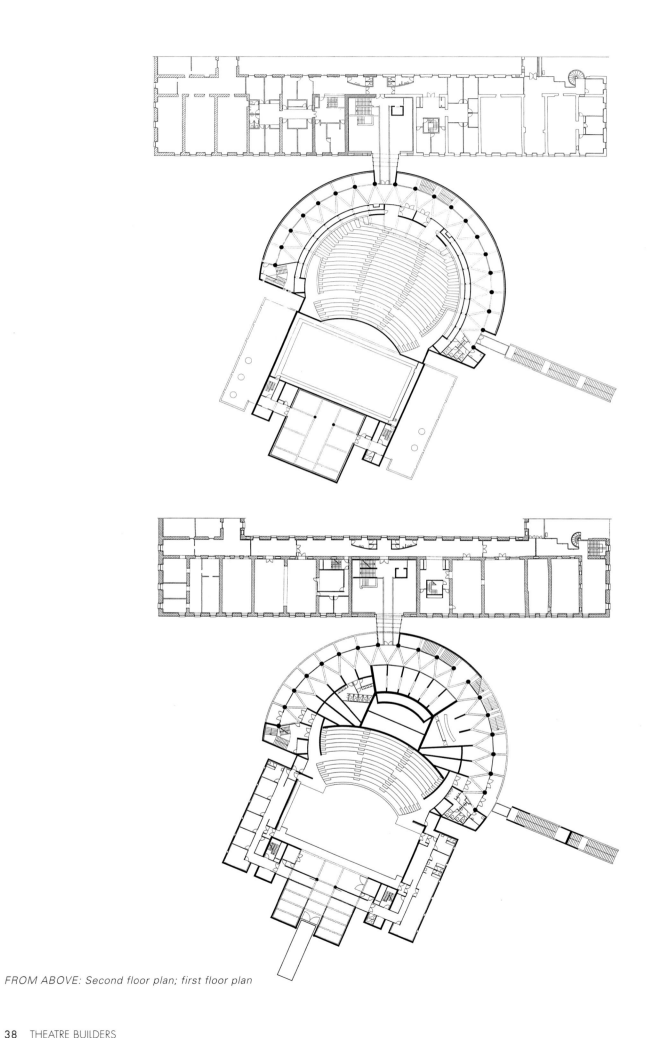

FROM ABOVE: Second floor plan; first floor plan

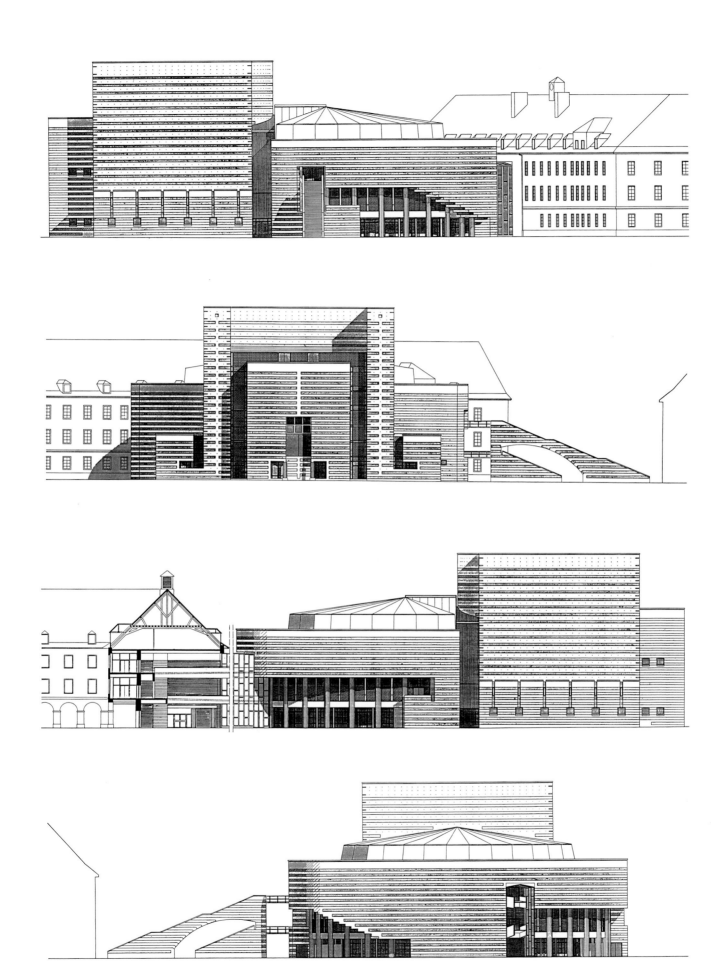

FROM ABOVE: North elevation; east elevation; south elevation; west elevation

MARIO BOTTA
PALAZZO DEL CINEMA AL LIDO
Venice, Italy

The commentary on Venice begun by Louis Kahn in his Congress Hall scheme in the early seventies continues here, with incontrovertible evidence, if it were needed, provided by Botta of his debt to his mentor. This debt could also be proven by earlier attempts, through a thorough analysis of his school at Morbio, or house at Ligornetta, among other equally obvious examples, which each rely upon the extension of a mural line to define territory, or to differentiate various characteristics of a region.

In this instance the territory is the Lido, the least textural part of the fabled island city, being most in need of urban direction. The only significant piece of context offered to the architect, aside from the seemingly limitless expanse of flat shoreline, is the Municipal Casino, built just before the Second World War, with its dominant art deco façade facing the sea, and a square entry projecting past the streamlined flat front to announce the foyer and central hall. Botta has taken this theme and combined it with Kahn's original *parti* for his unbuilt hall, adding 'prow'-like projections, albeit tongue in cheek. The placement of his hall, with the axis of the 'keel' spanning between a canal running behind the site and the seashore in front, gave him the opportunity to face the Via Candia and the Via Quattro Fontane, which run along each side, with a low arcaded element representing the 'berth'. Positioning the axis parallel to that of its art deco *alter ego* next door enabled Botta once again to demonstrate his unparalleled talent for establishing position, claiming territory, setting boundaries, and creating an organizing framework for future growth.

By pulling his mostly rectilinear footprint beyond the façade of the Municipal Casino, toward the Lungomare, and replicating the line of trees in a park opposite, Botta has achieved several important strategic goals. The first is that he has managed to evoke both the scale and the massing of the older building, by using its module, width and length, but by changing the shape of the inner halls and moving his building forward, has avoided any possible hint of direct derivation. Secondly, by his decisive move toward the sea, and gesture of formal landscaping, he has created a civic piazza in front of his neighbour which did not exist before; a gracious urban gesture that none of the other participants in the competition, with the exception of Carlo Aymonino and Aldo Rossi, even considered to be an important aspect of an intervention there. Of these three schemes, Botta's design is the most forthright, rational and modest of all the rationalists, in spite of the fact that Rossi recalls Roman massiveness and Aymonino attempted to reconstruct Terragni's unbuilt but much admired Palazzo de Congressi once more. Botta has intuitively realized that for the Lido to attract people, it must rival one of the most seductive cities on earth across the canal, and it presently does not. Jean Nouvel, ever sensitive to these matters, expressed this best in the description of his own entry by saying that:

Some cities are so beautiful, so attractive, so fascinating that they are fatal to their festivals, though they may be held some distance from the city centre, in closed buildings or in a place with no magic about it. The diagnosis is unequivocal: the existing site did not give one the impression of being in Venice. No one wants to come and shut themselves up here. Venice was, and always will be, a stronger magnet than its own festival . . . So, one has to be in Venice; the most one could set one's sights for is creating Venice, if possible. Venice is history

and the past. The old 1930s Palazzo del Cinema worthily attests to this fairly recent epoch, though it is remote if one considers the history of the cinema . . . Lido Island is part of Venice. But it is also distant, almost foreign. It has its own history based on modernity, enterprise, fun, fashionable vacationing and trade. It has its own memory, the high spots of which are luxury hotels, the casino and the original palazzo. The new festival facilities will have to fit into this special continuum.[1]

Botta has understood this need for transformation, in the context of the modesty required, as well as the history of the film festival itself, and the fact that Venice was the first city in the world to hold one in 1932. The 1937 Palazzo del Cinema by Luigi Quagliata, which the same architect enlarged in 1952 at the instigation of the director Antonio Petrucci, has now outlived its usefulness, but must not be disregarded, and Botta has honoured it.

Internally, the new palazzo is ingeniously divided into two symmetrically organized, bilateral halls orientated towards the Lungomare, with the main entrance, utilizing void created by the rake of the seating above. Characteristically, a small detail, the serration of the 'prow', facing the sea, makes it more distinct and lifts the pragmatic use of brick to another more formal level. If Venice is to rival Cannes, the growth of the festival should happen in a logical, measured way, with the heritage surrounding the event, and the city in which it is located, constantly in mind.

Notes
1 Jean Nouvel, *Domus*, (Italy) no 730, Summer 1991, p61.

FROM ABOVE: Sectional perspective; exterior perspective

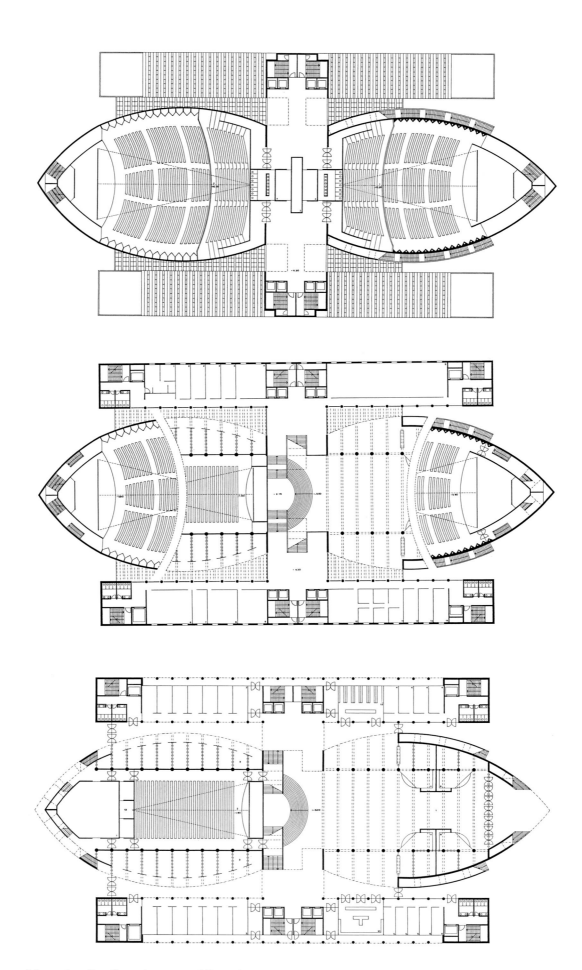

FROM ABOVE: Second floor plan; first floor plan; ground floor plan

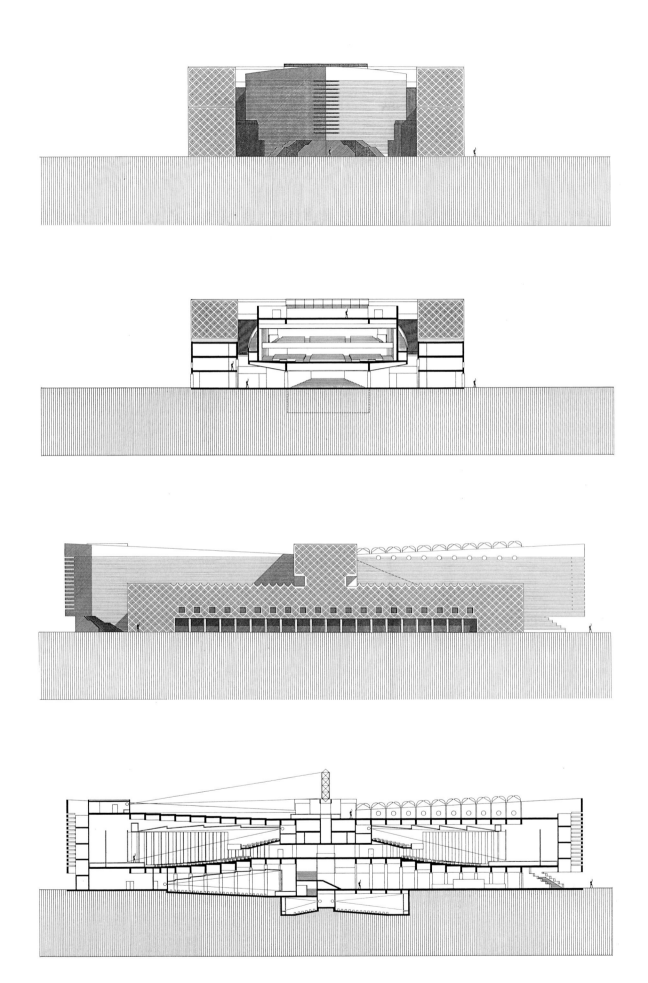

FROM ABOVE: West elevation; cross-section; south elevation; longitudinal section

FRANK O GEHRY
WALT DISNEY CONCERT HALL
Los Angeles, California

In a commission won in stiff competition against such formidable opposition as Stirling-Wilford and Barton Myers, the Disney Hall began life in contention and continues to generate it. Designated as the permanent home of the Los Angeles Philharmonic, the concert hall will occupy a prominent site at the intersection of First Street and Grand Avenue, adjacent to the existing Music Center of Los Angeles. While the other competitors mentioned sought to make broad urban gestures intended to continue linkages already established by the Downtown Strategic Plan making the hall the epicentre of cultural regeneration at the heart of the city, Gehry has focused more on the interplay with the music centre. It is a strategy similar to that taken in his design of the Aerospace Museum, where he ignored an opportunity to respond to the major intersection of Exposition and Figueroa in favour of turning inward to strengthen the pedestrian spine on which the museum is located. It is also consistent with his 'landscape' buildings of the late seventies and eighties, which created the *faux tableaux* of an acropolis in downtown Los Angeles and a New England village in Westwood.

Following the competition, although the design altered to accommodate changes in acoustical direction, the basic tenets remained the same: an open, accessible 'front door'; a pedestrian scale frontage along Grand Avenue, and a humanitarian approach toward the backstage area, treating musicians and staff with the same importance as those of the patrons.

The concert hall is located within a public park intended to soften the acres of asphalt and concrete which surround it. The entry plaza is at the corner of First and Grand, retaining the connection to the Music Center, with a secondary entry at Second and Grand as a main access to the gardens. Unlike most concert halls, the lobby is linear, reflecting the street pattern and increasing public access; a feature which is enhanced further by the large openable glass panes which allow unhindered entry. This area will contain such enticements as a museum of the philharmonic, Disney memorabilia, a restaurant, a pre-concert amphitheatre and gift shops, making it an attraction in its own right, with an underground parking garage feeding it from below.

The pre-concert amphitheatre is especially innovative, and is an attempt to establish a link to the public with performance-related lectures, educational programmes and impromptu presentations during the day. The intent, as in many projects included here, is to open up what has historically been regarded as the bastion of upper-class sensibilities; the concert hall as an impenetrable fortress of culture. This effect is further enhanced by raising the edges of the building's 'flowerlike wrapper' to allow the average Angeleno on the street inside; a bold move in a city where high levels of immigration and a volatile multiracial mix have created a palatable sense of fear, primarily among those who have patronised the concert hall in the past. Yet, this is typical of Gehry's social conscience, which can be identified as the motive behind his use of disreputable materials in the past which gained him a reputation as an avant-garde architect in the first place

The complex forms of the exterior walls required a massive departure from Gehry's usual approach. Computers, used to calculate the curves of the clay models in automotive design, were adopted to replace the tedious and partially accurate graphic projection currently employed by the office. Using probes connected to a console, designers were able to transfer the curves and folds of the concept model directly to the computer screen, conveying all the information needed to accurately map the cladding panels: originally this was to be French limestone but cost restrictions have necessitated the use of metal sheets. Since this breakthrough, Gehry's buildings are less fragmented, with smoother sweeping surfaces.

The two-thousand-four-hundred seat auditorium, within this computer-calculated wrapper, closely follows the necessary acoustical parameters with every effort made to achieve a feeling of intimacy. The orchestra is surrounded by wooden seating blocks and additional timber forms added inside the perimeter for visual and acoustic reasons, augmenting the sculptural aspect of the interior. Skylights and a large window at the back of the Hall will allow natural light to enter during performances held during the day, contributing to the new open atmosphere that Gehry wants to convey.

ZAHA HADID
CARDIFF BAY OPERA HOUSE
Cardiff, Wales

The new home of the Welsh National Opera was taken as an opportunity by the architect to address what she has identified as 'the mutually exclusive paradigms of urban design by attempting to be both a monument and a space'. While circumstances have unfortunately prevented its realization, it provides an important example of innovative design. To achieve this Zaha Hadid created a continuous linear form that acts as a foil to the oval harbour nearby, echoing the spirit of the Cardiff master plan, and is intended to breakdown the orthogonal arrangement of traditional theatres; a 'necklace' with the concert hall as the pendant and its subsidiary appendages as the jewels on the strand.

The building was envisioned as a strong figural landmark near the waterfront, with the main opening in the deformed perimeter carefully calculated to encourage public access, as well as outdoor performances, and to enhance views of the Inner Harbour and Cardiff Bay. This design allows the perimeter block to define the surrounding urban plaza and enclose the secluded internal space within a 'single continuum', a feature which is reinforced by raising the auditorium podium slightly to emphasize the complex when seen from the direction of the Pierhead. Similarly the plaza is extended, in a continuous warped plane, into the central courtyard over the entrance. This decision caused some controversy because it exposed backstage spaces that have traditionally been hidden from public view, and has also made the lobby a dark subterranean space.

The asymmetrical shape of the concert hall, which conforms to the distorted geometry of the perimeter necklace, was intended to focus audience attention toward the forestage, stage and orchestra pit, with 'perspectival' geometry used to ease viewing and give the audience a sense of the surroundings. The radial layout, as well as the different treatment of the balconies on each side of the auditorium, contributes to the visual liveliness of the room and establishes individual territories or 'places' inside the main space. The stalls are tilted slightly toward

the performance, increasing the auditorium's intimacy, whilst the dress and upper circles have the minimum slope allowed by sightline requirements to reduce the overall height of the seating, with maximum distances kept well within the thirty metre limit. Nearly all of the one thousand seven hundred and fifty seats beyond the orchestra pit have an unobstructed view of the proscenium and stage.

Despite the fragmented appearance of the design, the plan is in fact highly resolved and hierarchical, with theatrical functions arranged around the central court and office and support functions located around the perimeter. There are also direct, functional relationships between the seemingly spontaneous form and the operation of the backstage area, acoustical performance and structural design. For instance, the loading bays are positioned to provide unhindered access to the stages and to scenery storage. Such pragmatic considerations are also evident in the location of the soloist's and conductor's dressing rooms on the first floor above the stage door, with a vertical connection to stage left. Other dressing rooms are located next to and above these, all controlled by the stage door. Laundry and costume storage, above the dressing rooms, allows simple vertical access from store to dressing to storage and back up to laundry during the repertoire season. The dressing, warm up, practice and green rooms are used for visiting companies.

An obvious question, given the recent preoccupation with acoustically correct configurations, is the degree to which sound has been sacrificed to form, to which the architect and Arup Associates responded with the following arguments. The fundamental requirements of the brief have been met by providing a volume of $8m^3$ per seat, combined with suitable surface finishes to ensure a mid-frequency reverberation time in the range of 1.5^s-1.7^s. Limiting the distance, and providing clear sightlines to all seats, enables a strong direct sound with intimacy and intelligibility enhanced by early lateral reflections from the side walls and balcony fronts. The

balcony overhangs are designed to avoid acoustic shadows and maximize the free volume, while the asymmetric platform has been developed to avoid flutter echoes and limit oral colouration. The orchestra pit uses adjustable acoustic elements, lifts and rostra within the volume to provide an appropriate balance between orchestra and voice, for both romantic opera and the smaller classical and baroque repertoire.

Internal finishes to the auditorium were designed to ensure that the optimum reverberation time will be achieved. The walls and roof are of massive concrete, to avoid excessive low frequency absorption, and are combined with a strongly modelled ceiling to generate clarity. Acoustic flexibility, to accommodate other forms of performance, will be achieved by the use of retractable absorptive 'banners' to the rear of the auditorium. Seating will be chosen to minimize any change in the reverberation time with occupancy, final selection being confirmed by acoustic tests. Limited high-level absorption will be incorporated into the fly-tower to avoid excessive reverberation and provide an appropriate acoustic for the performers.

Control of intrusive noise to the auditorium is fundamental to the design. The 'necklace', in conjunction with a double skin outer roof, with a deep void, effectively protects the auditorium from external intrusions, while noise generating and sensitive spaces within the complex are separated. Internal sound is also kept to a minimum by selecting finishes to minimize impact noise; for instance the lobbies adjacent to the auditorium are carpeted and provided with an absorptive ceiling.

The ventilation and air-conditioning system for the auditorium will be designed specifically for low noise operation to ensure that a background level of PNC 15 ± 3 is maintained; achieved through the use of low flow velocities, inherently quiet under seat supply outlets and high-level extract. Particular care has been taken with the mounting of plant, ductwork and piped services to prevent bridging of vibration isolation and the transmission of structure-borne sound.

OPPOSITE: Rendered sectional perspective

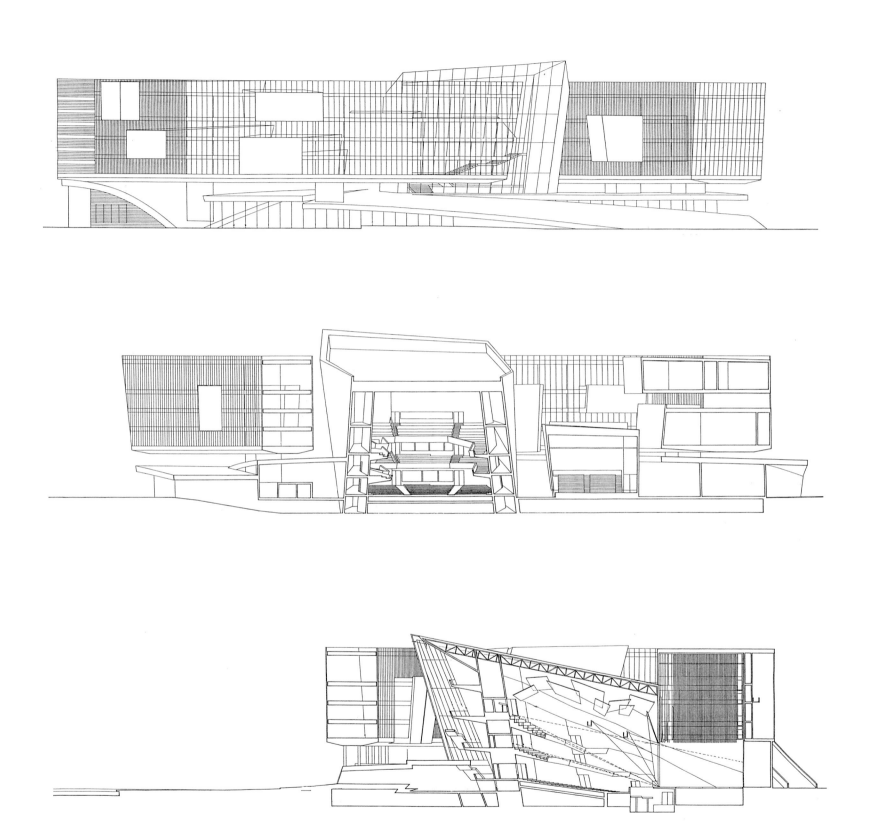

FROM ABOVE: Oval basin elevation; cross-section; longitudinal section

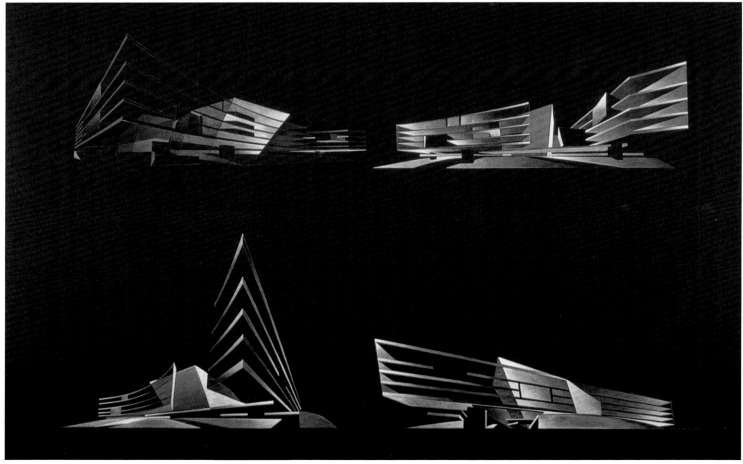

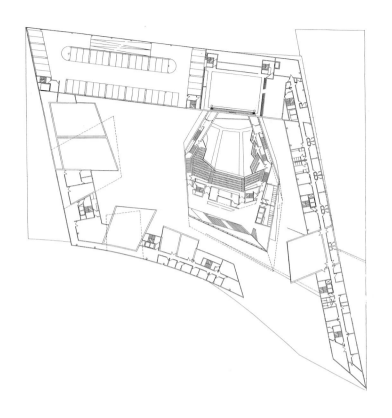

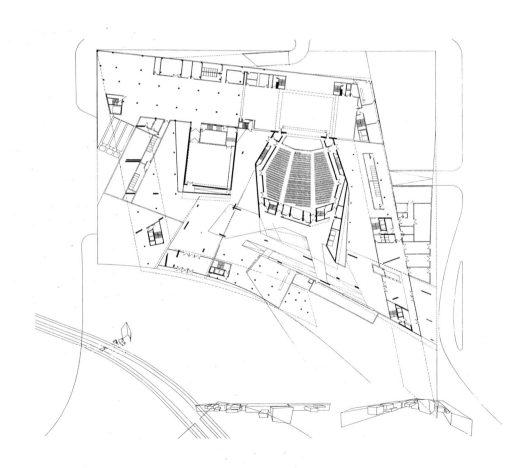

OPPOSITE: Auditorium development models; rendered perspectives; FROM ABOVE: First floor plan; ground floor plan

HARDY HOLZMAN PFEIFFER

THE HULT CENTER FOR THE PERFORMING ARTS

Eugene, Oregon

The familiar themes of theatre as a catalyst for downtown growth, the pairing of formal and informal halls to cover a wider spectrum of options, and civic co-operation to realize the possibility of urban identity, are all present in the Hult Center for the Performing Arts. Like Portland, the fortunes of Eugene, Oregon, rise and fall with lumber prices, which are connected directly to America's capacity for new homes. However, Eugene lacks such dense urban variety, and so architects Hardy Holzman Pfeiffer Associates (HHPA) had less contextual urban clues to follow, and had to invent its own. Selecting the metaphor of the ubiquitous pine forests that surround the inland city, the architects engaged the community, who had agreed to a eighteen and a half million dollar bond issue to build the centre, in the design process. The local performing arts organizations were also actively involved, and nearly forty of them, regardless of the level of use they planned to have in the future centre, were given an equal voice in guiding the concept. As architect Mildred F Schmertz stated:

To satisfy both the experimental groups and the traditional groups while keeping in mind the long-term goals of the community at large, we decided to build two rooms, the larger one formal and very traditional and the smaller flexible and adaptable. I think that the most important thing that we did was to convince the Eugene people that if they were going to build two theatres, the thing to do was to make them as opposite as possible – in size, in feeling and in function. In this way we gave them the widest possible range of performing choices.[1]

This democratic approach extended to the artisans as well, and the architects actively encouraged local crafts people to participate in the making of their theatre. Competitions were held and more than thirty artists were chosen to contribute work, ranging from the silk screen velour stage curtain to the bronze figures playfully placed throughout the complex.

The Silva Concert Hall, as the formal component was conceived as 'romantic' with seats ranged between a raked floor loge mezzanine and balcony that each have a different curve, with the upper balcony being the closest to the stage to avoid isolation and improve hearing. Roof and side walls are literally woven together to increase this impression of intimacy. Plaster bands with wire mesh borders suspended from pre-cast roof girders interlock, creating the inverted 'peach basket' space the architects visualized, and each band is backed with either reflective or absorptive material, to fine tune it, acoustically. The smaller Soreng Theatre, by contrast, is asymmetrical and flexible, with lighting visible on suspended gantries. The lobby that serves both spaces replicates a cascade pine forest, with many levels inside a soaring interior to allow people to see and be seen.

Notes

1 Mildred F Schmertz, 'Art for Arts Sake', *Architectural Record*, May 1983.

HARDY HOLZMAN PFEIFFER
BAM MAJESTIC
New York

The restoration of old theatres has played an important part in the resurgence of public interest in the performance of music and drama, and certainly deserves to be represented in any current architectural study. Construction costs are typically higher than in new buildings, as Arup's litany of unexpected problems encountered during their reconstruction of the Old Vic indicates, and the Bam Majestic was certainly no exception.

Faced with a tight budget, and an equally compelling desire to resurrect an important historical building, the architects took the unusual decision of intentionally leaving certain elements of the theatre in their deteriorated condition. The implications of this radical departure from other comprehensive and immaculate restorations, which now seem to be the order of the day, go beyond an obvious cost-cutting strategy and provide an astute commentary on performance art, effectively becoming a play within a play. This simple but effective strategy enabled the architects to direct the financial resources to the necessary new seating, lighting and acoustic control, and to fulfil statutory regulations, whilst making the history of the theatre a feature of its rebirth. Like the lines of an aging face, the walls provide a depth of meaning that allows the spectator to consider a past full of incident and adversity, gaiety and passion, excitement and solemnity: the complex variety that is an integral part of everyday life. The original fabric is left as a testimony to all that the theatre has endured during its long and eventful history, and, in the continuing debate on the gradations of restoration, it clearly articulates the view that sterile reconstruction destroys the spirit of historic buildings.

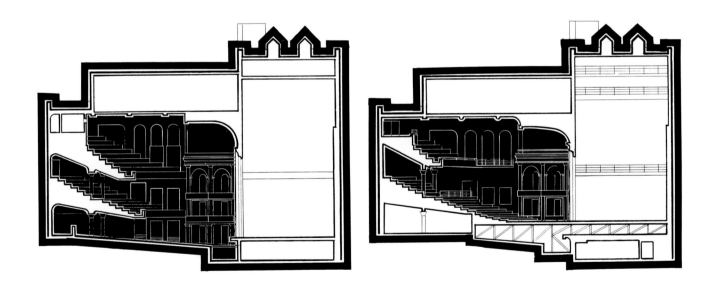

Sections before and after renovation

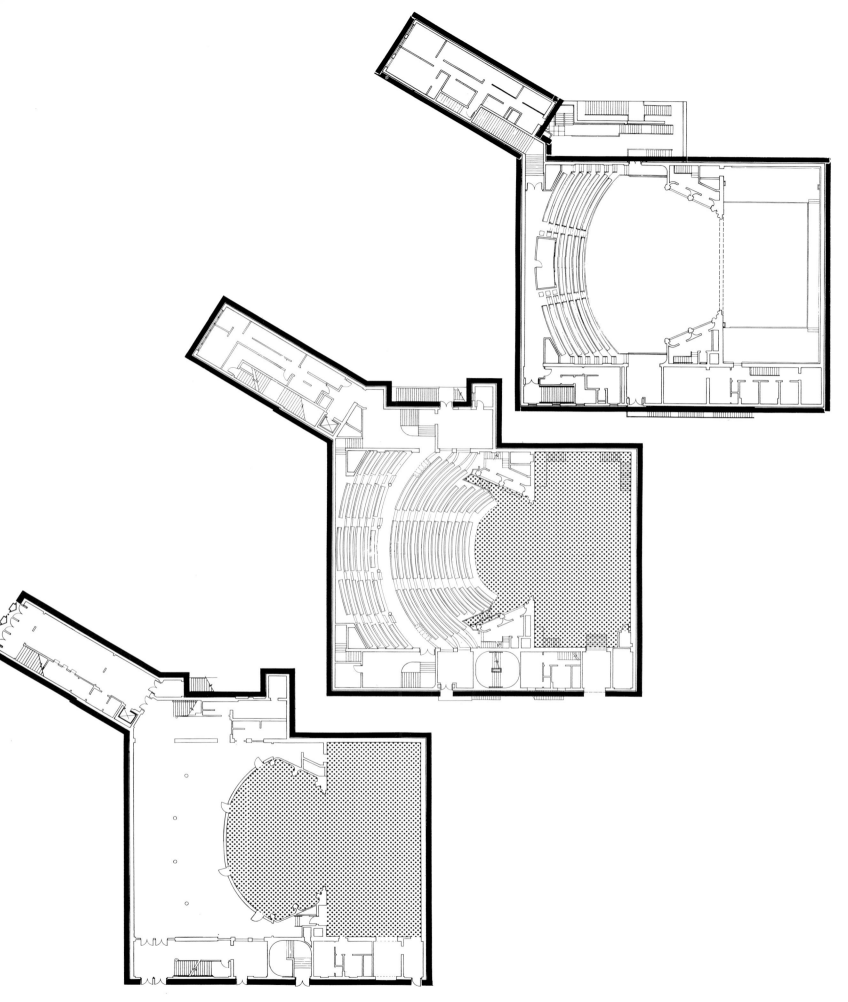

FROM ABOVE: Balcony plan; orchestra plan; lobby plan

MICHAEL HOPKINS
GLYNDEBOURNE OPERA HOUSE

Lewes, Sussex

Growing from the desire of Sir John Christie, in 1934, to provide a space for the performance of opera on his estate, at Glyndebourne House, this hall represents a particular national typology, rarely replicated elsewhere. Starting from what Peter Daley has characterized as a 'delightful ritual of country house picnic opera going', this hall presents the design dichotomy of formal informality, the high degree of sophistication presented by technical requirements carefully balanced by unhindered access to the natural environment surrounding the house.

Michael Hopkins and Partners has emphasized this balance by flipping the orientation of the seating toward the south, allowing the public more direct access to the idyllic grounds of the estate and creating ample space for the small city of support services required by a theatre of this size. In addition to the requisite scenery store, rehearsal stage and auxiliary rooms, these include the new Mildmay Hall and Wallop restaurant; the refectory components in a monastic site plan, in which the cathedral as the central element is given over to the performing arts instead. This comparison of ancillary services with a medieval town surrounding a place of worship is reinforced by the massive brick boundary wall around the hall, an elliptical ambulant which serves as an acoustic envelope around the horseshoe formed banks of seats. These are surgically inserted into a second, inner circle of services, including stairs and lifts that insulate the inner sanctum further, making it possible to maintain a high acoustical standard. The horseshoe form is appropriate in this ecclesiastical metaphor, since, as Derek Sugden has pointed out:

> ... the traditions of European opera grew out of the intellectual theories of the Florentine *Camerata* overlaid with influences of music and drama from the church and *commedia dell'arte*. Just as the *Camerata* grew out of an intellectual movement with the aim of discovering the essentials of Greek drama, so the opera house developed from the classical amphitheatre. The audience was soon enclosed and the walls brought sound to frame the action of the drama in a u-shaped

plan, ensuring visual and aural intimacy. From these beginnings, the Italian horseshoe developed and has maintained its pre-eminence for over three hundred years.

The architects, however, deny any intentional adherence to such precedents, their primary concern being the continuity of the intimacy of the preceding three-hundred seat hall. The new auditorium seems much smaller than its one thousand two hundred seat capacity would indicate, a feeling which is augmented by materials as well as form. The natural brick enclosing walls of the ambulant begin this reduction of scale. All external walls are solid load bearing brickwork, using traditional lime mortar, with no expansion joints. A handmade brick was chosen to match the house and made to a traditional imperial size. The external perimeter walls are a series of tapering brickwork piers with gauged flat arches spanning between. The intermediate floors of the perimeter offices and ambulants are made of pre-cast concrete beams and panels. The roof structures have wood or steel trusses supporting timber insulated panels, clad with lead using traditional details. The scale reduction is continued by the materials used in the interior of the auditorium, especially the balcony fronts and wall panels which are made from recycled pitch pine, much of it more than a century old reinforcing the image of the theatre as a much loved musical instrument resonating to the sounds inside. The acoustics in the new auditorium provide wonderful clarity, the volume and choice of building materials producing a good reverberance and a warm bass sound. It is approximately fifty per cent greater in volume per person over the old auditorium and has a reverberation time of 1.4 seconds compared to the previous one of 0.8 seconds, resulting in complaints of 'dryness' in the past.

In stark contrast to the material refinement of the auditorium, the stage and its auxiliary components reiterate the role of the theatre as a machine, in which nothing can delay production or be left to chance. The design of the stage, backstage and rehearsal stage allows the complex interchange of sets to occur on a daily basis. The stage is 18.5 m by 22 m wide, with a

proscenium opening approximately 10 m by 7 m high. The fly-tower incorporates double purchase flying, allowing access to the two side stages. The flying sets are a motorized system, configured to control thirty two hoists, variable or fixed speed, from a touch screen, microprocessor based control centre. The system moves lighting ladders – carrying a mass of 1400 kg – at speeds of 1.2 m per second with an accuracy of within 2 mm. Immediately behind the stage there is a large clear working storage space for four opera sets; 650 m² with a height of 9.25 m. The stage is separated from the backstage spaces by large acoustic doors which, when closed, provide a fire barrier of two hours and an aural barrier with sound attenuation varying from 34 decibels at 63HZ to 68 decibels at 4K. The largest door is the vertically rising rear stage door which is 17 m by 9.24 m high and weighs 20 tonnes. The backstage is directly linked to the loading bay and service yard. Leading off the storage area is a full sized rehearsal stage, with separate access and director's area. The rehearsal stage is acoustically insulated from backstage by a large, hinged, full height acoustic door. The space is naturally ventilated by openable glass roof lights. The loading bay provides direct access onto the backstage, with a lift down to the understage storage and plant.

In summarizing their participation, the architects and consultants alike inevitably refer to the tugging and pulling 'that took place between them to achieve the dazzling performances enjoyed in this singular setting each summer, placing this building at the top of the list of premier examples of theatre as a collaborative art'. Through it all, the architects managed to use this opportunity to continue to evolve several ongoing design themes, such as the use of indigenous materials in a truly contemporary way, combined with pre-casting wherever possible, to assure speed, quality control and the honest expression of materials and structural engineering work as an assertion of pride in craftsmanship. Architects and consultants have both won the day here, and the public are the beneficiary of their combined skill.

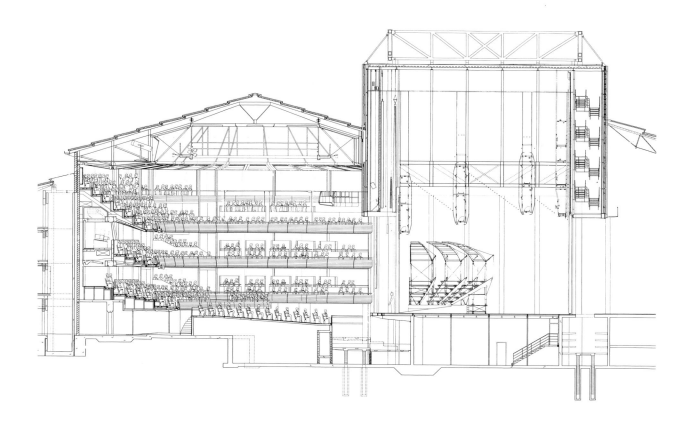

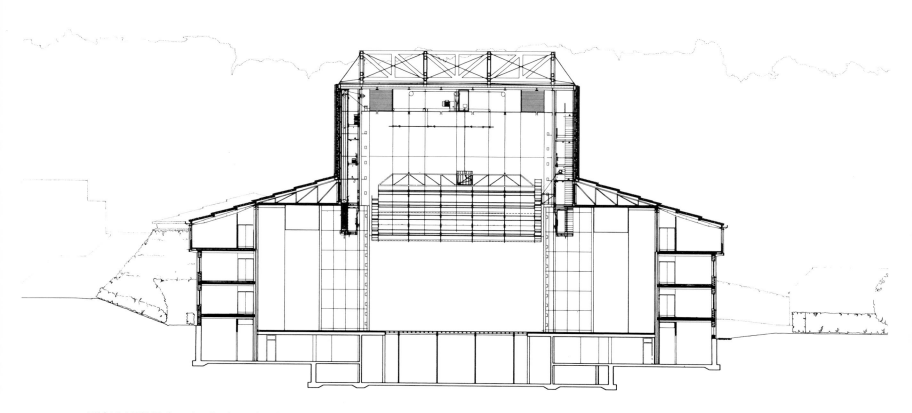

FROM ABOVE: Longitudinal section through auditorium and stage; cross-section through fly-tower

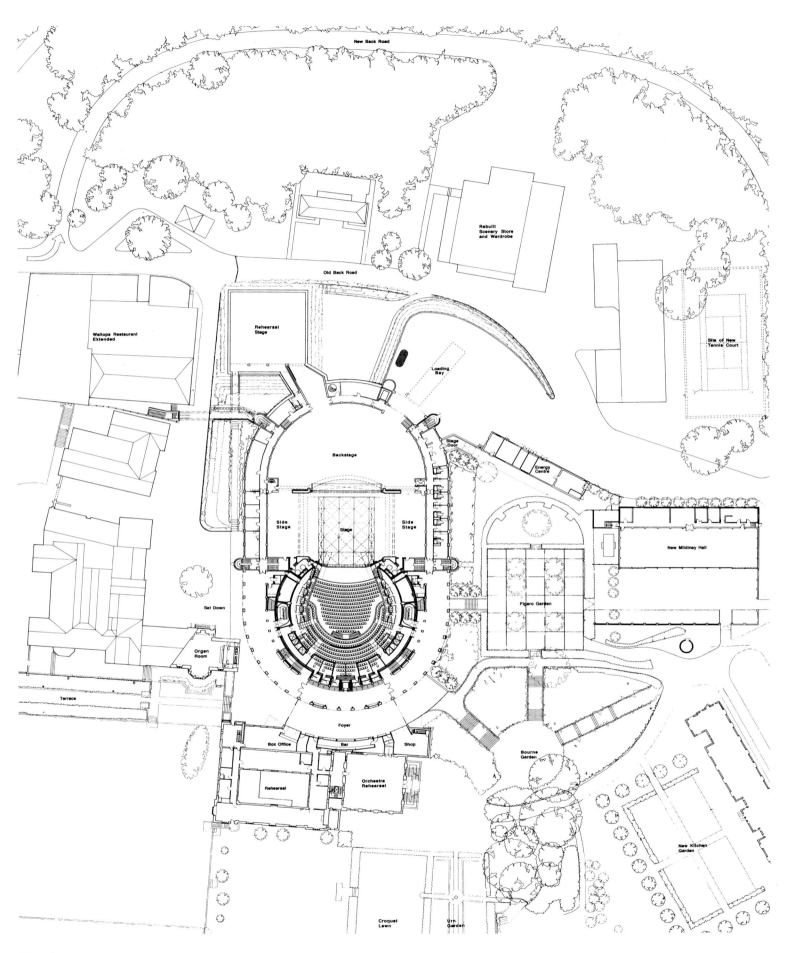

Site plan

New Back Road

Old Back Road

Rebuilt
Scenery Store
and Wardrobe

Wallops Restaurant
Extended

Rehearsal
Stage

Loading
Bay

Site of New
Tennis Court

Backstage

Stage
Door

Energy
Centre

Side
Stage

Stage

Side
Stage

New Mildmay Hall

Set Down

Figaro Garden

Organ
Room

Terrace

Foyer

Box Office

Bar

Shop

Bourne
Garden

Rehearsal

Orchestra
Rehearsal

New Kitchen
Garden

Croquet
Lawn

Urn
Garden

MICHAEL HOPKINS
QUEEN'S BUILDING

Emmanuel College, Cambridge

This small gem of a building, completed in the spring of 1995, provides a new lecture and performance space for the college, accommodating one hundred and eighty people with a raked auditorium and a surrounding gallery. Primarily designed for chamber music and small orchestral groups, the space can be adapted for lecture, cinema and theatre performances. A reception room has also been provided at the upper level to be used in conjunction with the auditorium and a new Middle Common Room. Seminar and small music practice rooms ring the building at ground level inside an open colonnade that acts as a buffer between inside and outside.

The Forecourt Building site fronts Emmanuel Street, between the Fellows' Garden and the Old Library. It is free standing and similar in size and scale to the Wren Chapel, breaking the orthogonal geometry of the Front Court and New Court with its apsidal ends. It is aligned on an axis with, and parallel to, Leonard Stoke's North Court Building across Emmanuel Court, which is intended as the link that will draw the building into the body of the college and as the beginning of a new sequence of spaces between the Fellows' Garden and Front Court.

Taking their cue from the Wren Chapel, the architects have faced the building in Ketton limestone, but have opened up the frame in such a way that the historical differences between the two structures are immediately obvious. Structurally, the compressive strength of stone has been maximized on the external walls and the spanning potential and mass of concrete has been used to full capacity for the floors. Steel and timber trusses, supporting a heavy timber acoustic roof have been finished in lead to complete an image of refined, assured and quiet strength.

The auditorium has excellent acoustics, already noted for clarity, warmth and excellent reverberance during musical performances. The narrow profile of the auditorium allows for excellent early lateral reflections and the high volume, set at just over 8 m³ per seat by the engineers from Arup Acoustics is perfectly suited to chamber music ensembles. The mid-frequency reverberation time has been designed to vary between 1.3 and 1.6 seconds, depending on how the room is used. A slightly higher value at low frequency has been designed to specifically support the bass response. The reduction in reverberation time required for speech, in the order of 0.3 seconds, is achieved by closing a line of drapes behind the platform and under the front edge of the balconies. The simple rake of the seating ensures the desired amount of intimacy between the audience and the performers and, to insure this, background noise from air movement in the auditorium has been limited to PNC20.

The curvature of the ends of the building has been used to best advantage to develop sound diffusion with undesirable focusing limited by modelling the concave surfaces. Screens will also be provided at a low level behind the performers. The roof has also been specifically designed to play an important role in the acoustics of the auditorium, with emphasis placed on the diffusion of sound which is achieved through the use of an exposed structure and modelling of the roof soffit. The shallow gallery and curved balustrade also help in distributing sound to the seating below.

For its size, this building can boast an impressive list of design talent whose combined skill was fairly tested by the configuration required by the site. In addition to architects Michael Hopkins and Partners and Arup Acoustics, Buro Happold served as the structural engineer for the Queen's Building. They were faced with the challenge of finding a way to use the Ketton Stone, chosen by Hopkins to blend in with the Wren Chapel and Westmoreland Building, as a bearing material, subjected to tensile forces because of the large openings required, rather than as a conventional cladding over a steel or concrete frame. One solution was to thicken the wall, but this would have required an excessive amount of stone. In addition, the auditorium has an exposed roof structure resting on twenty-eight columns around its perimeter and, although there is a solid concrete service core used primarily for transporting pianos, the columns rise unrestrained for over two storeys. To solve the problem, Buro Happold chose to pre-stress the columns – with a force twenty-five times the predicted loading – to offset any lateral loads and prevent tensile cracking. However, as the pre-stressing rods would have shattered the stone if applied directly, pre-cast concrete kneeler blocks were used at each floor level.[1] These blocks also resist the thrust of the arched voussoirs acting as lintels over the windows. The curved ends of the building required additional consideration since the thrust loads that are counteracted on the straight sides do not line up there, causing unwanted forces on the columns. These forces were offset there by tying back the columns to the concrete floor slabs, so that shrinking of the concrete over time will counteract any outward thrust. Large or small, each theatre project presents special problems that require the concerted efforts of a well co-ordinated design team.

Notes
1 CJ Buirgoyne, *Emmanuel College Magazine*, Spring 1994, p5.

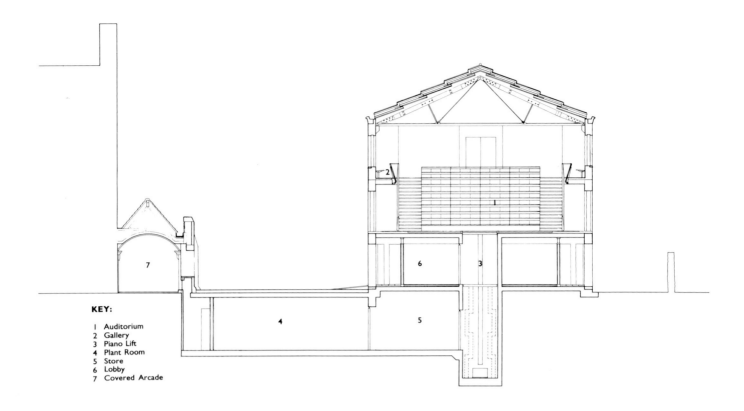

KEY:

1 Auditorium
2 Gallery
3 Piano Lift
4 Plant Room
5 Store
6 Lobby
7 Covered Arcade

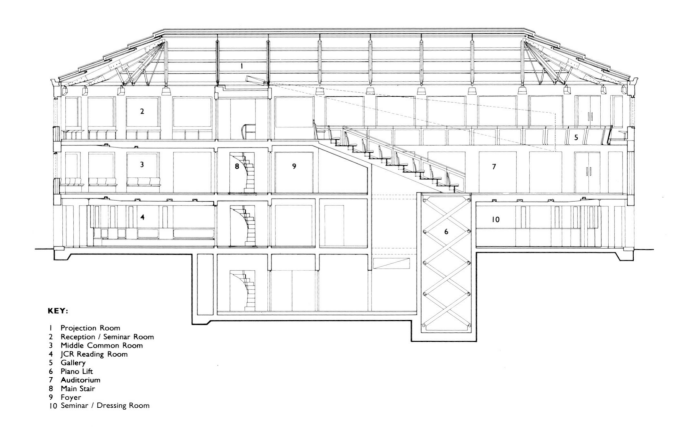

KEY:

1 Projection Room
2 Reception / Seminar Room
3 Middle Common Room
4 JCR Reading Room
5 Gallery
6 Piano Lift
7 Auditorium
8 Main Stair
9 Foyer
10 Seminar / Dressing Room

FROM ABOVE: Cross-section; longitudinal section

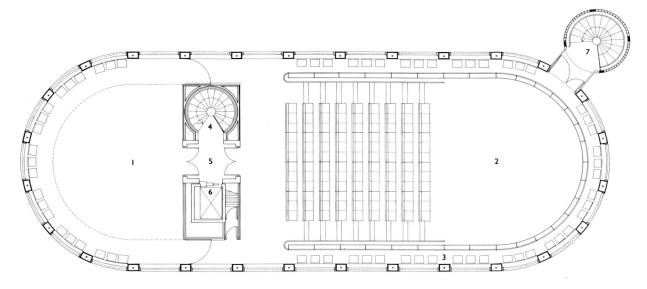

KEY:

1 Reception Room
2 Auditorium
3 Gallery
4 Main Stair
5 Lobby
6 Disabled Lift
7 Stair Tower

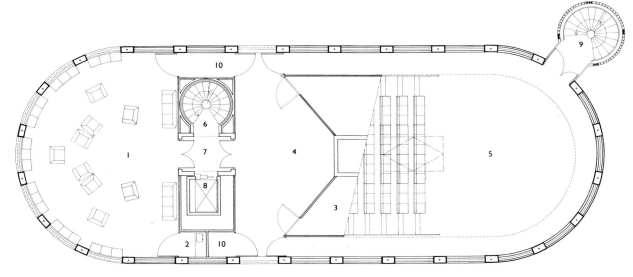

KEY:

1 Middle Common Room
2 Kitchen
3 Store Room
4 Foyer
5 Auditorium
6 Main Stair
7 Lobby
8 Disabled Lift
9 Stair Tower
10 Acoustic Drape Store

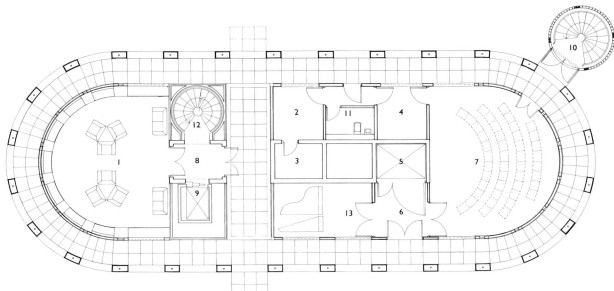

KEY:

1 JCR Reading Room
2 Music Practice Room
3 Music Store
4 Meeting / Supervision Room
5 Piano Lift
6 Lobby
7 Seminar / Dressing Room
8 Entrance Lobby
9 Disabled Lift
10 Stair Tower
11 W.Cs
12 Main Stair
13 Keyboard Music Practice Room

FROM ABOVE: Second floor plan; first floor plan; ground floor plan

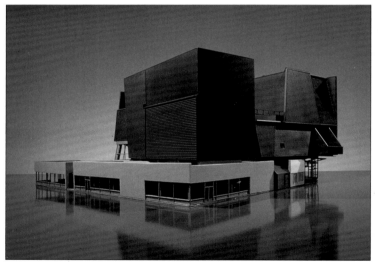
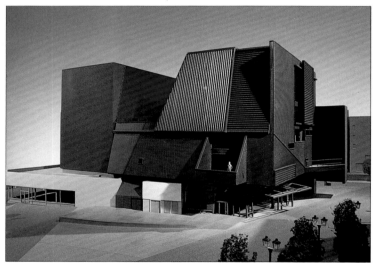

HOLT HINSHAW JONES
SAN JOSE REPERTORY THEATER
San Jose, California

Having gained international fame as the antithesis of Los Angeles in the sixties hit by Dionne Warwick, San Jose has since grown to be the third largest city in California and the eleventh in the United States. This theatre is located in the heart of San Jose's redeveloping core and is also a working home for the artists, craftsmen, technicians, management and staff of the San Jose Repertory Theater Company.

The neighbourhood around the theatre is predominantly filled with car parks and construction in progress and this project was conceived as the central 'cultural anchor' in a rapidly growing downtown area, characterized by a typical mix of retail and office space.

The eight block San Antonio Redevelopment Area is caught between the 'urban renewal' mentality of the sixties and seventies and more enlightened, historically based efforts today. Housing for the immigrant Chinese population that once lived there was bulldozed to create the 'superbloc' popular thirty years ago, with a Halprin fountain as a centrepiece, which became a symbol for the new downtown; demolished recently to make way for this theatre, signalling a significant change in planning sensibilities. Central to that change has been a master plan by Skidmore Owings and Merrill, including new state and federal office buildings, an art museum as another 'cultural anchor', a hotel, a three-hundred-unit housing project and a mid-rise building housing the offices of the Redevelopment Agency, which is funding this project using a combination of redevelopment area property tax revenue and bond issues.

When asked what lies behind their concept for a theatre to be placed within this volatile urban cocktail, Paul Holt recalls comparisons with other areas with similar temperatures, as well as Los Angles itself:

It is hot in San Jose, but it is neither as dry as a desert nor is it a tropical sweat house. Evenings in particular are pleasant, the perfect climate for living the mythical California lifestyle. The Hollywood Bowl comes to mind, and roller-skating in Venice. In San Jose though, the hills rather than the ocean define the horizon. They are more present than the ocean is in Southern California and more evocative, sporting gaudy colours at sunset and deep purple shadows afterward. San Jose's smog is less of a problem than Los Angeles' is too, so the hills remain visible as a comforting reminder of place.

For the most part, because the climate allows, the new downtown is growing up Disneyfied; special paving patterns, dining alfresco, cute but under-utilized electrified trains and the indiscriminate use of pastel stucco historicist imagery hint broadly at a mythical Mediterranean past. As convincing as Disneyland and as laid back as California – both theatres of sorts – a popular Utopia is acted out within the comfortable context of ye olde street furniture and the new style *calle*. For the most part, though, the real downtown clings to its suburban roots in defiance; the hissing of summer lawns slides into the disturbance of traffic and wind blown litter with the practised ease of what amounts to tradition in California.

In basic massing, the architects tried to reconcile the various forms interspersed with vacant lots that now surround the downtown site. The theatre is conceived as a 'magic box' containing and protecting the ephemeral theatrical experience, expressed as a cube hovering over a pinched-in base. This cube, achieved by placing a rehearsal hall on the theatre roof to break the singular profile of the fly-tower next to it, is rotated to proclaim the difference in character between the theatre and the urban grid around it. The cube was then carved away to reveal three distinct volumes related to the functions of the theatre, circulation and support facilities.

The six-hundred-and-twenty-five seat two level theatre has a flexible end stage format with a modified thrust capacity, which will also allow it to be used more easily by others after the repertory season is over. The dichotomy of a desire for both a proscenium stage and the intimacy with the audience usually associated with a thrust stage was resolved by placing an additional proscenium screen out over the audience, to blur the distinction between it and the stage and by using wrap around, non-box seating in the balcony, emphasized by a hoop lighting track, which is shaped to establish a sense of audience identity while at the same time allowing engagement with activity on the stage.

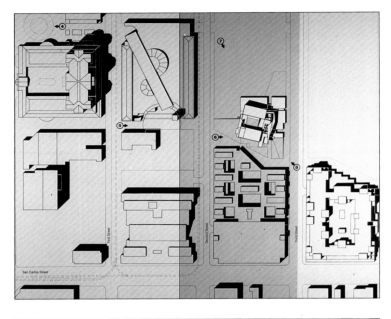
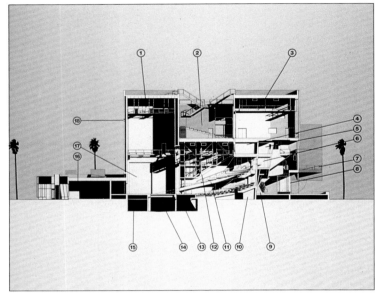

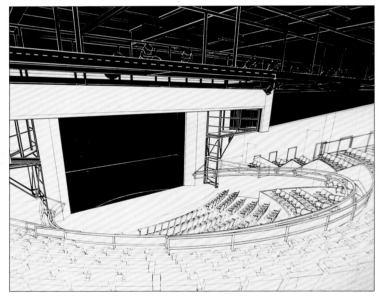

FROM ABOVE, LEFT TO RIGHT: Site plan; longitudinal section through auditorium; interior perspectives

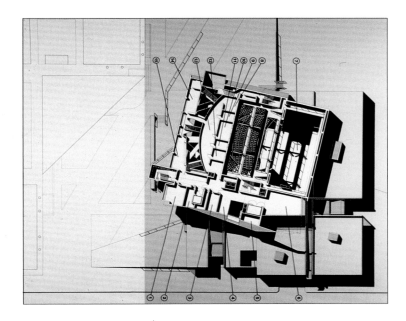
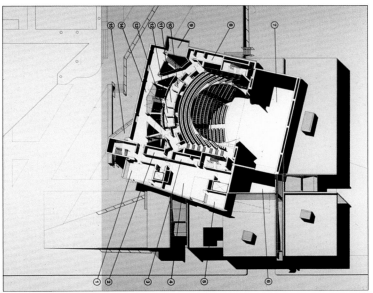
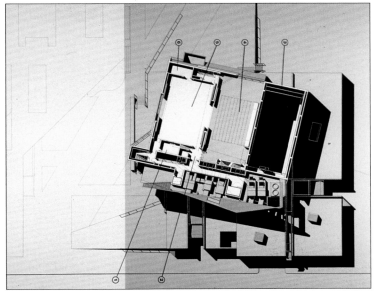
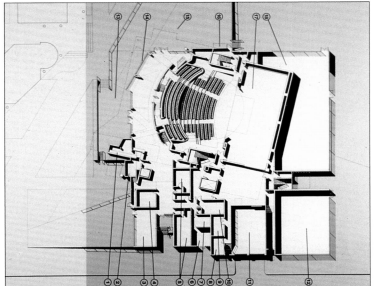

FROM ABOVE, LEFT TO RIGHT: Third floor plan; second floor plan; first floor plan; ground floor plan

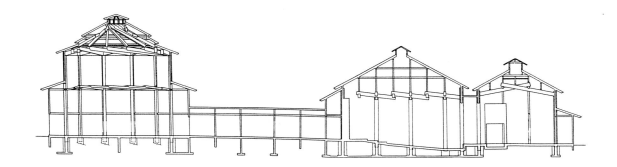

KAZUHIRO ISHII
BUNRAKU THEATER

Siwa, Japan

Kazuhiro Ishii loves to build in wood, considering it to be one of the most important materials of his architectural heritage. Problems of fire, rot, cracking and warping don't diminish his enthusiasm for it, or his determination to find timely solutions that will allow him to expand on an illustrious constructive history. This relatively modest *bunraku* theatre at Siwa has offered an ideal opportunity for exploration and creativity; Ishii is very familiar with the community and has had extensive experience building there. This chance encouraged him to investigate historical prototypes which would allow him to test the possibility that new ones would emerge. He is fond of telling the story of the massive temple at Todai-ji, which has recently been restored, including the installation of a new roof. When the old tiles were removed, the timber beams, which are over five-hundred years old are re-

ported to have sprung upward by several feet, once they were relieved of their customary load. Ishii cites this as proof of the remarkable resilience that cellulose displays, even after a long period of time. He paid particular attention to the techniques used in the Horyu-ji temple complex which is more than one-thousand-three-hundred years old, and has served as a model of bracketing and framing methods in the long evolution of temple design.

What he concluded, as a result of his study, was that the builders of the great wooden structures of the past had either used calculated innovation in their design, based on pre-existing models, or had relied on skilled artisans who did the same. He approached the village carpenters, discussed his ideas, and then left them alone to interpret them. The results surpassed his expectations, and in spite of a limited budget, Siwa has been the benefici-

ary of the mutual trust and respect that the architect and carpenters share.

A product pavilion designed as an annex to the theatre, houses a restaurant, lounge area and a space for the sale and display of speciality products from the region. The pavilion is laid out on what Ishii has termed an 'axial rather centripetal curve' for subtlety of line and to create a sense of enclosure without being restrictive. The parallel structural members are braced with horizontal angles, and depending on location, inside or outside the enclosure, the roof appears to be either warped or cambered because of the curve.

Ishii has made a valuable contribution to the search for a valid means of traditional expression that seems to preoccupy many Japanese architects today, making the preparation for *bunraku* a work of art in its own right.

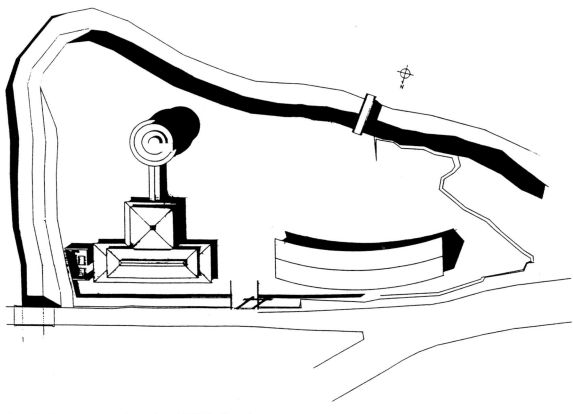

OPPOSITE: Longitudinal section; ABOVE: Site plan

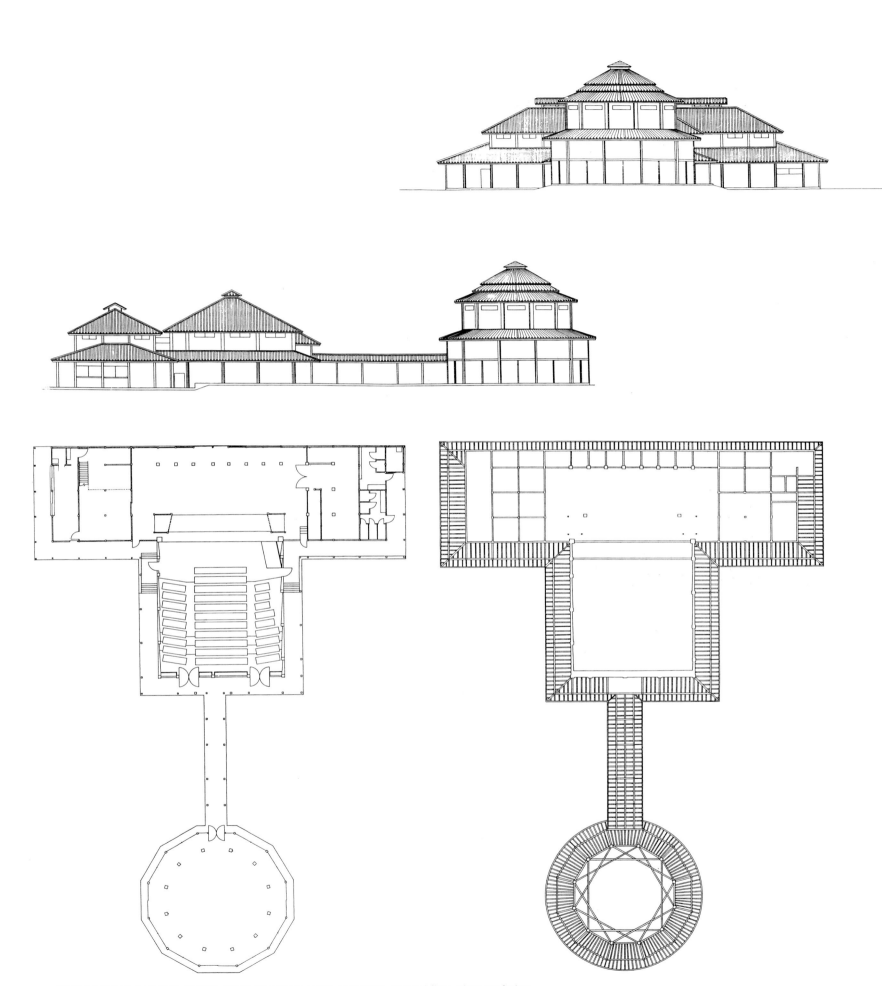

FROM ABOVE, LEFT TO RIGHT: West elevation; south elevation; ground floor plan; roof plan

KAZUHIRO ISHII
INTERNATIONAL VILLAGE CENTER
Yahata, Japan

Located on the lower slopes of Mount Sakakura, near Kitakyushu, this new complex combines the Hibiki Concert Hall, Yahatahigashi Community Center and an International Exchange and Information Centre into one serpentine glass container. Normally an enthusiastic advocate of wooden construction and investigations into contemporary expressions of traditional forms, Ishii has conformed to local precedent since Yahata is an industrial town where glass and steel are manufactured. The triangular site, south of the railway from Kitakyudhu, is three-hundred metres long, with a twenty metre drop in elevation from tip to base. Ishii has used the slope to emphasize the curvature of his building, and has angled the walls from base to parapet in certain parts of the lower configuration so that it seems to undulate along its extent.

The form was predicated not only by the materials required by the client, but also by Ishii's desire to unify the various diverse parts of the brief and to forward modernist precedents, such as those illustrated by Mies van der Rohe's Illinois Institute of Technology, and adapting them to the topography of Japan. As he explains:

Beyond a building which is essentially a square glass box, which seems to indicate the limitations of modern society, this glass structure assimilates its topography, reflecting changes in the weather and the seasons, becoming a kaleidoscope. Nearly eighty-five per cent of our country is occupied by mountainous areas, and topological architecture like this is suitable to it. The curving and gently inclined glass surface alternatively responds to the earth, the sky and the trees and its possibilities seem limitless.

The Hibiki Concert Hall is at the juncture of two twisted strands, above three levels of parking cut into the hillside. Reinforced glass is used for three of the curved surfaces in the space, which Ishii calls a 'concert hall for the CD age', supposedly because it is as hard and metallic inside as the glass and steel surfaces wrapped around it. Curved glass railings separate the balconies from the *loge* with few natural materials, except the wooden screen behind the low stage and its apron, allowed to break the brittle impression that the architect wants to convey. A *Kakyo*, or Japanese style room, is located at the tail-end of one of the crossed strands, connected to the lobby of the Hibiki Hall, which is really an historical replication inserted into the glass shell to avoid breaking the system that has been established; providing a connection to the past and token gesture to tradition. A sculpture called *The House of Music*, protected by a courtyard formed by an inner arc, is the only sign on the exterior that a concert hall is wrapped up inside the curving walls.

Tea ceremony rooms and *Kakyo* aside, the strict attention to detail, transmission of another culture through an adaptive filter and response to nature are what seem to convey the national character best.

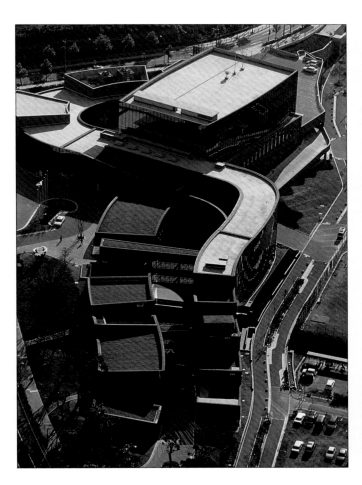

ARATA ISOZAKI
TOGAMURA
Togama, Japan

A festival sponsored by the Japanese Centre for the Dramatic Arts is held annually in the small village of Togama attracting an international audience that winds its way through the mountains to this secluded retreat. After the festival is over, the theatre is opened up to other companies who also come from all over the world to work here and be inspired by the quiet beauty of this isolated area.

Arata Isozaki has designed a series of structures, each carefully considered as part of an ensemble and positioned for maximum effect in a processional arrival sequence. The first of these was a given, an old grass *hozukuri*, or traditional farmhouse, that already existed on the site. Isozaki altered it to house the SCOT troupe formed by Takashi Suzuki, who perform a wide range of plays from *noh*, which is the earliest form of Japanese theatre, through comic interludes called *kyogen* to Greek tragedy. The farmhouse dates from the early part of the nineteenth century and Isozaki took a non-intrusive approach in restoring the exterior, placing a stage inside it and providing a back stage area closed off by sliding *shoji* screens. Winters in this province are cold and so the re-stored Toga Sanbo offers an enclosed pavilion for year round use, warmed by an underfloor system of heated rocks, as the farmhouse was in the past, placed under the stage area. The restoration has been carried out meticulously, with each detail taking on added significance because of

the minimalism of the architect's approach. The municipal requirements may have been viewed as restrictive by many other architects but Isozaki has typically turned it to his advantage, making the most of the area within the framework he was given. He has also replicated the rectilinear farmhouse form on the opposite side of the central square, or entrance foyer, rotated to negotiate a slope at that point and to add a twisting, dynamic massing to the set of buildings that extend outward from it like arms. The second arm, placed on the terrace below the theatre, contains dormitories for the performers arranged around a soaring interior space which extends upward to match the ridge line of the gable roof of the farmhouse. Typically dormitories conjure up images of hostels, but this block, like the theatre, serves a double purpose. This building also functions as a covered internal stairway, leading visitors ceremonially down the hill to the amphitheatre below. Located at the end of the lake, this is the fourth major component of this tightly formed ensemble, and as with its Greek prototype it uses the slope of the landscape to support its seats. However, the traditional wall behind the stage in the ancient example has been removed here to allow an unobstructed view of the mountains beyond, adopting the technique called *shakkei* used in Japanese gardens, meaning 'borrowed landscape'.

The main approach to the complex is by a road running along the western edge of

the Momose River, across a bridge toward the lake from which it is fed. The view from the main entrance bridge toward the ensemble is just as breathtaking as that seen by the spectators looking west, a linear sequential stacking of the various pieces of the puzzle, all mirrored in the still water of the lake. The effect is reminiscent of *beaux-arts* reconstructions of the approach to Delos at its zenith, revealing the Greek realization of the visual power of architecture layered in a line near the water's edge. Isozaki capitalizes on this power, extending the classical connection of the amphitheatre to another dimension of natural synthesis and mimesis, as Demitri Porphyrios has defined the word. This aspect of this relatively small project, of being able to be regarded in both use and approach in many different ways, with a variety of associations, lifts it above its provincial context, giving it a dream-like quality and universal application; the return of the theatre to its simple and quasi-mythical beginnings.

At a time when theatres are becoming increasingly complex, with a burgeoning list of requirements for space conditioning of all sorts, it is useful to consider the basic relationships from which this ensemble springs, enhancing the concept without high technology and expense. It is reminiscent of the circle in the sand from which theatre has evolved, and highlights that anything else added to that quasi-sacred act runs the risk of being superfluous.

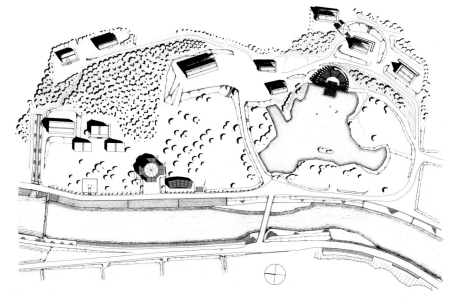

Location plan

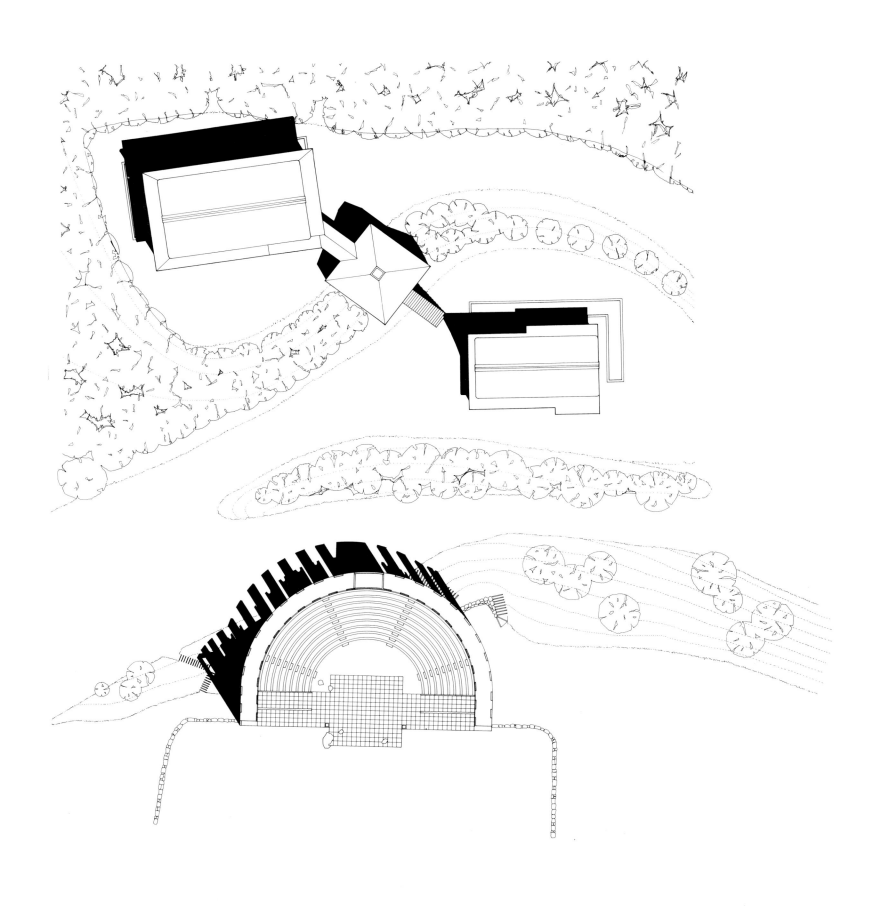

ABOVE: Site plan; OPPOSITE, FROM ABOVE: Amphitheatre axonometric; plan; elevation

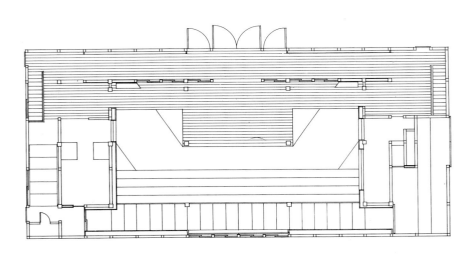

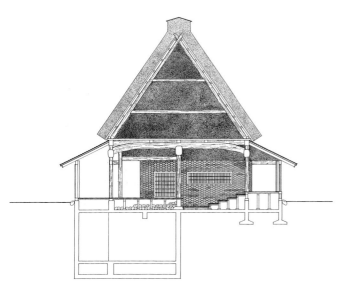

FROM LEFT: Plan; section

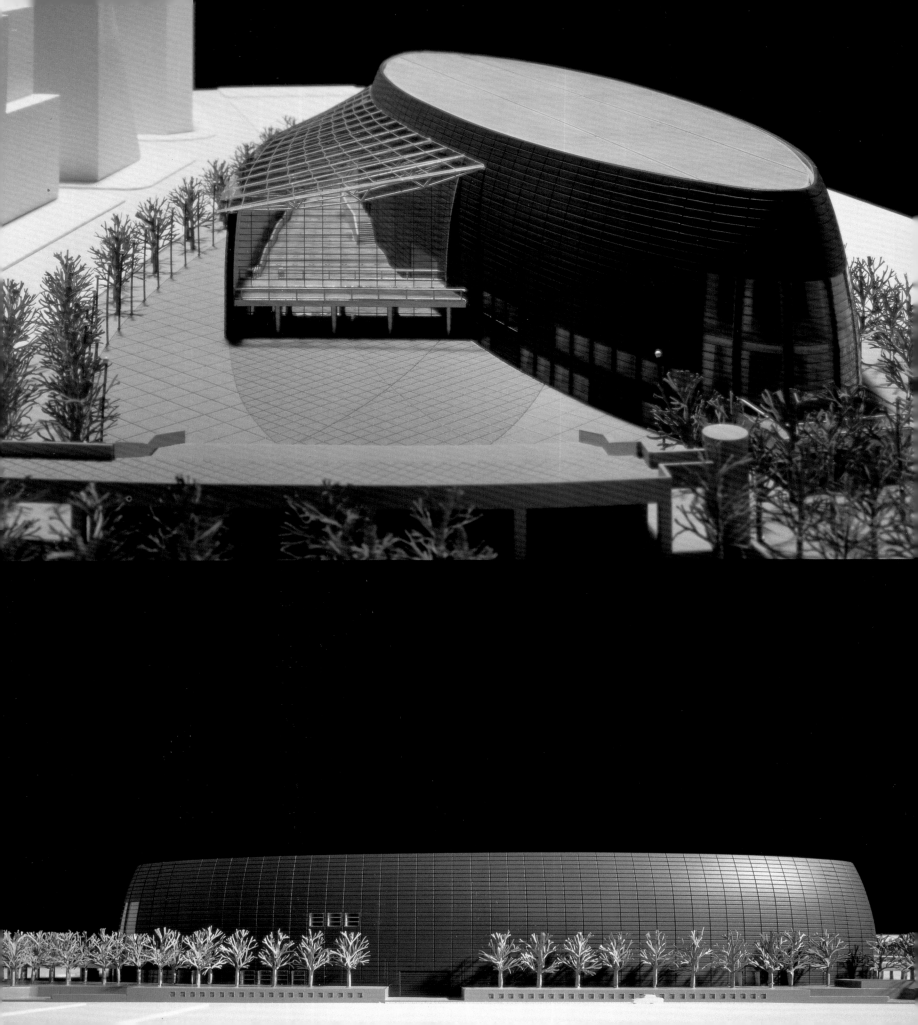

ARATA ISOZAKI
NARA CONVENTION HALL

Nara, Japan

Nara is currently in the throes of a massive redevelopment project called 'Silk Road 21', which is lyrically and improbably projecting the important commercial position the city had in the past into the next century. This image is heavily dependent on the Japanese railway, the city's contemporary lifeline, and therefore the site chosen for the Nara Convention Hall is adjacent to this line. It is a trapezoid plot, defined by a motorway that runs parallel to the tracks of the railway and the cardinal axes of the city, which have evolved from those of the ancient capital of Heÿo-kyo. The final, axial, elliptical form that emerged as the winning scheme in an international competition decided in the spring of 1992, reconciles the grids of both the ancient city and contemporary railway and is unified in a monumental response to the larger urban scale, in which it will be a singular symbol.

Isozaki established a plinth base for the entire site to reconcile a 2 m change from east to west and best accommodate a monumental, free-standing building. A level site also encourages pedestrian access from all directions around the Convention Hall, including the outside 'cultural plaza'.

The main approach to the hall will be from the train station, through the city park to the north-east of the site. The earliest sketches prepared for the competition show this and the organisation of a range of small, me-dium and large scale halls inside an elliptical form without articulation. Elaborating on this, as the design progressed, were explorations of a spatial link involving mid-sized halls to allow for future flexibility. Various types of seating were considered, including the concept of balcony seats on palettes, supported by framing columns that allowed these platforms to be incrementally projected out toward each stage at many levels, which eventually led to the development of movable seating; a light sub-system within a hard, structurally rigid shell. Carrying on from this basic idea, the main hall was designed as a multi-purpose, multi-focal space with a second stage to the rear of the main block of audience seating. Isozaki wanted to re-define the traditional relationship that has existed in theatres, of seeing and being seen, producing a 'dramatic space' that flows freely around multiple focal points. To allow this to happen, the proscenium can rotate or move up and down and the floor under the first level of seating is mechanized. The second level can also be raised and there is a deck to the rear that can be used as a sub-stage, or a foyer, if necessary. Acoustic and lighting systems have been made movable to accommodate such flexibility and part of the stage equipment has been left exposed, as a result. Rather than being conceived for its own sake, Isozaki anticipates that the multiple possibilities he has provided will foster new and dramatic forms of performances in addition to more conventional use.

In the earliest phase of his career, Arata Isozaki was not associated with the metabolist movement, that grew as a national alternative to modernism in Japan at that time. He took a different attitude towards form, which he feels should be independent of function. Architecture, for him, is 'a machine for the production of meaning' rather than a structurally expressive system of fixed and interchangeable components. Part of this meaning is cultural and the Nara Convention Hall is, perhaps, the best example to date of the efficacy of his search; a memorable image that is futuristic and traditional at the same time. This has not been achieved easily.

The curved section of the hall, meant to recall the large roofs of Todai-ji, Kofuku-ji, and Toshodai-ji, was originally to be clad in tile, but calculations of damage by differential shrinkage indicated a change to pre-cast concrete panels and a double shell, with the exterior skin supported by a steel truss. Manufacturing pre-cast concrete pieces to conform to a curved plan with twelve foci and four types of arc with radii that vary from 7.2 to 216 m has been challenging, a technological achievement equal to the symbolic role of the hall.

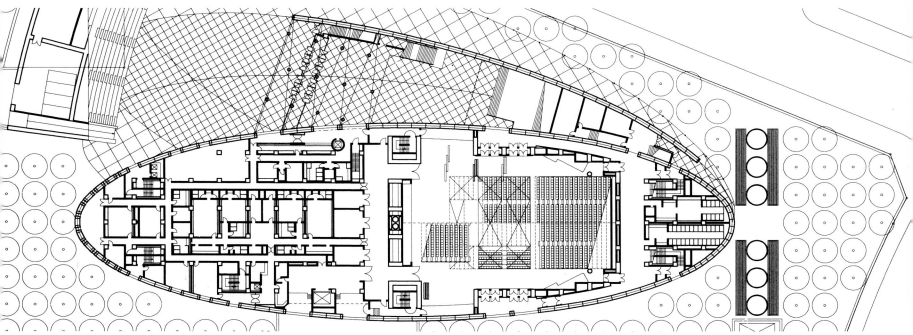

Ground floor plan

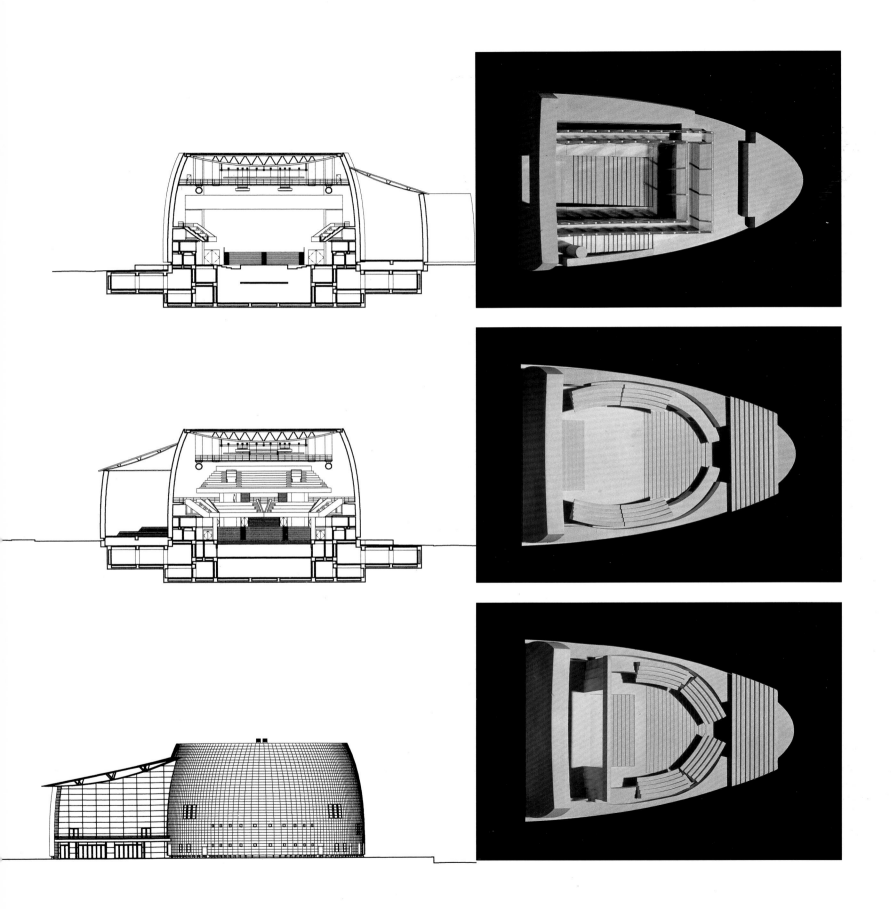

FROM ABOVE, LEFT: Cross-sections; north elevation; FROM ABOVE, RIGHT: Sequential cut away views of auditorium

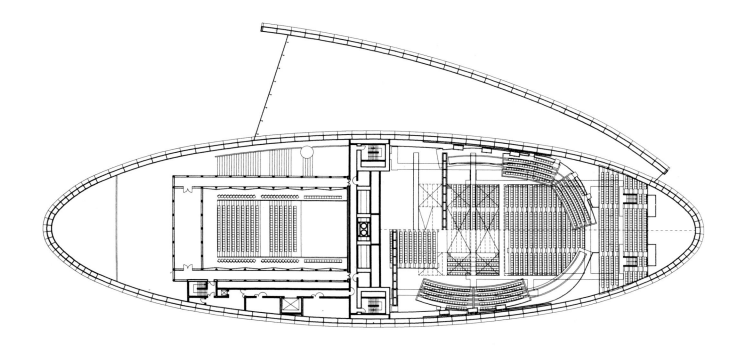

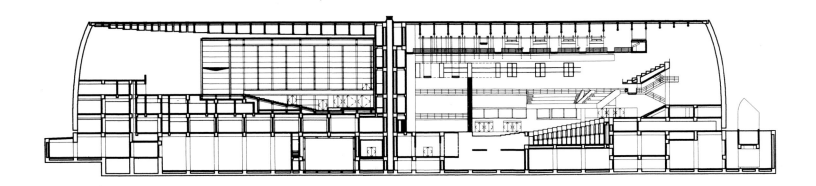

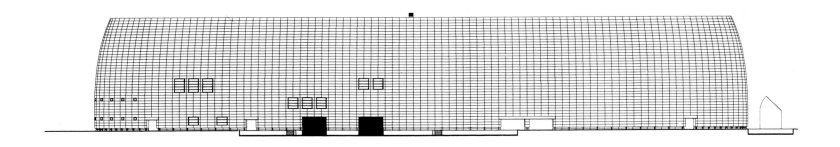

FROM ABOVE: Third floor plan; longitudinal section; west elevation

ARATA ISOZAKI
KYOTO CONCERT HALL
Kyoto, Japan

Kyoto is widely considered to be an urban repository of rapidly vanishing Japanese traditions: an architectural storehouse that is the antithesis of Tokyo; a place not yet overrun with individualized, modernized forms of personal expression so often found in the city to the north. From the huge Buddhist temples such as Todai-ji, which has just been lovingly restored, to the Katsura Imperial Palace, the impressive roster of national treasures seems endless and bound to give any architect with a commission to design a monumental public building in the city more than momentary pause. However, the image of wall-to-wall historical structures is not completely accurate, as many first time visitors find to their dismay. Isozaki's new theatre, completed in March 1995, is in an area where that fact is most obvious, and presented him with the perfect opportunity to pursue his favourite theme of the meaningful re-interpretation of tradition; to use this building as a touchstone for a new kind of expression that does not literally copy the old, but reflects its spirit.

His positioning, as usual, is highly skilled. The site, located to the south of a major intersection and at the edge of a transitional commercial and residential zone to the east, led him to locate the main entrance in the middle of the eastern side, breaking the building into two primary Platonic volumes; a circle and a double-square rectangle. The circle, with a six-hundred seat hall on the second floor, acts as a lobby on the first, with banks of doors leading onto a perimeter ramp that serves both the smaller hall above and the main

one-thousand-eight-hundred seat concert hall in the rectangle next to it. Streamlined fins reconcile differences in exterior elevation between the two volumes – as does a uniform roof line – and seem to spin out from the circle, which announces the building as it thrusts toward the intersection; logically assumed to be the major direction from which most people arriving by car would approach the theatre. This bold and visually successful elevational gesture, coming at a time when making entrances clear and easy to find is considered to be irrevocably functionalist and recherché in some quarters, is a hint of things to come, as are small details such as the various paving patterns used in the circular entrance hall, which lead people gently forward and upward.

The final goal of all this attention is the main hall, a classic shoe box with little embellishment used to disguise an aspiration toward perfect sound. In this shrine to music, there are references to the shrines of other times elsewhere in the city in its limited, almost severe palette, of materials and frontal focus. Except for the white plaster used on the walls of the upper half of the hall, stopping at a projecting cove that marks the transition to the ceiling, white oak seems to predominate on the floor and as a fascia on most surfaces in the lower half of the room, as well as on a pipe organ screen behind the stage. Four grey-green stone columns on each side wall run up to the bottom of the cove and serve to unite the two halves; the capitals of an indeterminate order that avoids immediate and specific association, are

purposefully understated. The seats match the colour of the columns, continuing the sedate, restrained quality of the space.

Paul Goldberger has succinctly unlocked the subliminal association here, by stating that:

What Mr Isozaki has done is to take . . . two seemingly irreconcilable models, Scharoun's Berlin Hall and the classical hall in the manner of Carnegie Hall or Symphony Hall in Boston, and meld them. The Kyoto Hall feels like Berlin straightened out, rejiggered into a traditional shape. The whole thing ought to feel awkward and unnatural, like an abstract painting retouched to take on representational form, but in fact the synthesis seems like the most natural thing in the world.

This interpretation is derived primarily from the materials that Isozaki has used; a choice that has added significance in comparison to the other shoe box halls seen in this selective collection. There is a tendency in many cases to try to soften the ideal container in an attempt to more closely approximate the plushness of the classical hall that Goldberger recalls; to pull away from the hard surfaces and straight lines that are specified by consultants today. Isozaki has adopted a different tactic. By the use of a fine hand and strict control of what fills the space, which may be said to be the Japanese connection here back to the past, he has complied with what the acoustician Minoru Nagata has requested and by exceeding it has placed the hall within a historical context and made it indelibly memorable.

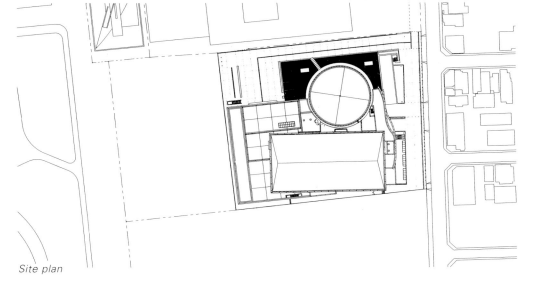

Site plan

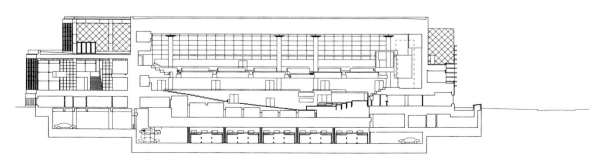

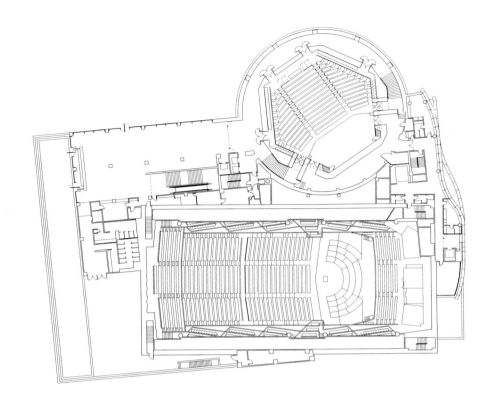

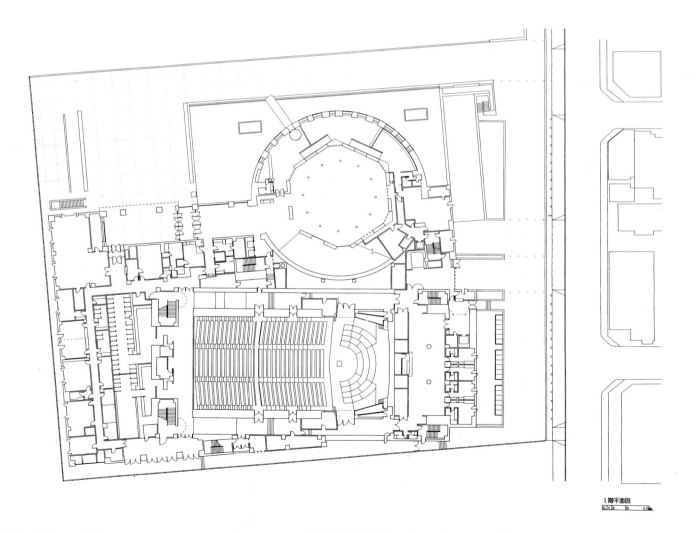

1階平面図

OPPOSITE, FROM ABOVE: North elevation; longitudinal section; FROM ABOVE: Third floor plan; ground floor plan

ARATA ISOZAKI
ART TOWER MITO
Mito, Japan

Of all of the major theatres completed by Arata Isozaki in urban areas recently, such as those in Kyoto and Nara, this complex in Mito, Ibaragi, most clearly replicates traditional European models of city piazzas; down to the Art Tower which is the campanile of this square. If such a parallel was intended, it would come as no surprise given the architect's consistent exploration of possible variations on themes from different periods. Although it follows the Tsukuba Civic Center by more than a decade, the Mito cultural complex invites comparison with it since the changes that have occurred over the last twelve years are notable in understanding this work.

When Tsukuba was completed, its liberal quotes from everything from Ledoux to Graques prompted Venturi, Meier and Moore to draw surprised commentary, following as it did the pristine purity of Gunma, Kitakushu and Fujima. In retrospect, it was simply a continuation of his ongoing attempt to locate the position that architecture does, or should, play in culture by clarifying concept and method, whether they are original to him or someone else. The empty piazza in that instance, a fractured replica of Michelangelo's Campidoglio eroded by a piece of the Piazza d'Italia, symbolized a city with no heart. At Mito, the four-square plaza is a response to a similar urban texture on all sides – as opposed to the definitive edges found in Nara and Kyoto – with the func-

tions clustered along three sides and the fourth, to the south, left open for pedestrians. This southern gate, relating to a wide street at the end of the site, is framed by three large oak trees, a significant change from their metallic counterpart at Tsukuba. The agenda, in the interim, has obviously altered for the architect. The metaphors are less stretched, more natural and humane, and directly related to a shift in social sensibilities that has taken place. The most obvious of these, the Art Tower itself, is a structural *tour de force*, with multiple meanings that begin to emerge after the initial sense of awe wears off; the most probable being a twisted strip of celluloid, which the perforations along the edge seem to reinforce. When seen at night, lit from inside and below, the tower is pure Hollywood, glistening like a fragmented metallic searchlight, twisting into the sky. At 100 metres high, it is more intentionally symbolic of Mito's centennial and the cultural rebirth of the city.

A theatre, concert hall and contemporary art gallery are clustered along the western edge of the site, intended by their proximity to encourage interaction and discovery. Seeming to delight in the restrictions he has created, Isozaki interlocks each of the parts with consummate skill, without concern for the potentially difficult planning conditions that he creates in ways that are textbook examples of the lessons Venturi promoted in *Complexity and Contradiction* thirty years ago.

After entering from the street, a central rectangular lobby, which is used as a conference hall on its upper level, serves both theatres; a circular hall on the right and the larger articulated concert hall facing the corner on the left. The circular theatre has seven long straight rows of seats facing a stage that can be pneumatically raised, with additional seating in two circular balconies above. Three lines of fixed panels form a backdrop for the thrust stage, which in combination with a raised square fly-tower, set up deliberate geometric interplay between the orthogonal and curved surfaces; conveying a sense of unity in the room and an equivalency between the performers and the audience.

Isozaki continues this tenuous balance in the concert hall as well, which is more elegant in finish. Three straight banks of seats, in this instance, are defined by smooth faced fan vaults, while the lights are contained in a large round dropped housing; the 'positive' opposite of the 'negative' square fly-tower in the theatre next door. One single marble column stands like a presence at the back of the stage, which in combination with the solid wood finishes that predominate and the smooth vaults and uplights, differentiate this hall from its neighbour. The fact that the acoustician Minoru Nagata also did the Kyoto Hall, proves that the collaboration between consultant and architect is far more flexible than Kyoto alone would indicate.

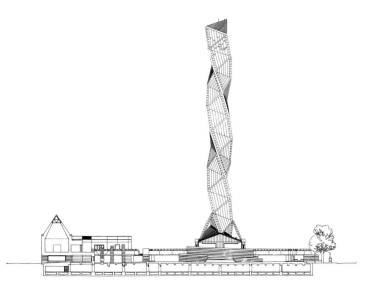

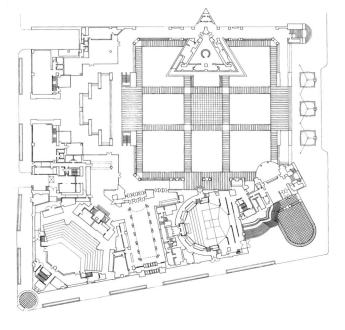

FROM LEFT: Longitudinal section; first floor plan

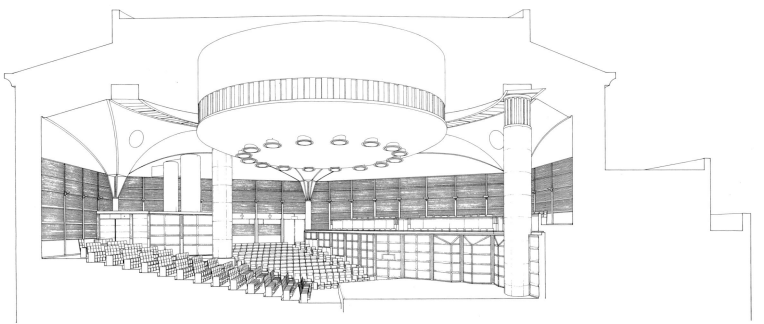

Sectional perspective of concert hall

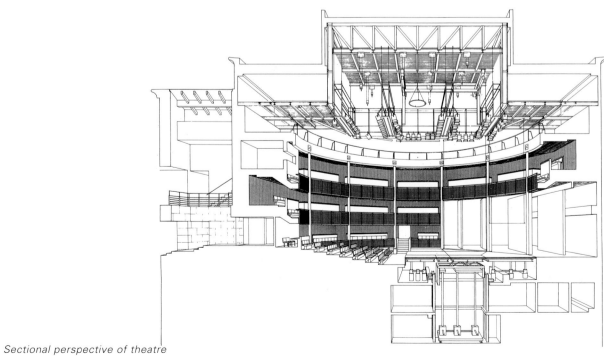

Sectional perspective of theatre

KISHO KUROKAWA
SAZANAMI HALL

Yamanami, Japan

Kurokawa has frequently written about symbiosis as the most recent phase of his work, which embodies tradition and a contemporary sensibility at the same time. The Sazanami Hall, which is one of his most recent theatre projects, was generated out of this idea, idealizing the historical importance of the need to perform.

Located in an open quasi-rural suburban area, this scheme is the sculptural and actual locus of a community centre, organized as a village around it. Rendered entirely in concrete and glass with terne roofs like the theatre, the surrounding 'village' is considered as a stylized *sukiya* grouping; small 'houses' arranged around a metaphorical temple, subservient to it and protecting it at the same time. A symbolic gate directs guests towards the parterre and formal entry; set slightly off the axis generated by the theatre which is opposite, across an internal court.

The first impression visitors have is that of having stumbled into a sacred precinct, as the interiors are as minimal as the external palette, with furnishings sparse and selectively positioned. The primary view is across a shallow pond – that occupies the entire central area – to the curved wall of the theatre, seen through butt-jointed silicone-sealed glass panels that run from the floor to a coved soffit, without any mullions in sight.

As far-fetched as the comparison may initially seem, this approach is reminiscent of the later residential work of Frank Gehry in Los Angeles: specifically the Schnabel House in Westwood, where a shallow, artificial 'lake' serves as a backdrop for the abstracted New England village that he has constructed. In each case the motive seems the same: a retreat into a fabricated, metaphysical fantasy in an attempt to leave a harsher, or more boring world behind; the

Schnabel House replicating a hagiographic American prototype to do so, whilst at Yamanami Kurokawa has distilled components that are quintessentially Japanese.

In addition to the *sukiya* village and temple, all of the recognizable Japanese elements are here, including Zen garden reductivist materiality and narrowly selected view. The extent of this distillation becomes most obvious in the theatre itself, which has a movable wall behind the stage allowing the mountain range to the north to be used as a borrowed landscape. This is the same technique used by Arata Isozaki at Togamura, a restored, century old farmhouse converted to a *moh* theatre. Yamanami and Togamura deliberately evoke both the beginning of the theatre and its original integration with the landscape, and the essence of Japanese architecture.

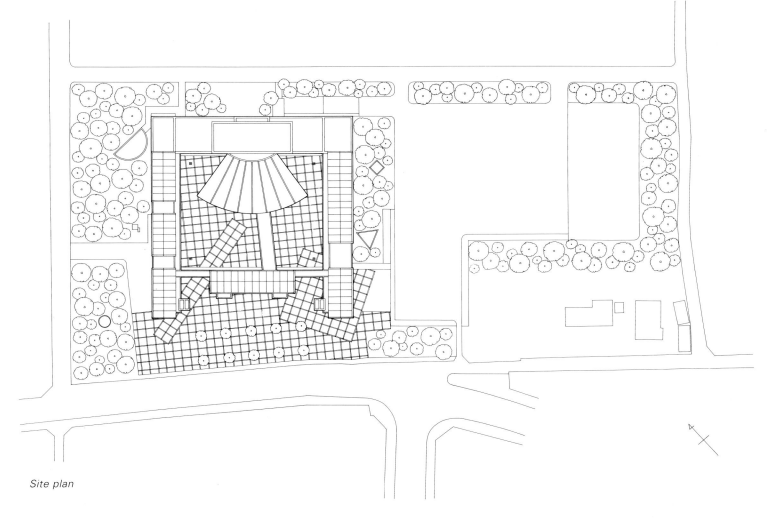

Site plan

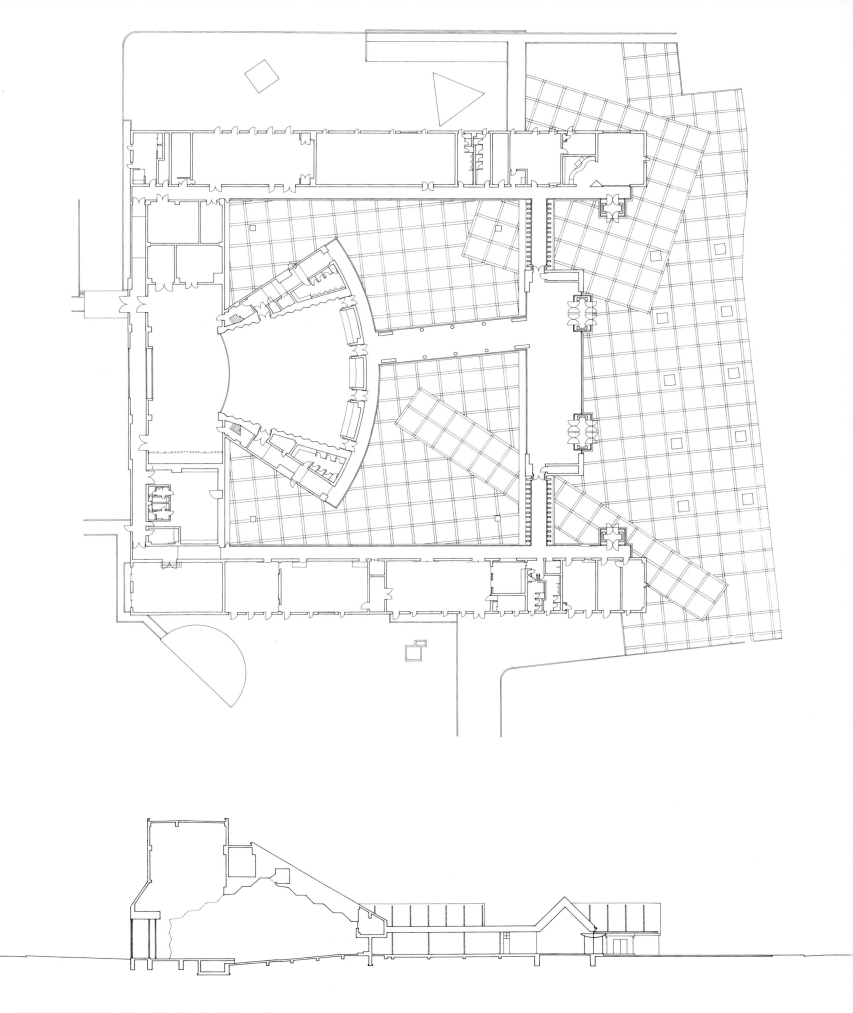

FROM ABOVE: First floor plan; longitudinal section

KISHO KUROKAWA
YAMANAMI HALL

Minami, Japan

This small theatre is the pride of Minami Yamashiro, the only village in the Kyoto Municipal District with a population of nearly four thousand, and was built as a venue for summer festivals. Despite its size this building includes a hall to accommodate traditional Japanese dances and also serves as a multi-functional community centre accommodating uses as diverse as a Japanese-style reception room, public health centre and research facilities.

Kisho Kurokawa has designed the hall in relation to the Kizu River nearby, with roof forms that seem to wave in response to the water, placed between two parallel walls. A second, lower block has a flat roof, with a linear, inverted barrel vault to protect against rain, that serves as a raised plaza overlooking the river, alleviates the crush during the festival season and acts as a

visual foil for the curving roof beside it.

Entrance to the hall, from parking to the north, is surprisingly formal, through tall, square structures with concrete bases and wooden tops, leading up to a pair of monumental stairs that penetrate each block. With these towers, Kurokawa has set up a duality, indicating his view of a parallel between the two volumes, and he has likened them to the stone lanterns commonly seen leading up to Shinto shrines throughout Japan. At night, these lend an air of excitement and high drama to the building's approach, raising the architecture to monumental status, and illustrating a practical way of stretching a limited budget. This pragmatism extends to the concrete bases which can accommodate stalls, again mimicking the shops traditionally found within a shrine precinct.

The foyer of the hall, which has also been designed to accommodate western style concert orchestras, is positioned to allow a final view of the Kizu River and the mountains in the distance, through a glass lined corridor that intentionally frames it.

Kurokawa is fond of pure geometrical forms, and describes the Yamanami Hall in the following terms:

. . . historical signs are transformed abstracted and fragmented, so that, like the geometrical forms, they become abstractions. In this way, all meaning is first eliminated and then intentionally re-allocated. These abstracted signs, because they have been fragmented and abstracted, have the potential to produce new meaning. In this way I believe that architecture approaches the realm of the poetic.

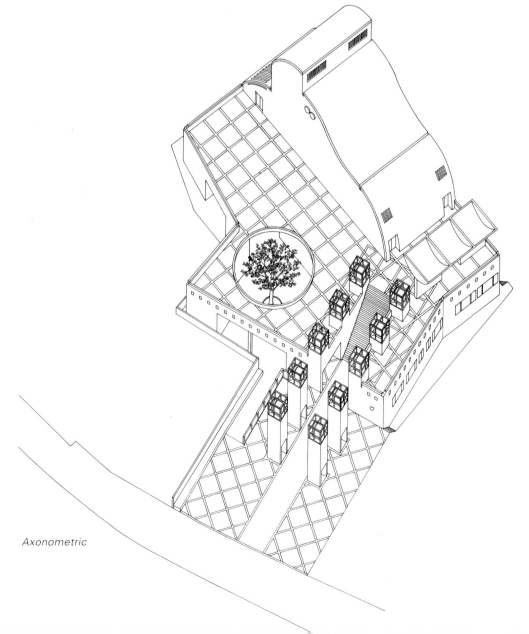

Axonometric

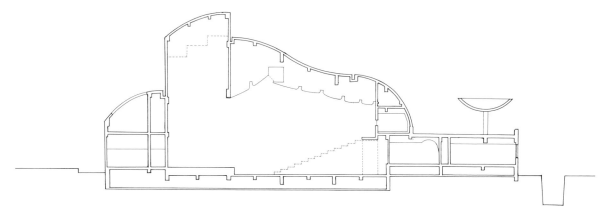

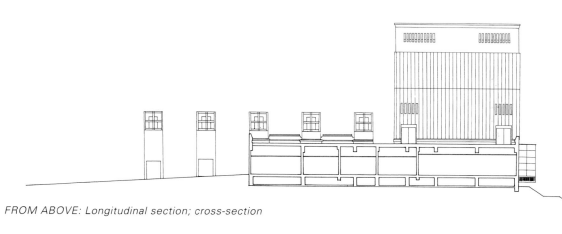

FROM ABOVE: Longitudinal section; cross-section

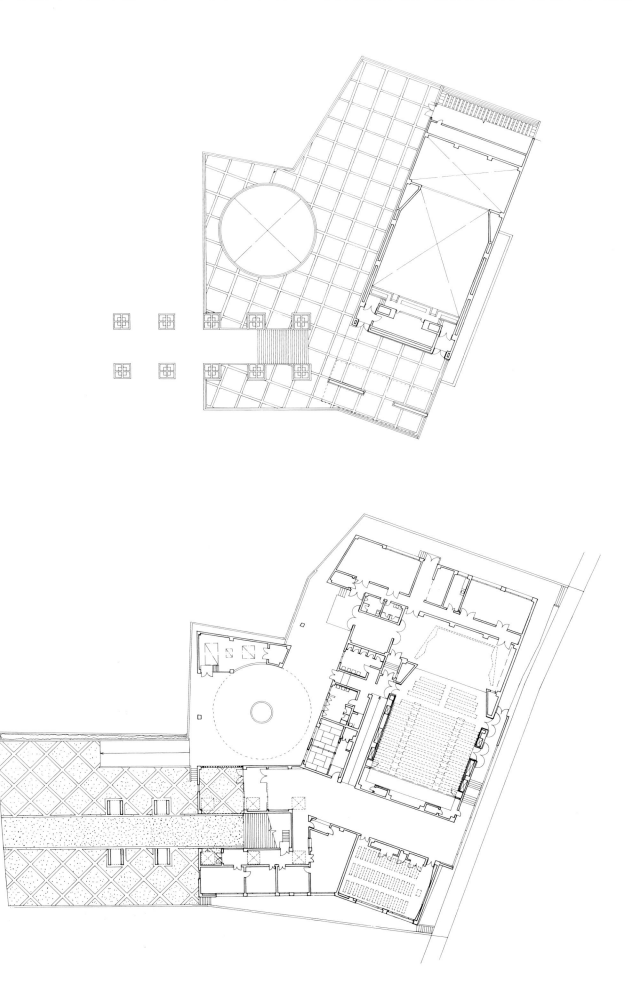

FROM ABOVE: First floor plan; ground floor plan

FUMIHIKO MAKI
KIRISHIMA INTERNATIONAL CONCERT HALL

Avia, Japan

Unlike many of Fumihiko Maki's more recent and influential buildings, the Kirishima Concert Hall was designed to respond to a spectacular natural setting, on a plateau in southern Kyushu. This area is a verdant paradise located with the Kirishima mountains to the east and Sakura Island to the south. The concert hall and amphitheatre have axes perpendicular to one another, but both face toward the surrounding peaks.

Intended to fit into this natural landscape, the concert hall gains presence from its distinct silhouette, but was intended to dispense, as much as possible, with the massive quality typical of the genre. It is used primarily as a music hall, suited for classical music, especially chamber ensembles and small orchestras, as well as providing the necessary amenities for music education and practice. The concert hall combines a leaf-shaped plan, that is a deformation of the shoe box type, with a key-shaped ceiling composed of triangular panels, to create a space that imparts a sense of unity between the stage and the audience. The design is also intended to have the acoustical merit of giving the sound an expansive quality that seems to envelop the listener.

When one approaches the theatre from the front, the road presents a continually changing panorama that has been carefully choreographed to emphasize a formal, processional sequence. Similarly, as the audience moves in from the foyer located on the periphery of the hall, vistas of the Kirishima mountains rise directly ahead, generating a sense of anticipation.

The rehearsal rooms surround a courtyard, intended to have the tranquil atmosphere of a music village set in the woods.

The field of vision opens out from this internal space toward the amphitheatre, strengthening the relationship between the two. Likewise, the sharpness of the ridge line on the main hall roof and the softness of the ridge line over the practice rooms are deliberately juxtaposed to balance one another, within the confines of the ship-like perimeter.

Following the direction of Professor Yoichi Ando of Kobe University, the basic proportions of the room are based on standard shoe box form, which is used as a general guide for fixing the width of the space, thus determining the duration of reverberation. In addition, to give the sound the required expansiveness, the degree of similarity between the sound as it reached the left and the right ears was used as an important acoustic index. After adjustments were made for other factors, the leaf-shaped plan and ship's keel section were proposed as a result of acoustic calculations that would carry the first reverberation to the listeners at an index level in the vicinity of 55 degrees. This design also had the advantage of enhancing the sense of a single shared space in which the audience are seated around the performers. Equally, the plan allows for the segmentation of the balcony seating whose right and left profiles step down toward the stage. This feature, along with the absence of overhanging projections, results in an interior which possesses a unique dynamism and strength of focus.

In order to provide acoustic energy to the entire space, sound-deadening materials were used as little as possible and the idea of covering the entire ceiling with triangulated panels was employed in order to produce a smooth sound to gently sur-

round the whole audience. These were an important design motif in this project as well as an acoustical device. While mediating the complex plan and ship's keel section as a complex polygon, lightness was emphasized through the three-dimensional overlaying of the triangles.

A festive space was sought that was both impressive and sumptuous, yet abstract in form and not reliant on decorative devices. The left and right side walls were given highest priority as the components of the acoustic system actually lean toward the audience. Gentle diffusion of the sound was another condition the hall had to meet, and was accomplished by using vertical ribs that created unevenness in the wall; mathematically calculated to simulate a random state within a given cycle. These were treated with a natural wood finish to create an interior with the warmth of a musical instrument, harmonizing with the rich acoustics of the hall.

Asked if the metaphor here which is so unmistakable, was developed on purpose, Maki attributed it to the dual prerequisites of the entry sequence, designed to maximize the appreciation of an unparalleled site, and the desire for exemplary acoustics. Given the numerous possibilities of this open setting, it is interesting that Maki, who is more accustomed to severe, urban constraints, chose to impose his own restrictions, and that unfortunately these have resulted in one of his least eloquent solutions, much less memorable than his spiral building, for example. The final form here, that so obviously ignores the beauty of the natural setting it is supposed to augment, is perhaps the ultimate warning of the effects of allowing acoustical considerations to govern all others.

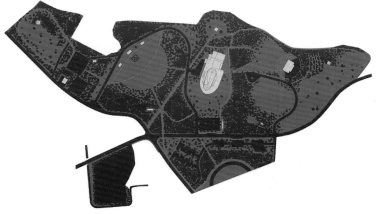

Site plan

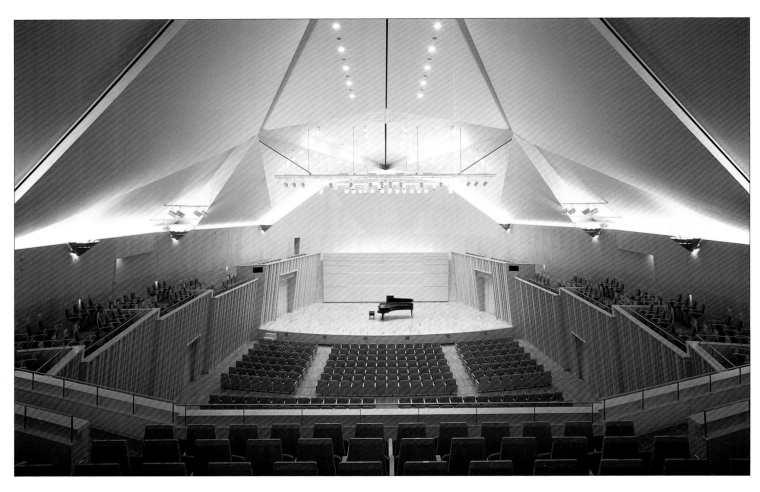

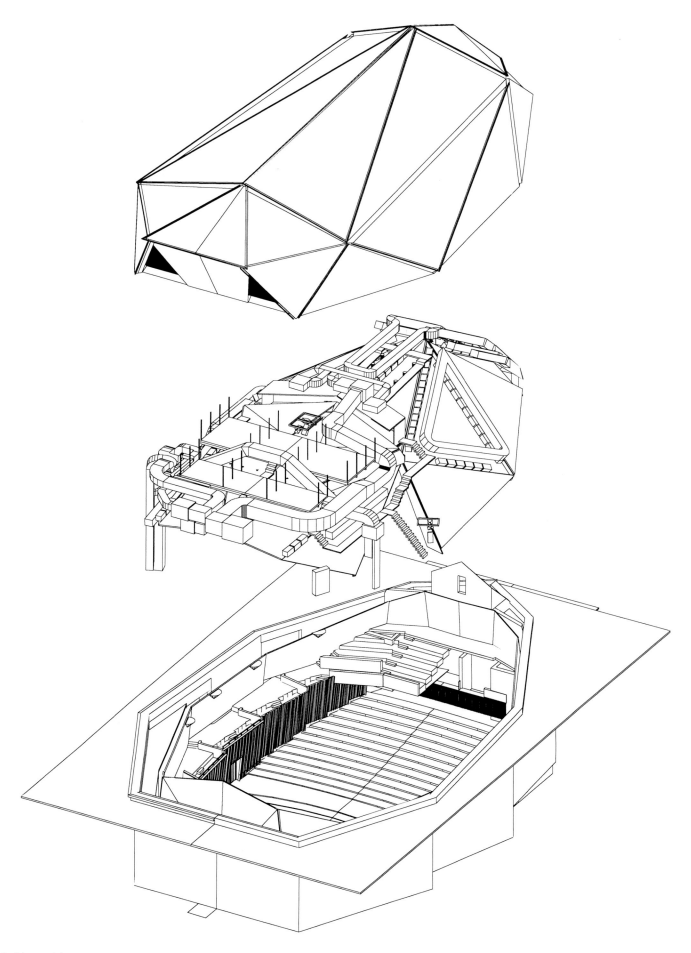

Exploded isometric

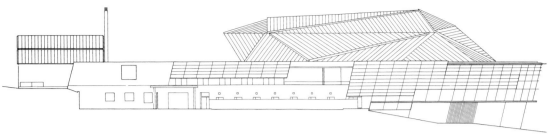

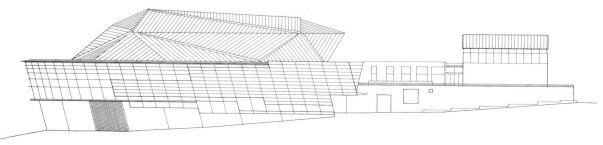

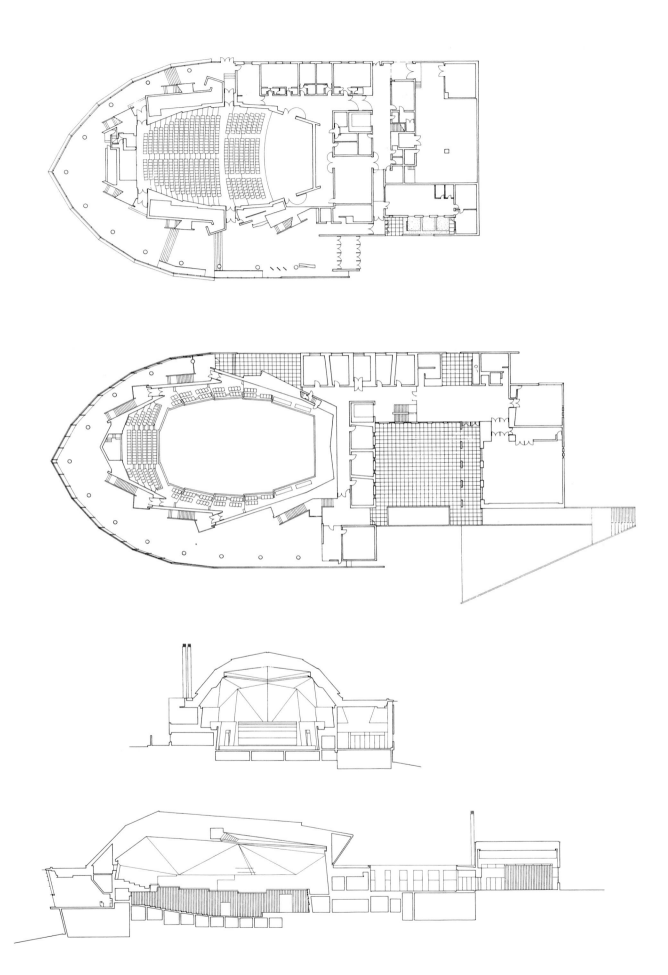

OPPOSITE: Front and rear elevations; FROM ABOVE: First floor plan; ground floor plan; cross-section; longitudinal section

FUMIHIKO MAKI
MUSICON BREMEN

Bremen, Germany

An entry in an ideas competition, this proposal responds positively to the historical richness of one of the oldest and largest cities in Germany with a population now hovering around half a million. In a preliminary study, the design team discovered that Bremen serves as an economic and cultural centre for a region of over three million, but, in spite of its grand musical history, has an existing concert hall that can only accommodate one thousand hundred. This has meant that great symphony orchestras bypass the city, which is deprived of such cultural exposure.

Supported by the city, the charity Friends of the Philharmonic started raising funds and finally organized a limited competition for a new concert hall, the Musicon Bremen. One of the main purposes of this was to explore the feasibility of the site, as well as to provide an inspiring scheme that would spur public interest and help to raise further funds.

The site is located outside the medieval centre, just north of the main train station; a setting which marks the basic conflict and inspiration of the design. Developing the idea of what they have called the Musicon in the Park, the Maki team has used the line of procession through the station building to establish a significant connection between the Burgerpark, the most important recreational area of Bremen, and the medieval centre of the city. Yet, as this axis is more interrupted than emphasized by the unattractive Burgerweide fairground and the new pedestrian Klangbogen, the scheme only links the convention hall with the station.

The greenery along the Gustav-Deetjen-Allee was considered as an appendix to the Burgerpark which was related solely to the train underpass east of the station. To counteract this the design team has proposed extending this area into the competition site and the Burgerweide fairground. In order to maintain continuity the Gustav-Deetjen-Allee will be closed to public traffic.

Within this newly defined space, the Musicon is conceived as an independent volume, a pavilion in the park. By relating the outside areas to the building, every side of the Musicon is activated. At the same time, the long and simple form creates a clear spatial definition for the Burgerweide fairground. The linear arrangement of functions permits a low 18 m silhouette, leaving the tree tops of the eastern greenery visible from the Burgerweide. The design team intentionally avoided a complex, volumetric expression of functional requirements, choosing a clear arrangement of three independent highly discernible units instead; the foyer, concert hall and outdoor performance area. They felt that this arrangement had the advantage of variety and flexibility. The proximity of the foyer to the convention hall is intended to encourage shared events, whilst the plaza maintains the separation necessary for the independent expression of the Musicon.

Placing the public areas, foyer and terrace at the ends of the building heightens transparency. At the northern end of the site, the main entrance to the Musicon, the new retail shops and the existing gallery of the convention hall create a lively plaza, a communicative centre between the Burgerpark and Burgerweide fairground. The foyer with its roof terrace and restaurant can be used for small concerts, performances, exhibitions and receptions, and has been conceived as an independent public space; a contemporary plaza. The artist's area with its spacious rehearsal and tuning rooms has a separate entrance on the second floor and can be used or rented out during the summer for workshops, academies or small concerts. Finally, during festivals the terraces, concert hall and foyer can be used together as one platform. The concert hall opens up to the terraces and renders the entire building open to the public.

These terraces are an additional example of the team's aim to make the theatre a transparent public space. They have a strong relation to the park and at the same time they are connected to the concert hall by glass foyers, mediating between the hall and the surroundings. As a result, they can be used in multiple ways, as intermission terraces, or for small open-air concerts independent to the main hall.

During festivals, terraces, concert hall and park can be used together. Performances on the Burgerweide are visible from the terraces of the Musicon and conversely, images projected onto the louvred façade of the theatre can be viewed from the lawn. Another screen on the terraced area can transmit the performances from the hall simultaneously to the outside, giving many people, especially at expensive concerts, the opportunity to participate in the musical event. The park to the east will be revived and become a 'sound garden', with sound cubes complementing the existing sound poles which are part of an acoustic installation lining the Klangbogen to the west. A small amphitheatre will provide an additional place for performances. Together with the terraces and the new Burgerweide the reinterpreted park will become an extension of the concert hall.

With its variety of usages encompassing the general public as well as visitors to the philharmonic concerts, the Musicon could become a new, less monumental symbol of the city of Bremen. However, since discussions about the final character of the new concert hall are still ongoing, detailed designs have yet to be finalized. Instead, the Maki team has attempted to allow as much flexibility as possible in its proposals, so that each individual component can be independently developed without detracting from the overall architectural concept.

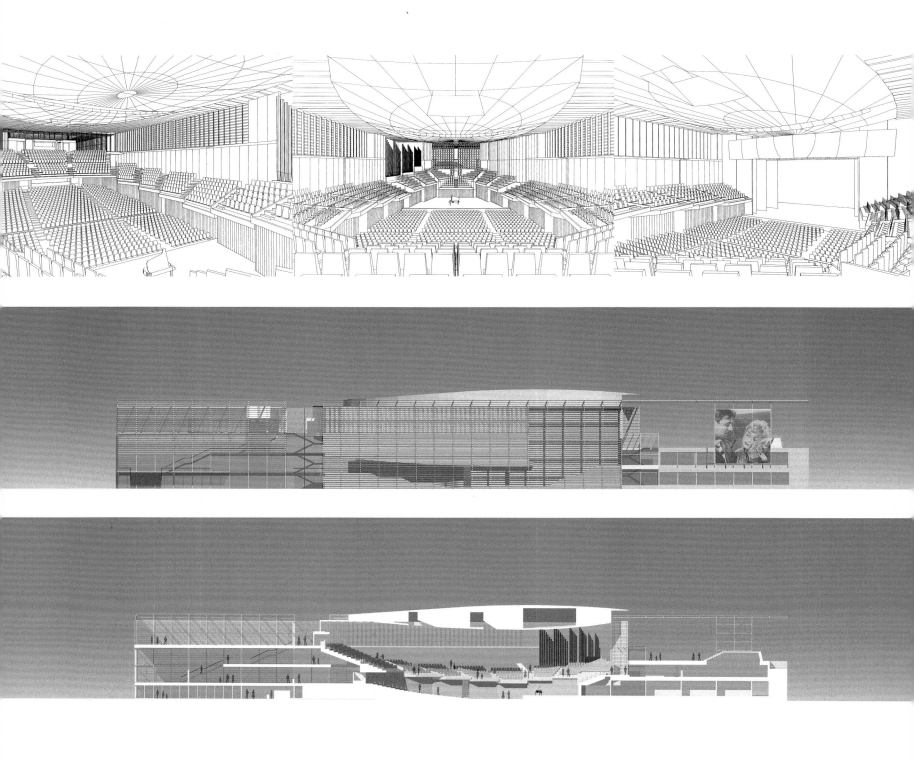

FROM ABOVE: Interior perspectives illustrating auditorium and stage formats; side elevation; longitudinal section; OPPOSITE, FROM ABOVE: Second floor plan; first floor plan; ground floor plan

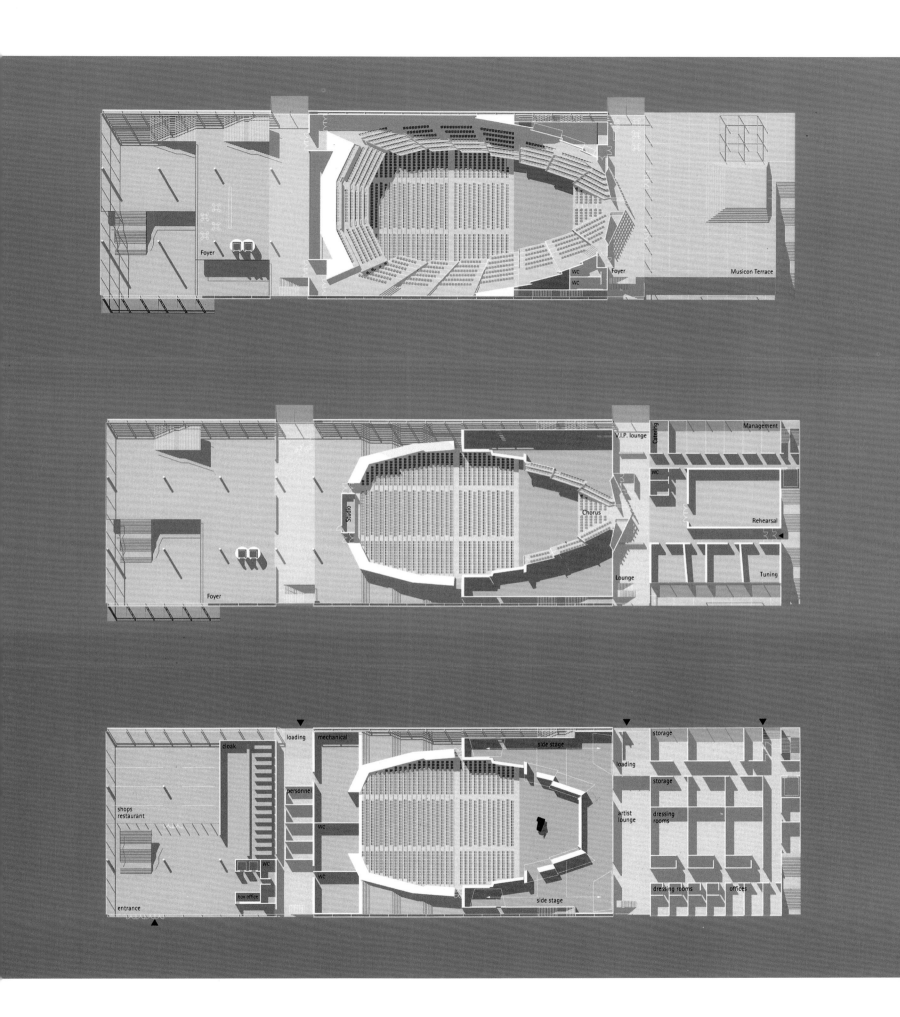

Foyer

WC

WC

Foyer

Musicon Terrace

V.I.P. lounge

Catering

Management

WC

Studio

Chorus

Rehearsal

Lounge

Tuning

loading

mechanical

side stage

storage

cloak

loading

storage

personnel

artist
lounge

dressing
rooms

WC

shops
restaurant

WC

box office

dressing rooms

offices

entrance

side stage

MOORE RUBLE YUDELL
CENTER FOR THE PERFORMING ARTS

Escondido, California

Consistently seeking to establish historically significant connections to whatever surroundings are provided, Moore Ruble Yudell have sought to align themselves with two major influences here. The first of these is a pre-existing master plan for Escondido by Pacifica Architects, who designed the City Hall nearby using a Mission Style emphasis in 1988. The architects, and especially Charles Moore, who founded the Los Angeles firm and was deeply involved in this project prior to his death in 1994, were also keen to evoke the earlier work of regional master Myron Hunt, who also specialized in the Mission Style. Looking especially to Hunt's Throop Hall of 1910 at the California Institute of Technology and the Pasadena Public Library of 1927, they adopted a similar vocabulary of weighty bearing walls, hipped roofs, arcaded *passarelles* and integration with carefully landscaped gardens, adapting this language to a more broad based project than Hunt ever had the opportunity to realize. To offset what might otherwise have proven to be oppressive, unrelenting massiveness, compositional surprises have been introduced much in keeping with the barely suppressed, zestful approach also seen in the earlier work produced by this office, in what typically comes across as sheer joy in

the knowledge that they understand what people respond to. These surprises which transfer from the exterior elevations into the generation of plan forms, include large looping arches, intersecting lines and layered volumes, which screen interior spaces from both heat and noise. The architectural massing of the centre, which includes a one-thousand-five-hundred-and-thirty-two seat lyric theatre, four-hundred seat community theatre, art centre with museum, studios and small library, and conference centre, has been intentionally manipulated to reinforce that screening.

The lyric theatre has been placed at the intersection of Valley Parkway and Escondido Boulevard so that its fly-tower holds the corner and the roofs of the spaces connected to it cascade down to the garden area protected by the L-shaped form of the complex. This grassy quadrangle, designed to look as informal as possible and yet echo the oval lines of the performance spaces, mitigates between the campus and the complex, breaking into smaller courtyards as it dissipates along both arms of the centre. This sense of using the building form as both a wall to the main street and an arcaded village facing the campus they protect, pervades the complex making the interior elevations

appear to be a stage set that prepares those approaching it for the performances they will see inside. The question, of how to architecturally deal with the common feature of a high box-like fly-tower and lower roof over the seating – in a way that goes beyond modernist, functional expression – has been a preoccupation for many of the architects presented in this book, and has been solved in this instance by incremental sealing and cascading forms.

The focal point of the Escondido complex is the one-thousand-five-hundred-and-twenty-four seat concert hall, intended for symphonies, opera, drama and musical theatre. The architects and their acoustic consultants, the Talaske group, decided to seek a combination between a classic, sweeping opera house form and a shoe box concert hall with an adjustable stage. The acousticians paid special attention to the sound reflection patterns within the first quarter second in an effort to create a lively atmosphere in the room; using CAD modelling and a 1:24 scale model of the auditorium to fine-tune reflection characteristics, with digital signal processing software used to replicate the acoustic environment. The result of these tests was a reduction in the depth of the balcony.

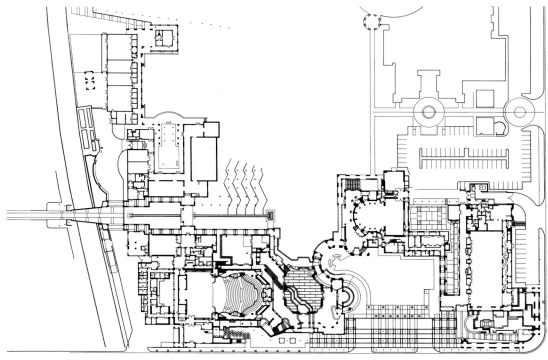

Site plan

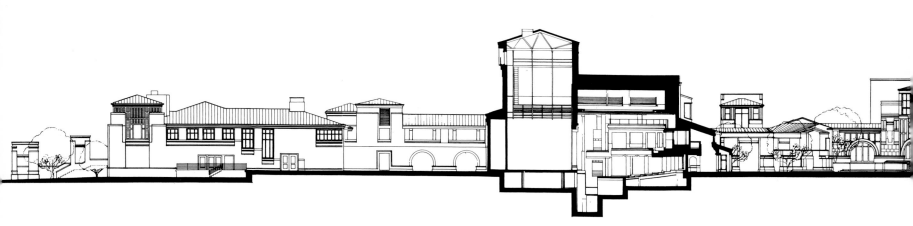

ABOVE: Lyric theatre; BELOW: Site section including lyric theatre

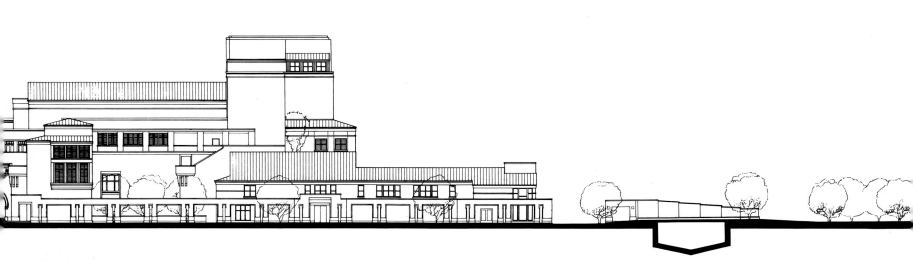

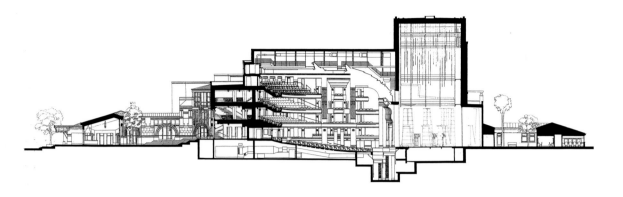

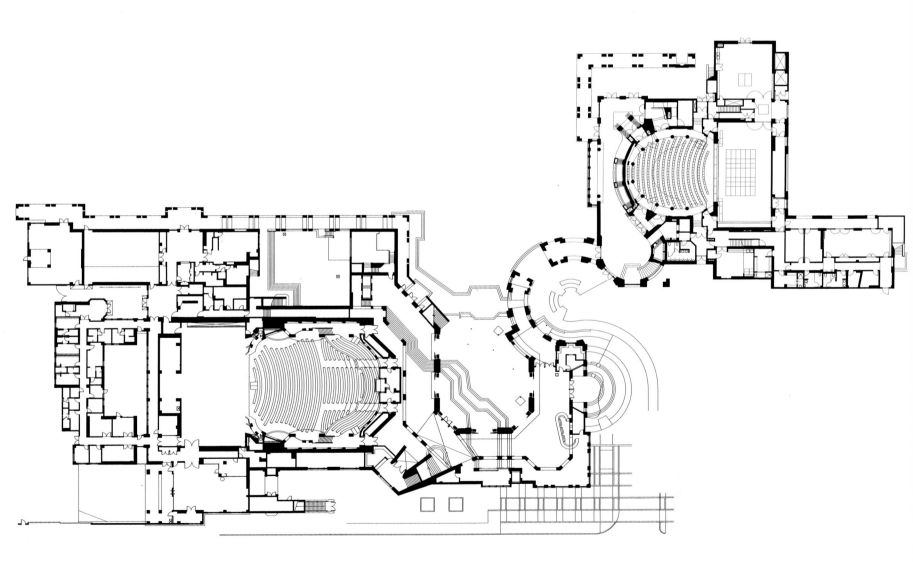

OPPOSITE: Concert hall; FROM ABOVE: Section through concert hall; ground floor plan including the lyric theatre and concert hall

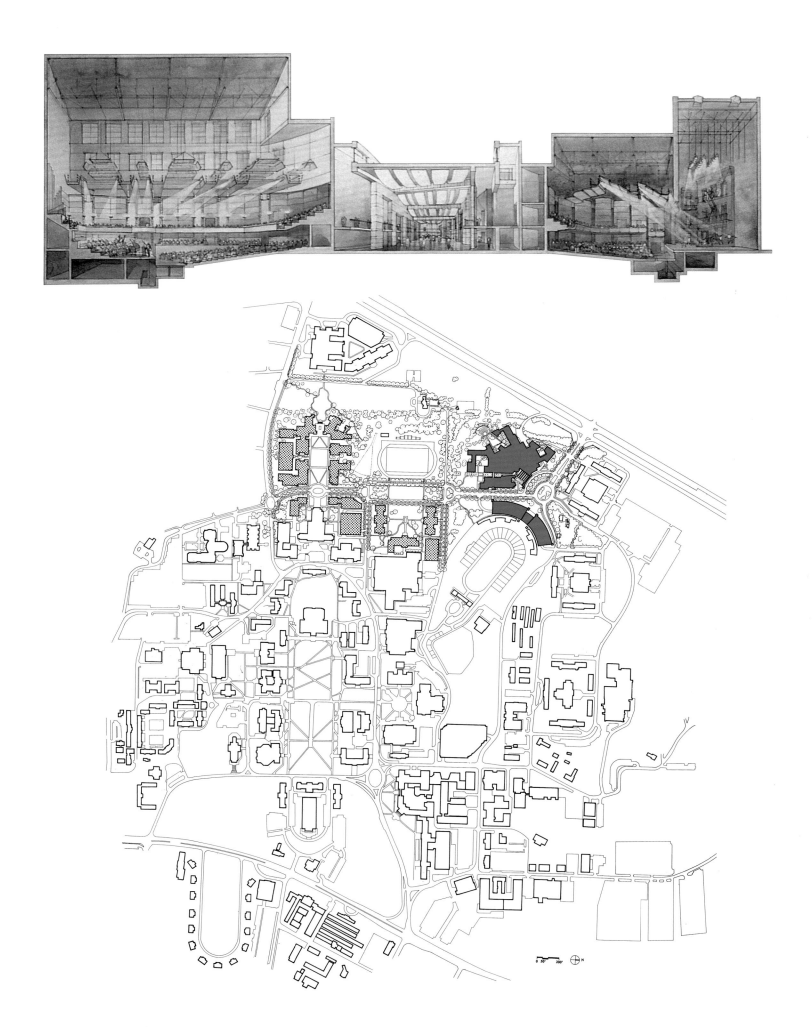

MOORE RUBLE YUDELL

CENTER FOR THE PERFORMING ARTS

College Park, Maryland

Designed to replace the Tawes Fine Arts Building, which now houses the University departments of Music and Theatre, this new centre will echo the dual educational and cultural role of its predecessor but has a widely expanded agenda. Despite stiff competition, Moore Ruble Yudell won this commission because their design most closely reflected the expressed wish of the University that it fit the existing campus plan, and establish both real and potential connections with the surrounding community. The consistent willingness and facility that this firm has shown in tackling similarly complex problems in the past, and its well documented concern with the perpetuation of historical urban patterns that still have meaning today, gave it a decided edge in this instance. The jury found the other entries too monumental and lacking the integral scale necessary to effectively mitigate between campus and community.

Considering the wide variety of spatial requirements included in this building, ranging from a one-thousand-two-hundred seat concert hall, three-hundred-and-fifty seat recital hall, six-hundred-and-fifty seat proscenium theatre, two-hundred seat dance studio and two-hundred seat experimental theatre, with fifteen classrooms, thirty-one laboratories, forty-six teaching studios, more than one hundred faculty and staff offices, a performing arts library and a one-hundred-and-twenty-five seat restaurant, the architects' achievement is all the more impressive.

The Moore Ruble Yudell design is intended to be an integral cultural complex in its own right, and yet also provide a master plan for future growth. This framework directs the orderly growth of the West Campus, establishes clear connections to the Main Campus, develops a rich hierarchy of gathering places and buildings and ensures that the Centre for Performing Arts is a coherent part of the evolving whole.

This 300,000 square-foot building benefits from the close functional relationships among its parts, having a varied and intimate feeling of scale. Accordingly, the building is configured as a kind of aca-

demic village. The open spaces and courtyards are shaped to establish points of entry, enhance views from the buildings, provide a variety of social and activity spaces and be complimentary. Courtyards related to academic functions are typically south-facing for warmth and light, while studios such as dance and music benefit from soft north and east clerestory light. While each programme's uses are clustered for clear functional adjacencies, there are zones where they meet and share social stairs, lounges and courts. This allows for both departmental identity and casual cross-fertilization among the performing arts. The library occupies a central functional and symbolic role with access from the public plazas as well as directly from the music department. It has one floor for ease of movement and function, with views to two courtyards.

The major public entry is focused around the landscaped North Circle. Entry courts to the library, music, theatre and dance spaces are contiguous but have differentiated identity and scale. The vehicular and pedestrian approaches to the theatres are clear with ample room for dropping off and waiting. Service areas are screened with landscape and grade changes. Locating structured parking to the south provides some six hundred spaces on four levels. An arcaded connection allows for direct covered entry to a balcony level of the lobby, whilst a second arcade provides similar access to the academic areas. This building also serves as a buffer to the sports facility to the south.

A grand processional sequence has been orchestrated from the arrival at the entry plaza, anchored by a marquee tower, through a clerestory-lit lobby which serves as a piazza for all major performance halls, continuing on to the restaurant and out to a dining court and landscaped amphitheatre beyond. Along this sequence each hall has a strong identity and its own portico. Balconies for each hall overlook the lobby, adding the chance to see and be seen in this grand space. Plaster canopies soften and reflect the clerestory light. The rich

character and diversity of the plazas, the lobbies and courtyards allows for flexibility of social and performance events.

The performance halls are shaped to encourage a close relationship between every member of the audience and the performers. They are seen as places to enhance lively communication at an intimate scale. To that end the geometry of the spaces meets the technical and acoustical requirements while maintaining clear short sight lines. The halls allow filtered clerestory light for daytime performances, with the flexibility for total darkness when desired.

The architects and their consultants used the wide variety of performance spaces available in the programme as an opportunity to implement a concept of spatial tuning or variable acoustics. This approach by necessity varies from hall to hall, and the geometry of each space was married to the acoustic response required.

The concert hall, built high and relatively narrow with massive materials, is meant to surround a capacity audience with the sound produced by an orchestra and chorus. However, when large ensembles rehearse, or smaller groups perform, interrelated systems of adjustable absorption elements and overhead sound-reflecting panels surround the performers adjusting the acoustical response of the room. On a smaller scale in the recital hall, similar variable acoustics systems will provide the right kind of support for musicians and tailor the listening experience to the audience.

In the proscenium theatre, the fixed acoustical environment is oriented toward opera and ballet with forestage reflectors that carefully balance the loudness of the pit orchestra with the needs of the singers and dancers on stage. Amplified musical programmes, such as musical theatre or other popular forms of entertainment, and theatrical productions that feature voices which are not electronically amplified, will take advantage of the adjustable absorption system that promotes intimacy and speech intelligibility.

FROM ABOVE: Sectional perspective showing concert hall and proscenium theatre; site plan

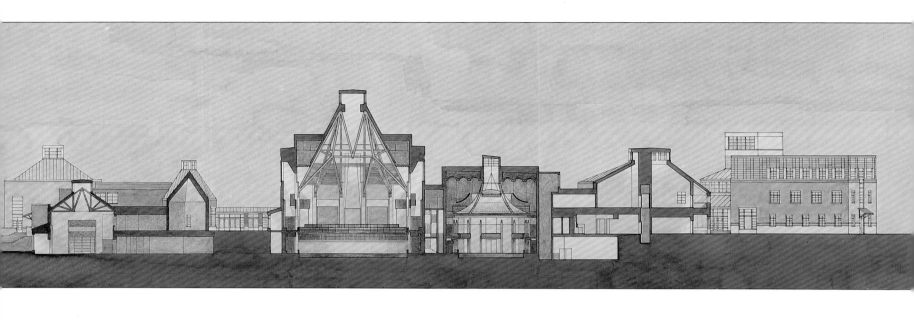

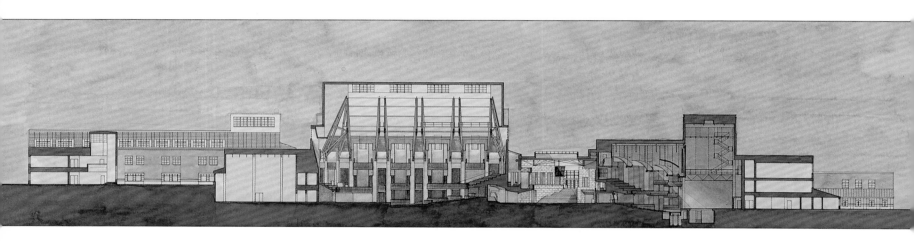

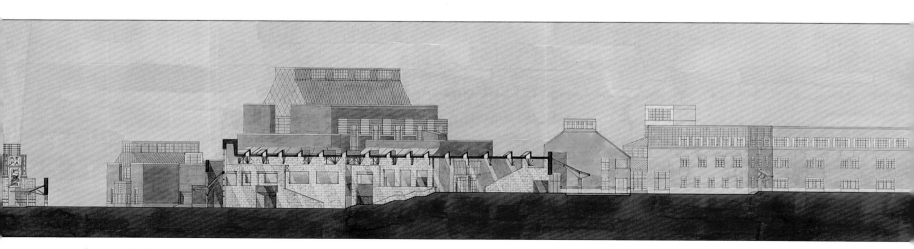

FROM ABOVE: Cross-section through concert hall and recital hall; longitudinal section through concert hall and proscenium theatre; section through processional sequence

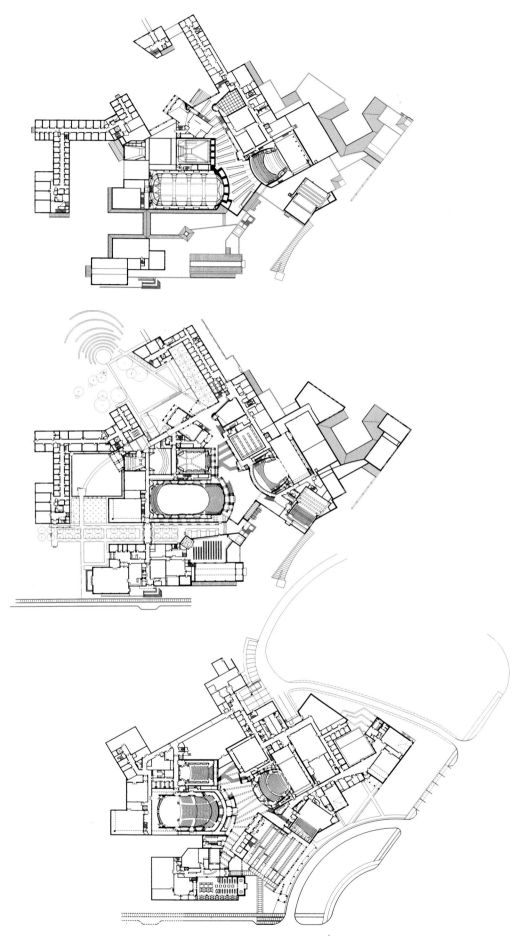

FROM ABOVE: Second floor plan; first floor plan; ground floor plan

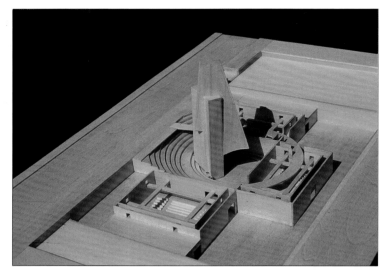
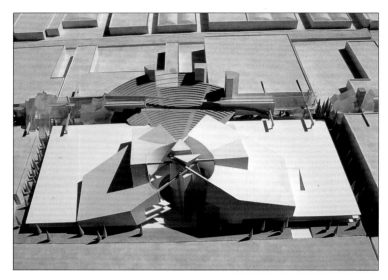

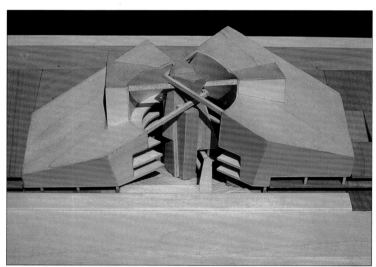
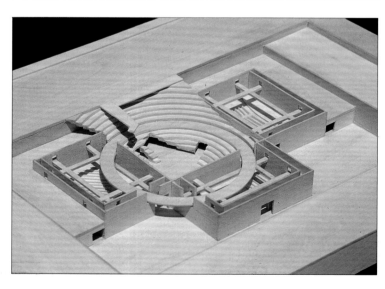
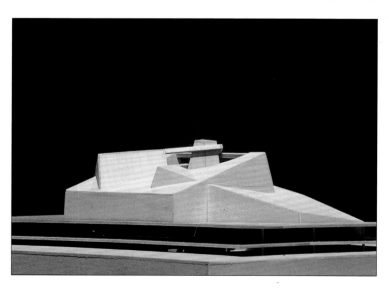

ERIC OWEN MOSS
THE WARNER AVENUE THEATER

Culver City, California

As in the example of the Green Umbrella Theater in the same area of Los Angeles, Warner Avenue begins with a circular form, which has been further fragmented into segments, but it is surmounted by a tower, rather than the upside-down abstracted bow-string trusses, used to mirror the pre-existing structure of an industrial shed.

An overview of Moss' recent work indicates a marked preference for the circle, which is found in several residential projects, as well as the Ince Theatre where a hemisphere has been elevated above the ground and separated into pieces. In terms of working method, Moss is a maverick ideologically opposed to total reliance on computer-aided design; his progress sketches for this project, as with all others, reveal the methodical development of a design idea from a pre-selected geometrical form and its continual manual refinement. In this respect, he moves against a growing trend found in several other avant-

garde offices in Los Angeles, such as that of Frank Gehry or Morphosis, where computers have taken on increased importance, as discussed in the explanation of the evolution of the Disney concert hall design in the introduction to this book.

Moss' work benefits from his ability to visualize space without artificial intelligence, and to continuously shape those visualizations graphically. Warner Avenue is the latest instance of his thorough knowledge of geometry; a skill which many architects forget as soon as they satisfy an academic requirement for it. In a sense, he continues the traditional persona of architect as geometer, the human repository of sacred knowledge as exemplified by Isidorus of Miletus and Anthemius of Tralles, the builders of the Hagia Sophia and the unknown designer of Chartres. Unlikely as Warner Avenue seems as a possible contender for similar architectural greatness, close inspection shows a

kindred process at work; the search for ways to break existing conventions, find new forms and provide a suitable background for yet-to-be-discovered methods of performance.

Grouped together with the Green Umbrella and Ince Theaters, the Warner Avenue project represents radical formal experimentation in a genre that may generally be seen to be moving in the opposite direction today; towards increasing rigidity, within envelopes strictly dictated by acoustical considerations. Even the most cursory historical overview of theatre design, however, indicates that such radical experimentation has always been the rule rather than the exception, and inflexibility at any stage in the growth of an institution is a precursor to atrophy in the next. Moss' efforts in this arena may disturb purists, but it is a refreshing and healthy counterpoint to the shoe box cult seen elsewhere.

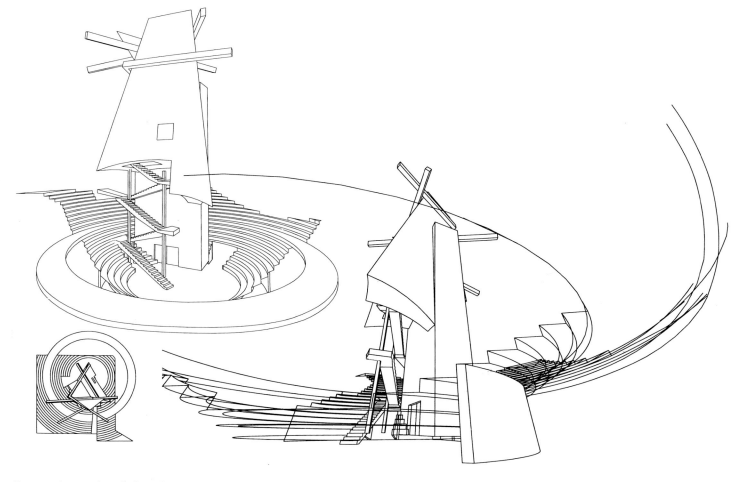

Perspectives and roof plan

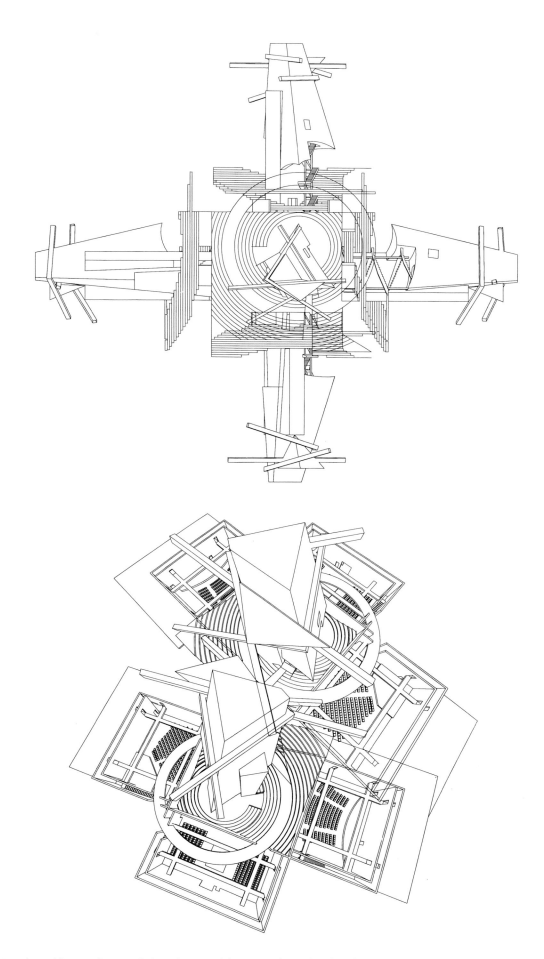

FROM ABOVE: Theatre plan with superimposed elevations; aerial perspectives showing the interior

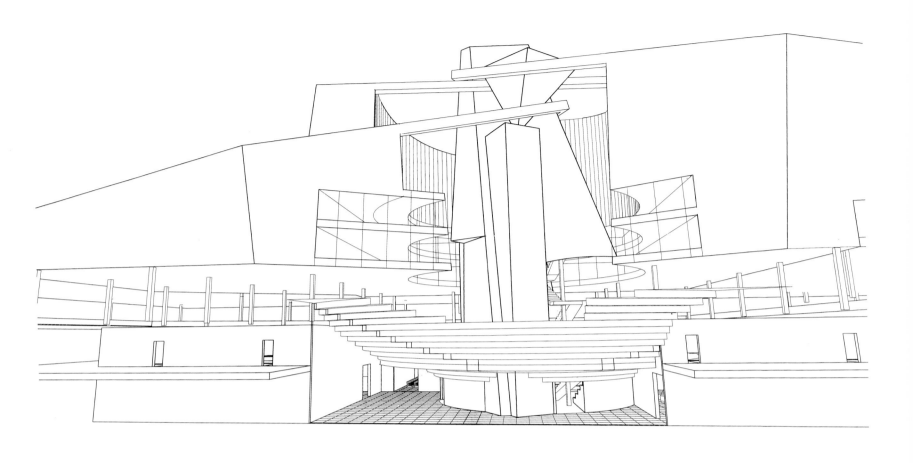

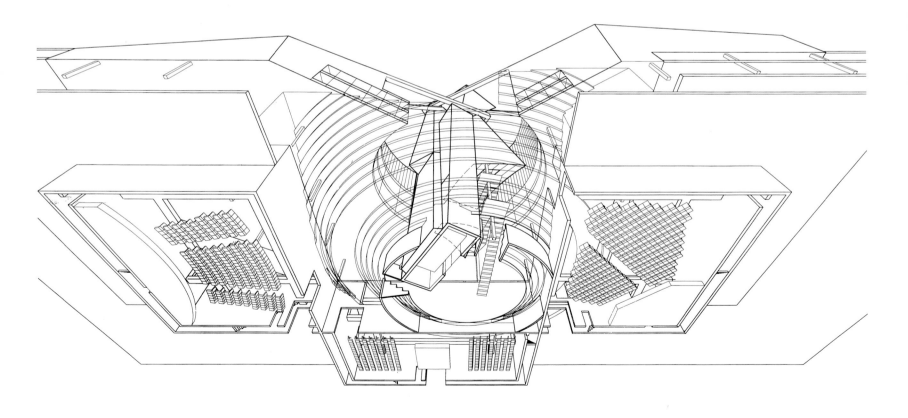

FROM ABOVE: *Interior perspective; worm's-eye view*

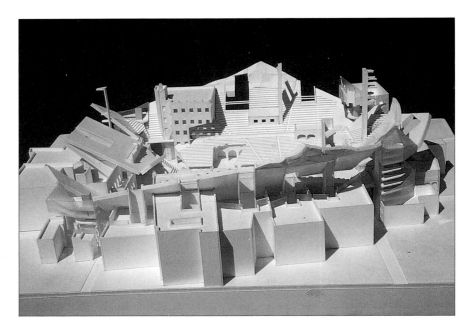

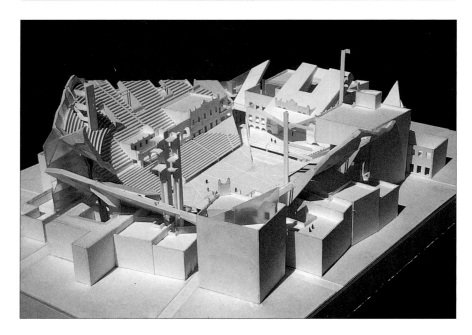

ERIC OWEN MOSS
NUEVA VIEJA

Havana, Cuba

The inevitable and long awaited transformation of Cuba and of its capital Havana draws closer everyday. The repressed desire for transformation is enormous and, when it comes, it will be of a high magnitude socially and ideologically, as well as physically. The Plaza Vieja proposal by Eric Moss reflects and symbolizes this anticipated change and is extreme in its reaction against the spectre of the past. Considering this, and taken in that spirit, its excesses are understandable if not totally believable when re-examined in the cold light of day.

The plaza is located roughly in the centre of the mandala-shaped city, favouring the easterly, port-side of the north-south axis. Moss has labelled it the 'erogenous zone' of old Havana and advocates drastic surgery to allow the sensory overload that is soon to hit the country to be experienced fully, without rejection. Hoping that this project will be the catalyst for a whole new initiative in Cuban city planning and architecture, he advocates an 'attack' on the old plaza and major alterations to the traditional core.

Dating from the seventeenth century, the Plaza Vieja began as a park surrounded by several large, single family houses. In the eighteenth century the area became an open market and carnival site and one hundred years later, the area was demolished and the market moved out to the perimeter. In 1900 it was replanted with trees and landscaped as a park and, just before the revolution, it achieved its present form, surrounded by contiguous arcaded buildings, with a large garage built under the raised plaza.

Moss' proposal implodes the present plaza, placing a forum/theatre/stadium, which he visualizes as a multi-purpose arena, inside the deteriorating site. While the function of the plaza, as a place for public gatherings, will remain the same as it has for four hundred years, the architect intends to substantially erase the existing colonial architecture, leaving only a few pieces of it intact as an image of the past. Moss sees the real tradition of the plaza as defining public expectations, rather than a static architectural form derived from outside sources; the changing functions of residential enclave, park and market square that it had over the centuries, providing evidence of redirected public purpose. In this sense, the architect sees this proposal as being consistent with the pattern of change and continuity of purpose that has characterized the area.

The buildings surrounding the plaza are three- to six-storey structures, which typically have large central courts, and are configured according to the pre-established block grid of old Havana and this aspect of the grouping was identified as a second target. Moss resolved to 'rupture' that grid and to re-form a portion of it into a new, more loosely organized street which cuts through the old structures connecting the central courtyards around the square, turning them into public gathering places. In a new hierarchy of order, the plaza becomes a large-scale public space and this outer, pedestrian street is a smaller scaled secondary sequence of spaces, related to the square but quite different in character.

Moss has described his design in the following terms:

The proposal is an aesthetic act and socio-political act. The new structure intervenes in an old neighbourhood leaving a physical skeleton of the old sociology, but suggesting a new social prospect. City buildings cut the new bleachers. Bleachers slice the old buildings, and the severed remains must find new aesthetic and social purpose. Space is now defined above, below, or through the bleacher plane. And the serpenting 'dissolve' . . . makes exterior fronts along what once was the dark archeology of old colonial buildings. The project intends to be historically naive. It assumes the world can change, can become something it's not. It never assumes we know the city in perpetuity, that the city knows us well, and that we merely reshuffle recognizable pieces. The project remodels, revises, re-interprets, renews. It doesn't simply bulldoze. But is not afraid to bulldoze. The project looks askance at the bloodless colonial architecture, but doesn't entirely deny that architecture a residual place.

As a part of that residual place, an existing building at the north end of the old plaza arcade will become a stage incorporating a new proscenium structure which curves over the roof of the original building. A new orchestra pit will be cut from the roof of the garage to be located just to the south of the stage. Performances can occur on the stage, or anywhere else within the plaza; the complete realization of a long held dream of full, social participation.

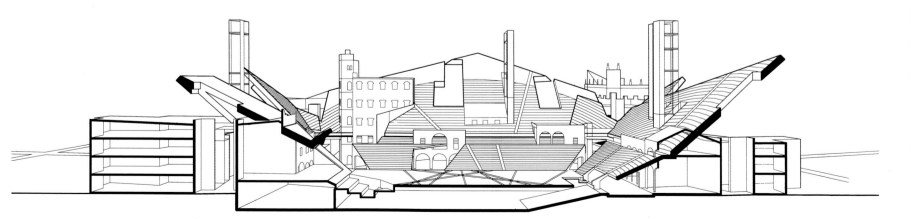

Sectional perspective

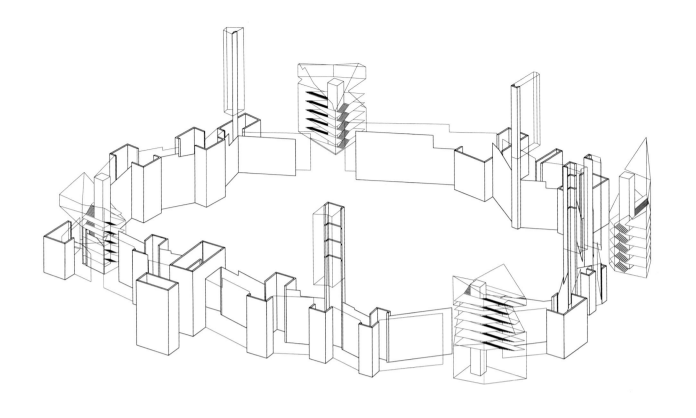

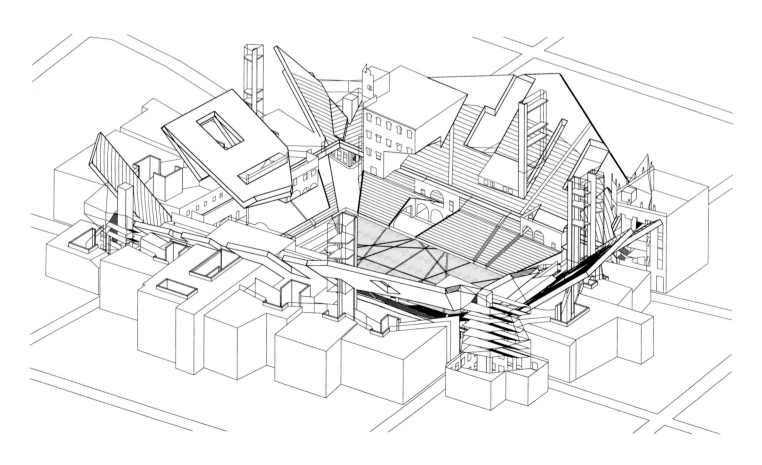

Sequential axonometrics

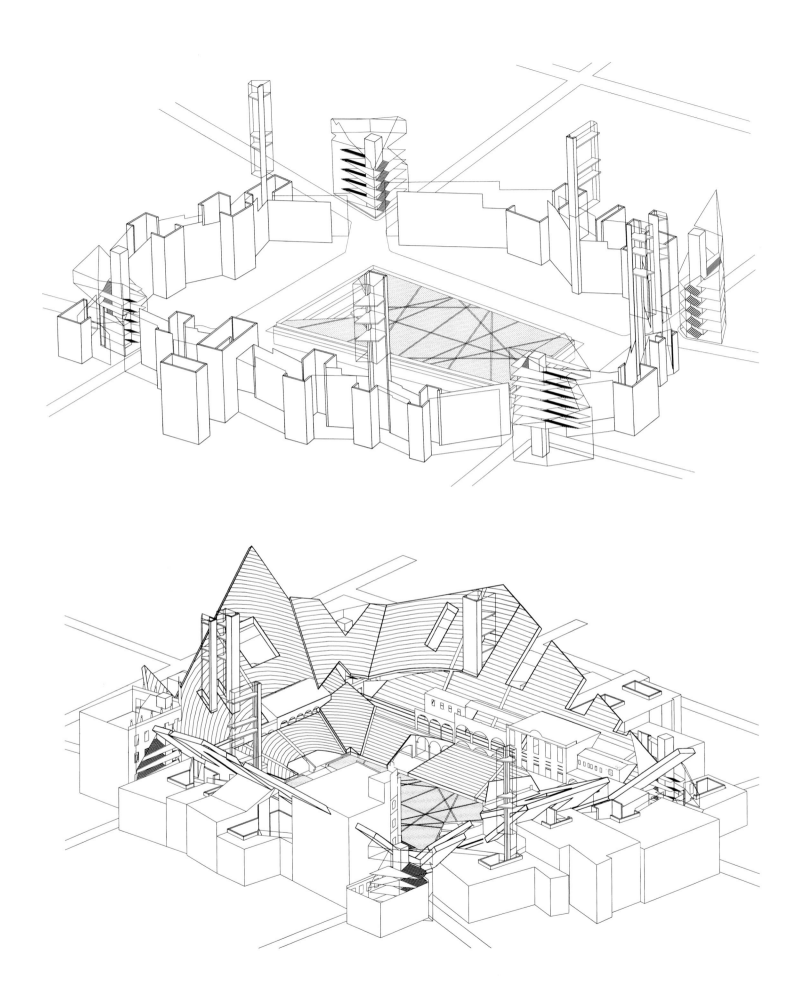

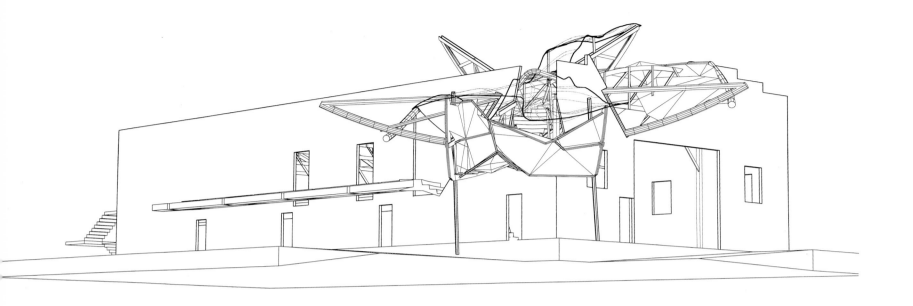

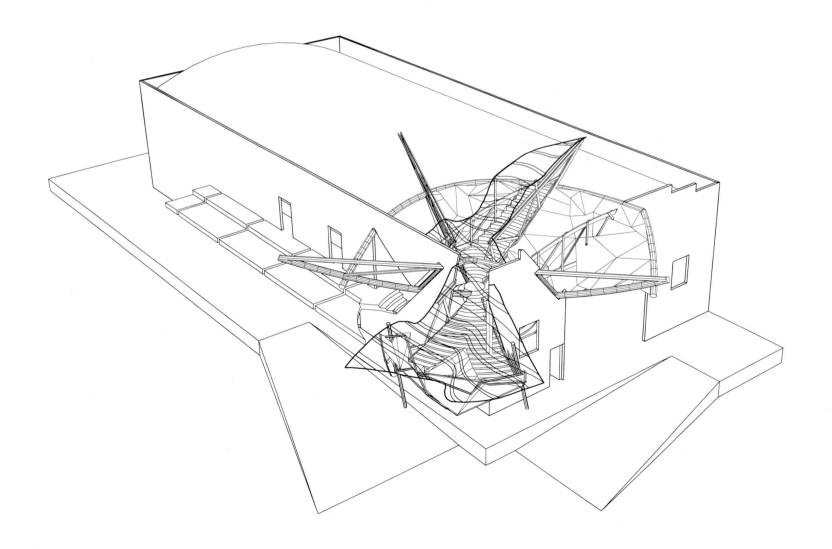

ERIC OWEN MOSS
THE GREEN UMBRELLA

Culver City, California

Eric Moss has established himself in the enviable position of being able to re-configure an entire sector of Los Angeles, in an area where the motion picture industry was first established and now continues to grow once again. The industrial shed is a predominant building form in Culver City, located between the centre of Los Angeles and the Pacific, and these typically consist of a straightforward, rectilinear envelope, covered by a curved roof held up with wooden bow-string trusses.

Frederick Smith, the developer for many of the properties which Moss designs in this area, is decidedly enlightened but pragmatic nonetheless, and a consistently successful formula that he and Moss have hit upon is to use architectural pyrotechnics to attract public attention, create visual identity and sell leasable space in what is otherwise a simple retail and commercial zone. The Green Umbrella addresses all of these requirements, evoking the show business continuum of Culver City, the increasing wish for a public forum in Los Angeles, and the growing need to use mixed-use development to make that slowly expanding forum financially viable in an increasingly competitive market-place. Moss has effectively blended both public and private aspects of the scheme, allowing relatively unhindered access to the theatre whilst retaining the privacy of the offices in the remainder of the building; creating a symbiotic, profitable relationship for each.

The bow-string structure that the architect found in the existing building has been appropriated as a symbolic form, and used as a sculptural device to signal the entrance. Several new trusses, turned upside-down and inserted at odd angles, like spokes in an imaginary wheel, correspond to the theatre below, literally turning the corner of the shed into a separate building.

As the national counterweight to New York, Los Angeles, at the end of the twentieth century, is in the process of adopting the persona of its east coast *alter ego*, with many intriguing parallels. New York, for example, was the immigration gateway to the United States for much of the nineteenth century, with the majority of those sailing past the Statue of Liberty to Ellis Island coming from the other side of the Atlantic. Los Angeles has taken over this role, accepting many new immigrants from the south and east, and its function as the new gateway to America, while still lacking a contemporary equivalent of the Statue of Liberty, is undeniable. Frank Lloyd Wright is credited with saying, during his first visit to Los Angeles, that it seemed as if the entire country had been placed on its edge and that everyone that was loose had rolled toward the Pacific. Los Angeles has now moved beyond its primary function as a centre for the dispossessed, or the embodiment of the 'American Dream', attracting those who felt compelled to find it in one of the many scenarios that it offered. Instead, people from outside the

country, lacking the luxury of the disillusionment that many Americans now feel about the dream they once had, of an easier, prosperous life in a physical Utopia, have been more than willing to appropriate it for themselves and to work hard enough to make it happen.

This significant change has caused Los Angeles to be labelled a 'social experiment', and the trends that emerge from Southern California these days are less related to fashion than they are to more substantial discoveries of ways that many diverse peoples can live together. That feeling of experimentation, pervades every aspect of life in the city, at all social levels, and may be accurately read in contemporary architecture, especially through the work of particularly sensitive architects such as Eric Moss. The Green Umbrella Theatre is yet another sign of this new inclusiveness, and the general determination to resist the pervasive fear that sometimes seems to grip the city. It moves the theatrical tradition that New York has boasted of for so long to a new plane, rather than continuing on with more of the same as others have done in the refurbishment of many of the older theatres that still exist in Los Angeles' own version of a downtown Broadway, which, not coincidently, goes by the same name.

Culver City, needs watching as an indicator of a different direction, whilst the Green Umbrella is at the forefront of finding a new role for an ancient institution.

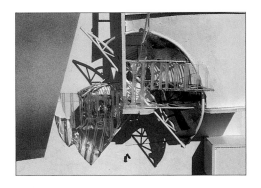 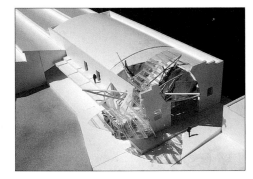 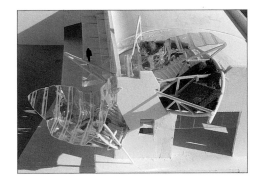

OPPOSITE: Exterior perspectives

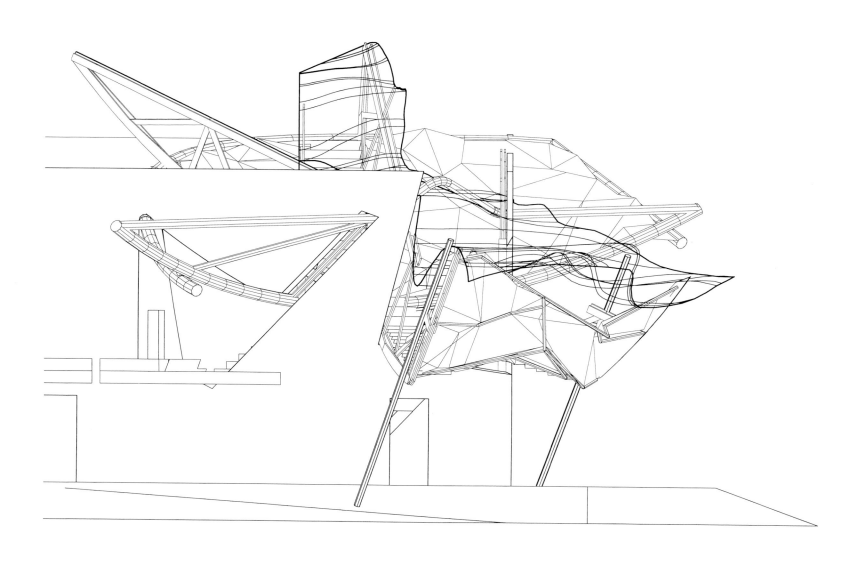

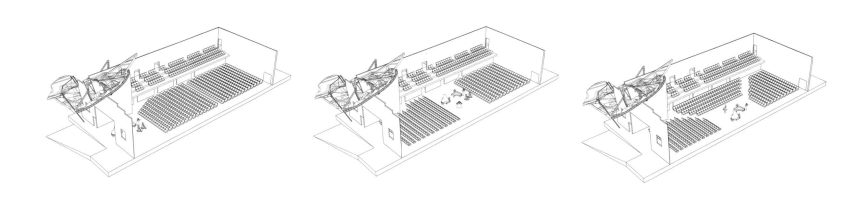

ABOVE: Detail of canopy; BELOW: Seating arrangements

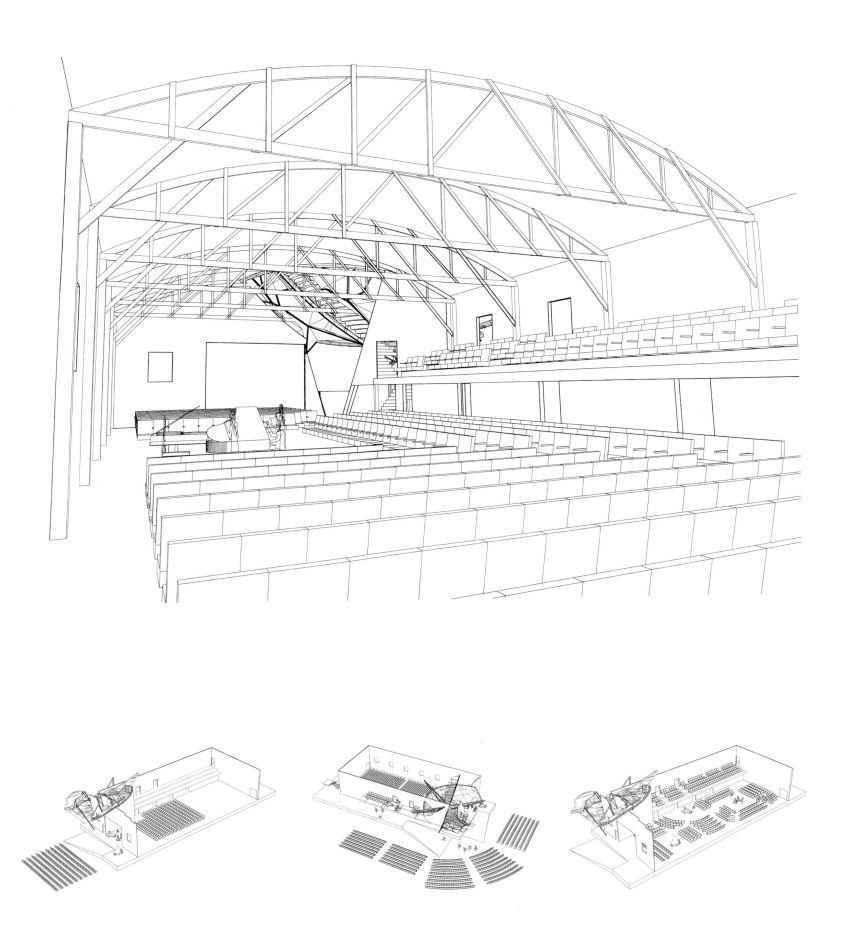

ABOVE: Interior perspective; BELOW: Seating arrangements

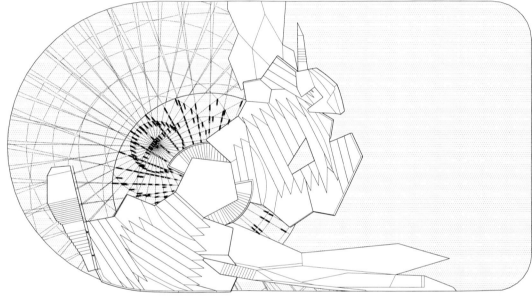

ERIC OWEN MOSS
VESEY STREET THEATER
New York, New York

In dealing with the difficult parameters presented by a traffic island in Battery Park, New York City, near the Hudson River, Eric Moss opted for a diagrammatic fulfilment of the public and private zones of the site, allowing for multiple use. The project is a round open-air theatre, with an outdoor projection platform and large video screen that can accommodate various scales of performances day and night. Moss has visualized this as an enlarged version of Speakers' Corner in Hyde Park, London, a public podium where opinions can be freely expressed by anyone; 'a forum for purveyors of current wisdoms to stand up and yell'.

The outdoor stage is flanked by two stairs that provide access to an enclosed backstage, while two large spaces below ground are contiguous to the stage space, with roofs formed by the bleacher seating above. Vertical glass walls, which slice through the bleachers, divide and enclose these rooms, to make the activity below ground visible from a park nearby. The two rooms are capable of dealing with a variety of uses, depending on how the neighbourhood around the theatre eventually evolves. These could range from town meetings, open discussions, lectures and films to commercial facilities such as retail shops, restaurants and clubs in the future.

Moss has connected the submerged precinct with the upper level by two 'excavated slots', the first of which continues the line of Vesey Street to the west. The second extends north in anticipation of people who may walk to the complex from a new office building just being completed in the vicinity. A third axis runs diagonally from the north-east. Moss aligned these excavations with shadow lines cast by the bleachers, which will be east-west at noon on the winter solstice and north-south at six in the evening on the summer solstice. He disclaims neolithic recollections in such alignments, believing it to be unlikely that theatre users will realize or care about the solar source of these cuts in the surface of the park. He has done this:

To move the design beyond simple utility. The relationship to a theoretical shadow (not actual because the surrounding buildings preclude its literal appearance) and to elemental conditions of earth, sun and sky . . . manifests the need for the presence of the subject matter in the life of a city, and simultaneously an inability to deliver it unambiguously. The slots will remain enigmatic, but will be fun to play in.

The construction of the theatre itself is as complex as the architect's diverse motives in orienting circulation, involving the intersection of a partial sphere and another made of pentagonal concrete plates, which hold the bleachers. The two spheres have slightly different geometric centres, both of which are intended to be distinct from the turning radius of Vesey Street. The intention is to introduce disturbance and disharmony, rather than harmony. By offsetting these centres, so that dissonance will transmit a subliminal essence of resolution, Moss has provided a fundamental geometric order of sphere and penta-sphere, but by blurring the relationship of the seating, stage, projection screen and circulation shafts to them he wants to make a clear reading difficulty.

A portion of the first, partial sphere has been removed next to the five sided outdoor stage and landscaped to continue the surrounding grass onto the theatre. A series of lines, coinciding to longitude and latitude, is etched on the surface of this 'excavated earth bowl', meant to describe the underlying organizational order of the spheres and their centres to those who pick up on the disjuncture and are aware that a geometrical strategy is at work. At points where these lines intersect on the bowl, perpendicular steel pipes of average human height project from the curving surface. These pipes surround the stage from the western and southern sides and can also be used for exhibits. This double use emphasizes the impromptu character of the entire complex. The grass recollects a traditional, park like surface and may be used for picnics, but may also attract demonstrators, drawn by this highly visible location and convenient open space. The theatre, screens and subterranean rooms also invite unexpected uses by local residents and office workers nearby. Moss has treated this as an urban sculpture with many facets borrowed from the park. He also feels that:

The image of the object along view corridors, from the Hudson and from adjoining office buildings is equally important. The view from above should be astonishing, intriguing, enervating. The theatre should be both recognizable and enigmatic. The legibility, the meaning, will vary from observer to observer over the course of the day, over the course of the year. So the theatre will not only serve those who exploit its utility, but will perpetually provoke those who simply look.

Plan of auditorium

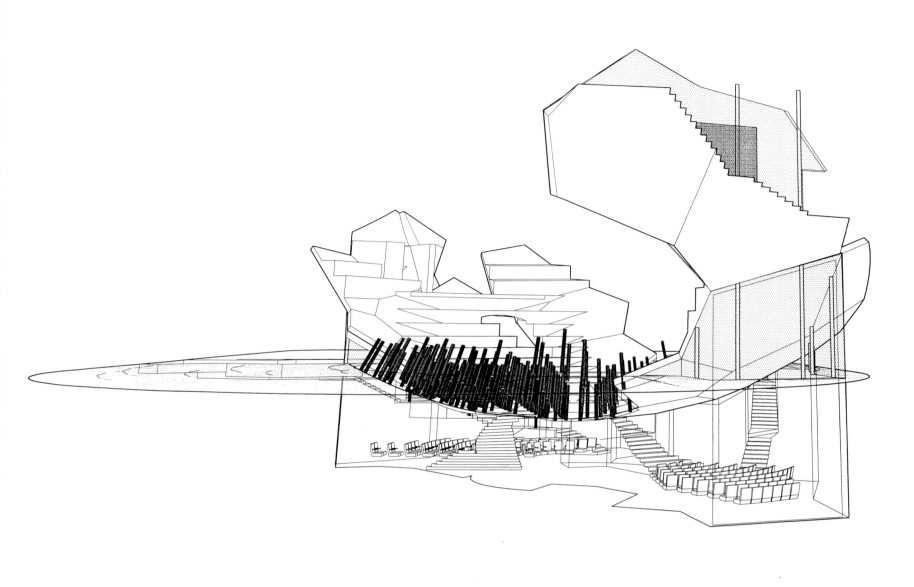

  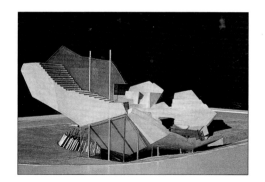

Elevation

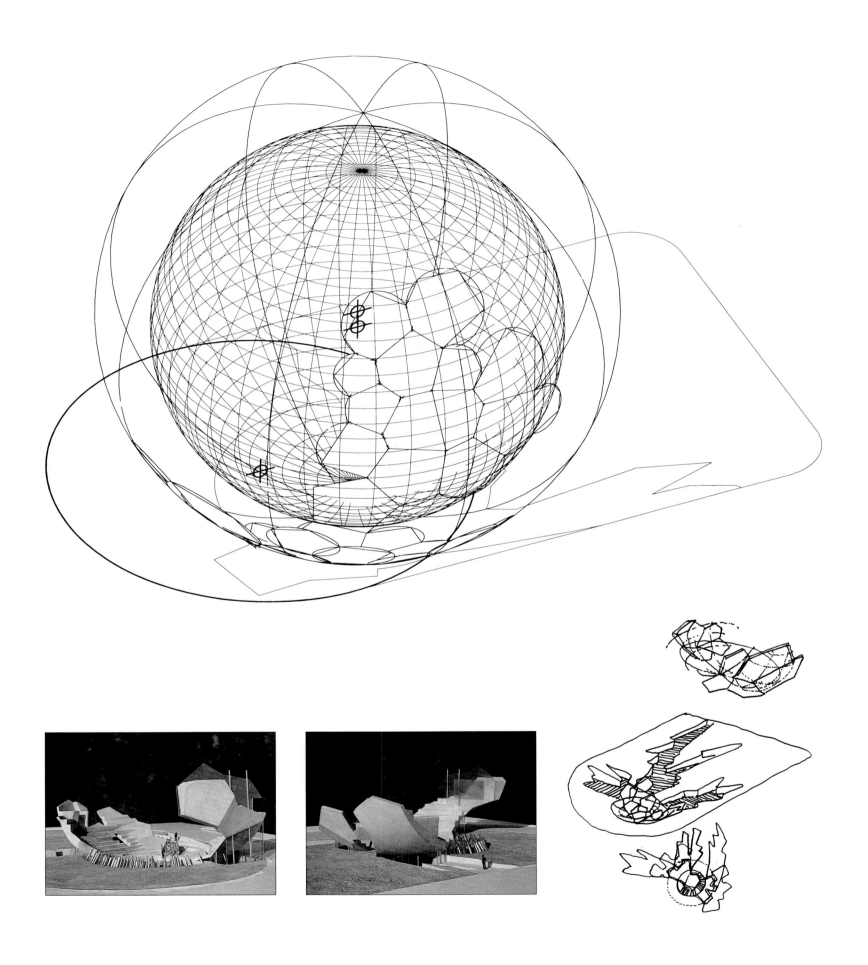

FROM ABOVE: Constructional geometries; concept sketches

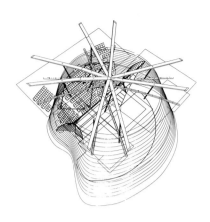

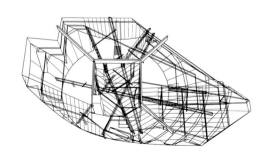

ERIC OWEN MOSS
CONTEMPORARY ART CENTRE

Tours, France

This competition entry for a hall dedicated to Francis Poulenc in Tours is instructive as an unconventional approach to conditions that generally elicit a more conservative design response, indicating new possibilities in theatre design. Here Eric Moss has once again attempted to 'rewrite' the constructed history of the area surrounding the site, picking up clues from the many layers of which it is composed, as a counter-commentary on public expectations of what a theatre should be, and transferred this concept of dislocation and reconstitution into a literal site planning strategy. To this end Moss proposed the excavation and reconfiguration of the ground plane from the Rue Clouet and the Parc Mirabeau to the Rue du Petit Pre in a series of contiguous, gently sloping grass plains, differentiated by concrete retaining walls. These plains, which alternatively slope between the northern and southern edges of the site, intersect roughly near the middle, creating an irregular valley which slopes from west to east. This first act, of what Moss refers to as a 'rupture' of the site to produce a new landscape, provides a fresh foundation for four new structures which will bridge over it.

At the east end of the site, the Centre for Contemporary Creation begins as a cone which tilts toward the Rue Clouet. An imaginary vertical plane slices through this cone at the property line, leaving the cut volume inside the invisible legal boundary and the original Euclidean profile becomes difficult for all but the most practised eye to determine inside the transformed object. A museum component is expressed as a helix, with its unequally sized floors spinning clockwise around an orthogonal block that is roughly square in plan and contains the café. Intended as the social hub of the centre, this café is accessible from the Parc Mirabeau to the east, as well as internally from the west and is surrounded by meeting rooms, an information facility and a bookshop, in addition to the kitchen with its accompanying service areas. The café roof is glazed, as is its east wall, which visually connects it to the park. This glass roof is supported on the top chords of three hairpin trusses that also carry the main floors of the building. These are slotted as they leave the café to allow people there to see activity at all levels and a truss chord passes through each slot. The café block, on an axis with the theatre at the opposite end of the site, is intended to dominate the massing of the museum roof. The main roof has three elements, which slope from the building perimeter to meet one of the major concrete walls.

The public entry to the Centre for Contemporary Creation faces west, with tilted glass planes that extend into the building, shaping the entrance area. Pedestrians enter at ground level and move up a stair to the exhibit space. Above this are the educational centre and lecture theatres, with the administration offices at the top which overlook the park.

The theatre comprises the second major portion of the complex, dominating the western end of the site as a counter-balance to the museum to the east. It was designed in steps, the first of which was the formation of a vertical Euclidean cylinder, as in the design of the centre it opposes. Moss intended a metaphor of compression to make this form seem as if it was being 'squeezed' or 'attacked' by the existing buildings at the perimeter of the site to create an impression of 'disingenuous difference' to the historical fabric adjacent to it. The second design move was to insert part of a sphere under this cylinder to form a curved soffit beneath it, followed by the insertion of two walls placed perpendicular to one another, which support these stacked forms at ground level. The final compositional gesture was to position a cube over this vertical assembly, dividing it into several sections which accommodate production requirements, access and seating. The cylinder protrudes through the sides of the cube to allow the curved forms to predominate.

A glazed lobby at garden level serves both the theatre and the museum, creating a visual connection between each component in a pragmatic and symbolic gesture intended to re-define two institutions which have a roughly parallel historical time line. Both are served by a three level garage placed below the new central landscape. From here, there is direct access to the glass enclosed entry, which faces a paved plaza for outdoor performances, and then to the theatre lobby above by stairs or elevators and on into the theatre itself. The auditorium has three adjoining tiers of seats, and from north to south, each slopes more steeply, providing three different perspectives of the stage. The box, extending from the central, conical section, provides additional seating, as well as a projection and lighting booth. The roof of the Theatre is also supported by trusses, which radiate out from a position roughly equivalent to the right centre of the stage. The top chord of each truss bends twice in section, once in plan, conforming to the changing geometrical profiles around it. The section profile of the curve determines the shape of the ceiling over the seats, with acoustic panels, catwalks and lights suspended from a grid.

Had it been chosen, the Tours Contemporary Art Centre and Theatre may have been modified slightly by consultant considerations, but its underlying formal geometry is so strong that it definitely represents the most obviously 'architect-led' case study of all those included here. It also contradicts any preconceived notions of required formal relationships in this genre, and provides valuable insights into ways in which those preconceptions may be exploded.

OPPOSITE, FROM ABOVE: Aerial perspective; worm's-eye view

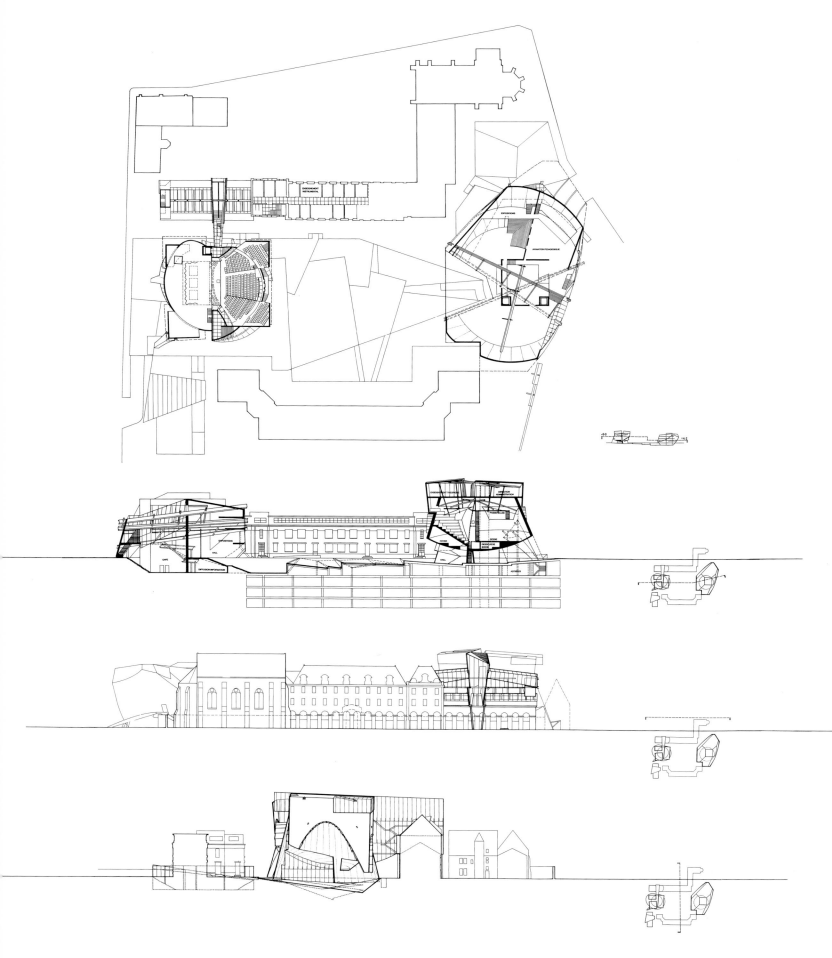

FROM ABOVE: First floor plan; section; elevation; section through courtyard

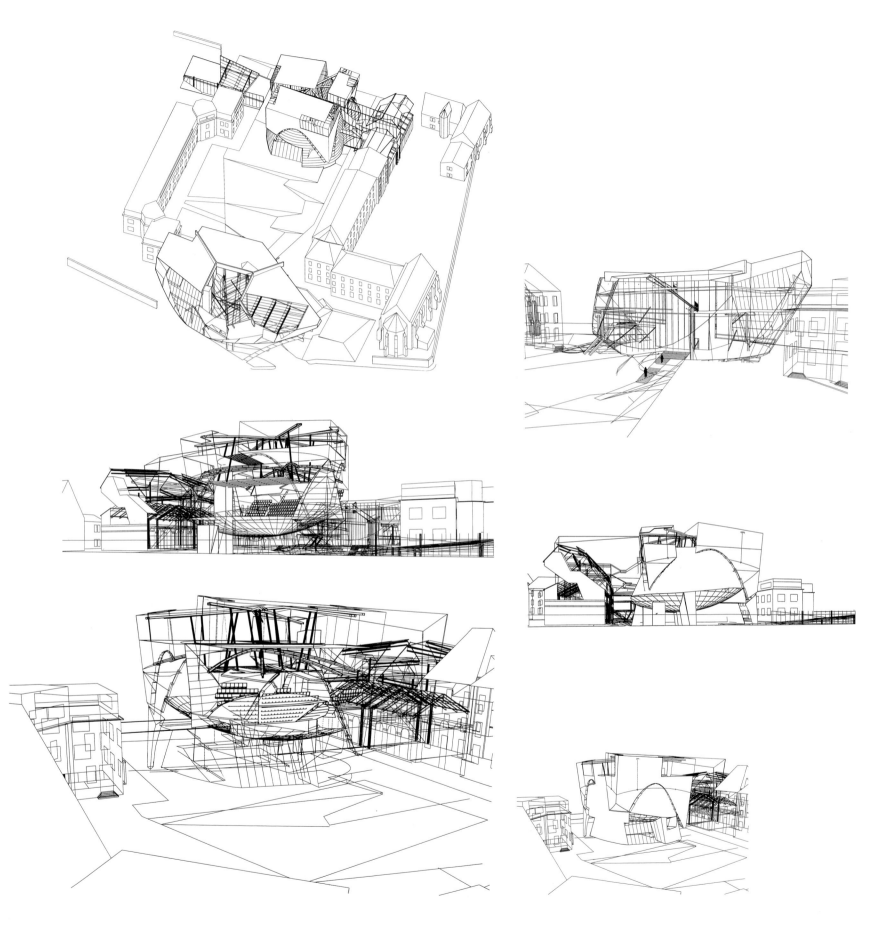

FROM ABOVE, LEFT TO RIGHT: Aerial view of overall scheme, cutaway to reveal internal structures; exterior views

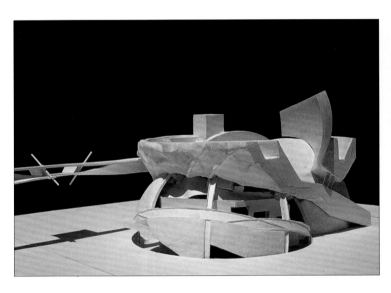 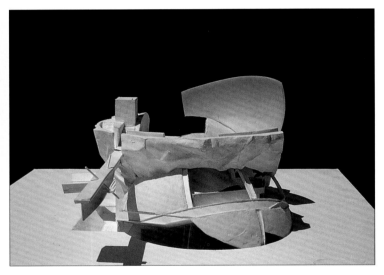

 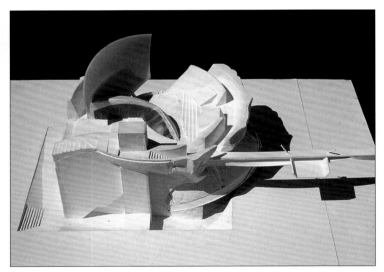

ERIC OWEN MOSS
INCE THEATER
Culver City, California

As one of a group of new performance venues being included in the 'connected points' palindrome – that Fredrick and Laurie Smith envision in western Los Angeles – the Ince Theater represents a return to the original concept of the genre, in spite of its avant-garde aspects. The Smiths believe that theatre has lost its initial spontaneity, as well as its cultural significance, and has been relegated to dealing with topics that are historically obscure or irrelevant to its contemporary context. In tandem with Eric Owen Moss, their goal has been to return to a basis of social recognition that they see as missing from other similar institutions.

This initiative takes on an added significance given its location; in the early days of the Hollywood movie industry, the MGM Studios stood here, something which created a distinct social ambience. The new theatres are intended to contribute to this tradition of creative innovation, utilizing the same technological expertise that film producers now increasingly rely on for spectacular special effects.

This all fits in with the direction of the new urban paradigm they are planning: an 'electronic city' without houses, inhabited by commuters working in the entertainment industry. Unfortunately, it is a decidedly different alternative to the strategic plan for downtown Los Angeles that has been put forward – a civic framework organized according to more predictable guidelines. Culver City, in which the Ince Theater plays a critical role, could not be further from the tenets of this new urbanism, since it is generated from the same impetus that created Los Angeles. Rather than relating to public spaces, pedestrians and regional styles, this theatre, like its siblings the 'Green Umbrella' and Warner Street, is internally focused and dependant on the automobile for its audience; an amorphous cybernetic entity answering to a continuing commercial reality.

The 'contest' now being played out in Los Angeles between this constantly changing electronic Utopia and the master planning principles, based on consistency and the death of 'autopia', has global repercussions. As a symbol of the former, the Ince Theater is of great significance.

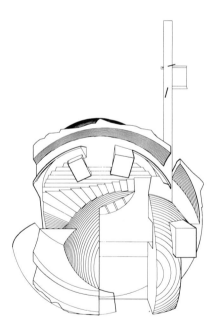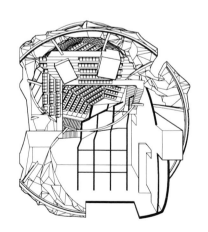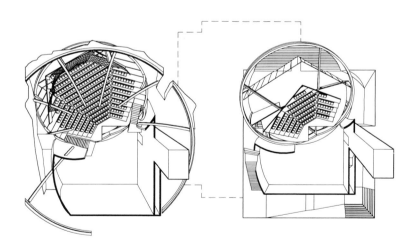

Sectional perspectives illustrating interior

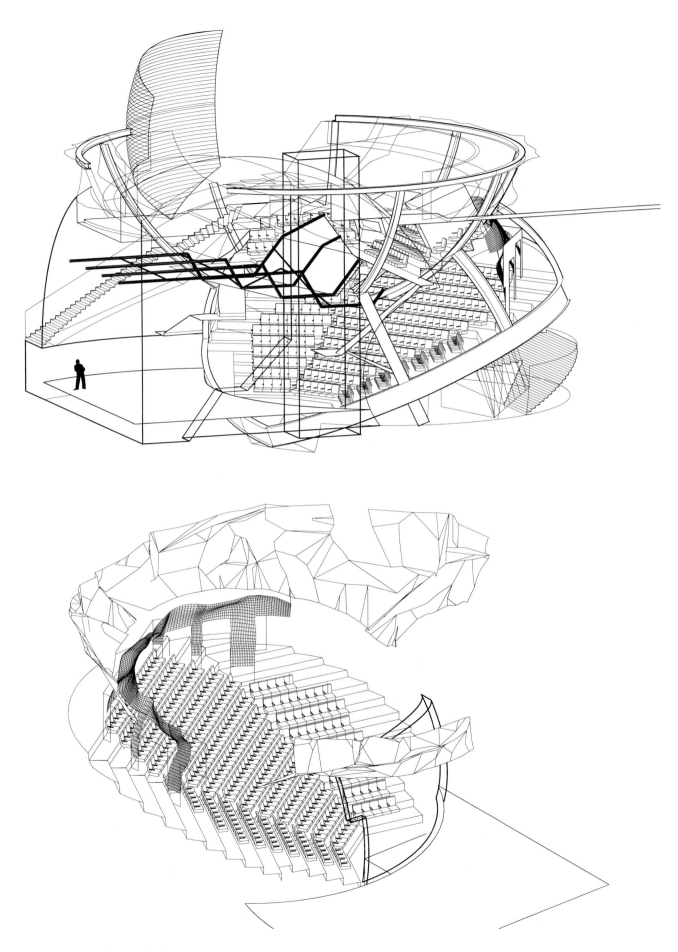

Interior perspectives illustrating auditorium

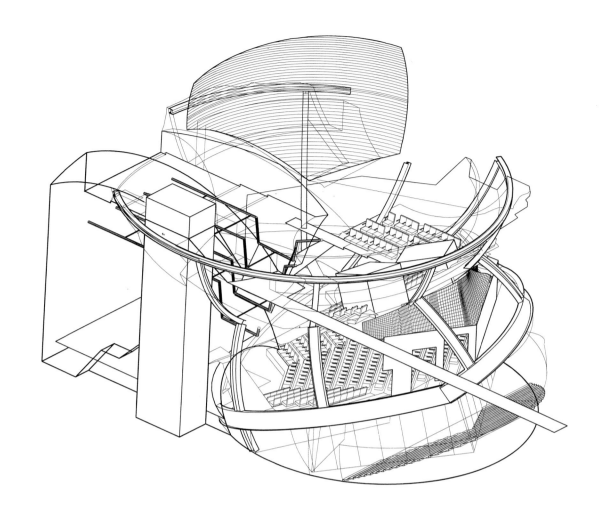

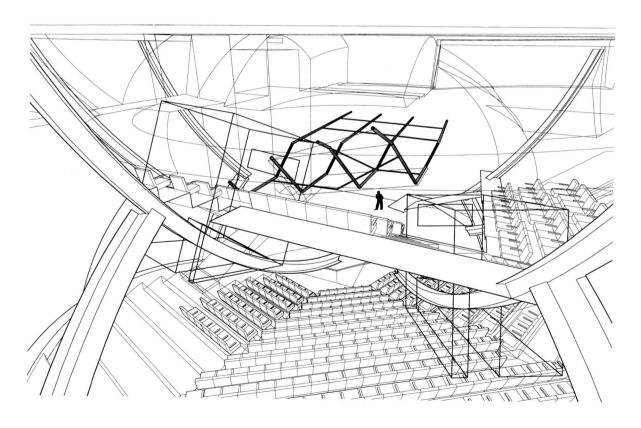

BARTON MYERS
PERFORMING ARTS CENTER

Newark, New Jersey

There have been many proposals for this arts centre which was first announced in 1987, and was originally conceived as five buildings on a six block site between Broadway and the Passaic River in Newark. The New Jersey Economic Development Authority (EDA) was instrumental in the initiation of the project, piecing together fourteen separate properties to make up a viable eleven acre site, finally realized in December 1991. The centre is part of a larger urban renewal area, that includes Newark Housing Authority property along the riverside, intended for a mixed-use development that will feed into it. The EDA financed the cost of acquiring the property for the centre itself, about twenty million dollars, through the sale of bonds. It in turn leases the property to the state, which pays an annual rent of about two million dollars. The state subleases it to the art centre for a token dollar a year.

From the beginning then, this project has been envisioned as part of a wider, highly complex real estate development puzzle, and is meant to rely on a potent mixture of uses to attract people to it. The first phase of the centre is focused around a two-thousand-seven-hundred-and-fifty seat multi-purpose hall and additional five-hundred seat studio theatre, as well as spaces for rehearsals and classes and two restaurants. It has a five-storey high glass atrium, used as a lobby but which can also accommodate banqueting facilities. The four tiered larger theatre has a ceiling which retracts, and when down, combines with the fly-tower to act as a reverberation chamber. It has an underfloor air supply system designed by Ove Arup & Partners, the first of its kind in the United States. Because the centre is only one mile away from a large railway station and on the flight path of Newark Airport, maintaining

all acoustic standards was difficult, but achieved by establishing an 'acoustic zone', which separates the hall from the rest of the centre. There is no resident company, and so this is a 'road-house' like Cerritos. Cost consultants played an important role in the final realization of the project as options began to become more tangible, with trade-offs made when financial considerations became clearer, ending at nearly sixty eight million dollars. The architects have treated the centre as a 'beacon to the city', a present and future locus of urban activity at a civic scale, combined with a pedestrian scale at ground level to encourage a lively integration with its neighbours.

Once again the onus of proof has been placed on a performing arts centre to establish a sense of community where it has not existed in the recent past, and this attempt seems to be working.

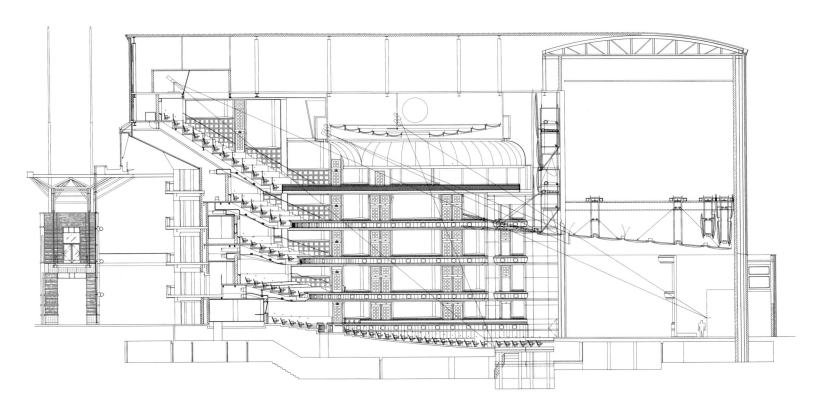

Longitudinal section

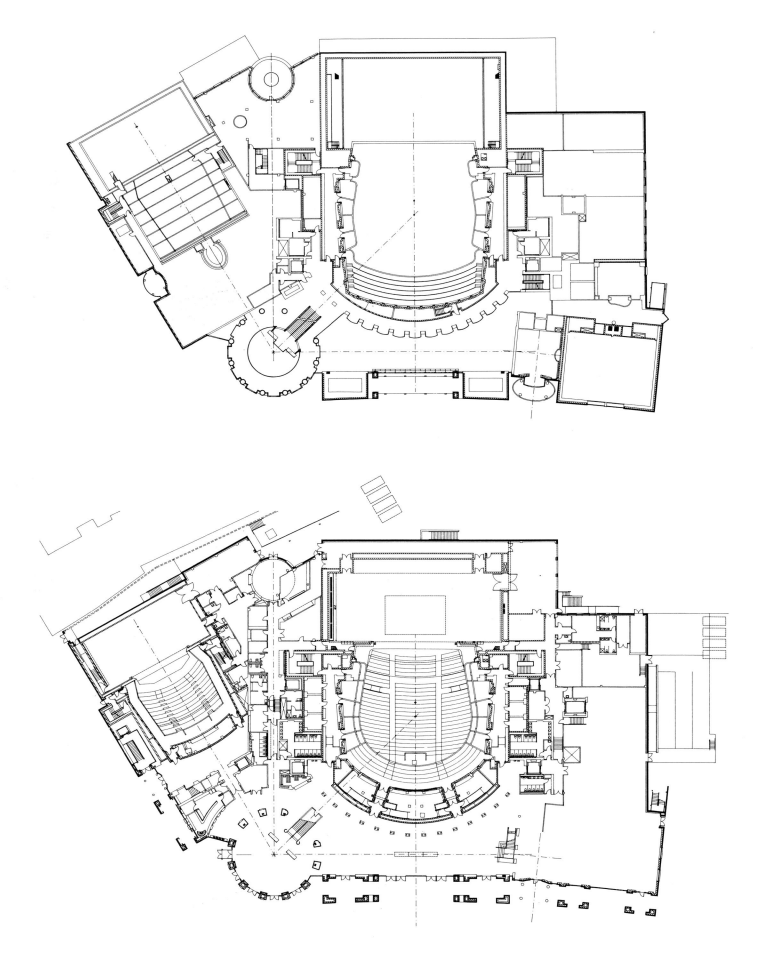

FROM ABOVE: Fourth floor plan; ground floor plan

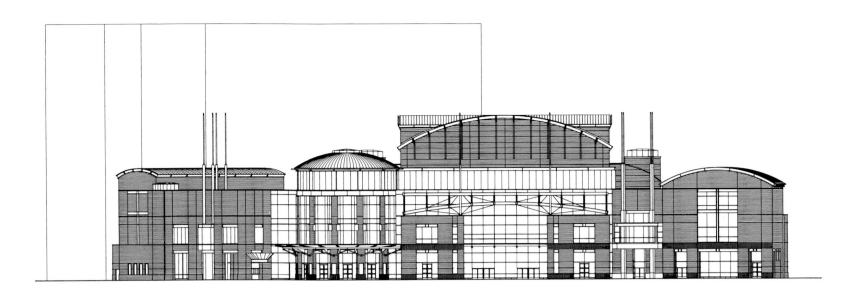

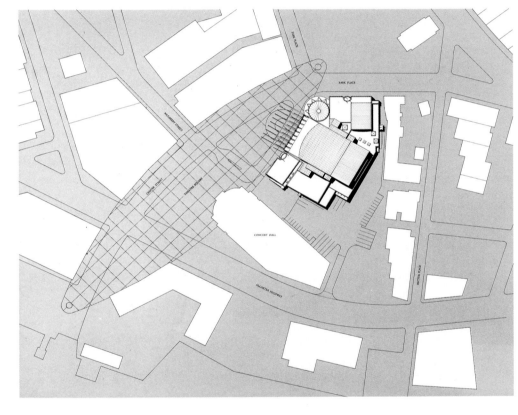

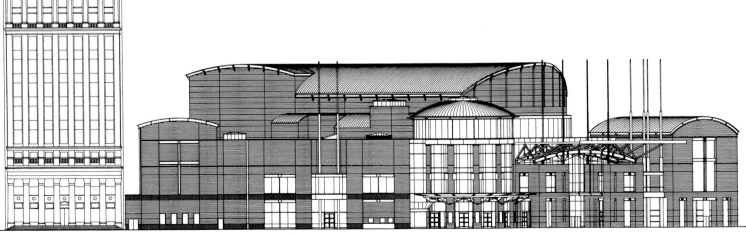

FROM ABOVE: South elevation; site plan; west elevation

BARTON MYERS
CENTER FOR THE PERFORMING ARTS
Cerritos, California

Cerritos, which is just inside the southern border of Los Angeles County, is a prosperous, rapidly growing community that, like several others present here, has attempted to establish an identity through the construction of a theatre; completed in 1992 at a cost of over sixty million dollars. In determining the need for a centre here, local leaders realized that downtown Los Angeles is half-an-hour's drive away and that the closest competitor would be the Orange County Performing Arts Center, twenty miles to the south.

Cerritos has grown as a commercial area, thought of by many non-residents as home of the Auto Square, which is an enormous market-place for used cars that has helped fund the Performing Arts Centre, as well as a regional shopping mall connected to the San Gabriel Freeway. The centre is possibly the most important piece of a one-hundred-and-twenty-five acre town centre development surrounding city hall; a programme estimated to cost five times more than the theatre, and which includes office use and a new hotel. The Cerritos Redevelopment Agency has funded this scheme through an incremental tax on commercial development and the Mayor at the time the programme was launched in the mid-eighties made no pretence about the purpose of the Arts Centre when she said, 'culture adds value to commerce'. Cerritos, then, has been pragmatically planned as a focal point for future urban growth and a catalyst for increased economic prosperity, a textbook example of an edge city of the type immortalized by Joel Garreaux.

To clearly signal the role of the theatre in helping perpetuate a national dream that many have felt to be dying in the state that mythologized it, Frank Sinatra opened the complex by singing there for five nights in a row. These expectations are evident in the design and the heavy emphasis on technology that has been used as an attraction. The theatre is promoted as being completely flexible and able to be changed, within ten hours, into one of five configurations; ranging from a six-thousand-three-hundred-and-ninety square-foot flat floor, through a one-thousand-seven-hundred-and-fifty seat concert hall, one-thousand-five-hundred seat arena and equivalent lyric opera theatre, to a drama hall of nine hundred and fifty seats.

The technology required to achieve this high degree of flexibility includes side towers, which contain three levels of box seating fitted with perforated bags. When filled with compressed air, these raise the towers off the floor and allow them to be floated into a new position, either flat against the side walls for concerts or diagonally for drama. Five floor lifts control the options of a forestage, orchestra pit, an extension to the orchestral seating area, storage of seating racks under the stage, or transformation of orchestral seating into a sound mixing area. In flat floor mode, when the seating towers are positioned flat against the walls, an acoustical ceiling called 'the flipper' drops to conceal the fly-tower and convert the space into a continuous hall. The flipper, which weighs twenty-seven thousand pounds, moves downward to create an arch for drama, or can be set at an angle to provide a second proscenium arch for the lyric configuration. Tracking side panels suspended from the ceiling adjust the proscenium, which is nearly one hundred feet high to forty-five feet wide when used for opera.

Unlike Myers' theatre in Portland, there was no context here, making his first priority 'to create a sense of place', or more prosaically to establish some degree of urban texture in what was essentially a car park. The tactic adopted is a cityscape of blocks, towers and courts, clustered in ways that magnify massing. Courtyards are a well established architectural tradition in Southern California, reiterated more recently by Frank Lloyd Wright and Rudolf Schindler, before a progressive distancing from nature began in the fifties. Myers echoes Bertram Goodhue's exuberant participation in the Panama-California Exposition in San Diego, now popularly known as Balboa Park, as well as a more generic reference to the mission style. Volumes, such as the ever problematic fly-tower, have been broken down to contribute to the impression of a city within a city and banded patterned stone work in combination with smooth white stucco, polished red granite, French limestone, patterned ceramic tile and spires sporting coloured banners, all contribute to what has been referred to as a 'carnival like' complex. This gaiety continues into the interior and was described by Leon Whiteson thus:

> The auditorium scores . . . its quality of lighting and its subtle palette of colours and finishes. The architects have played down the cleverness of the mechanics in favour of an ambience that recalls a delightful Italian baroque *teatro communale* with its boxes and balconies.[1]

Notes
1 Leon Whiteson, 'Stage Presence', *Architecture*, May 1993, p77.

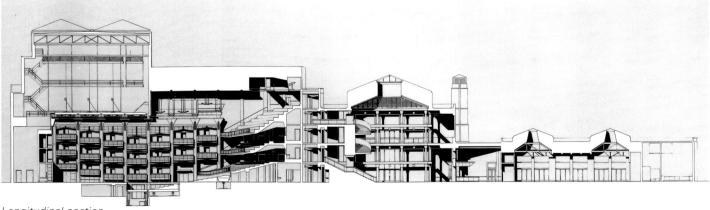

Longitudinal section

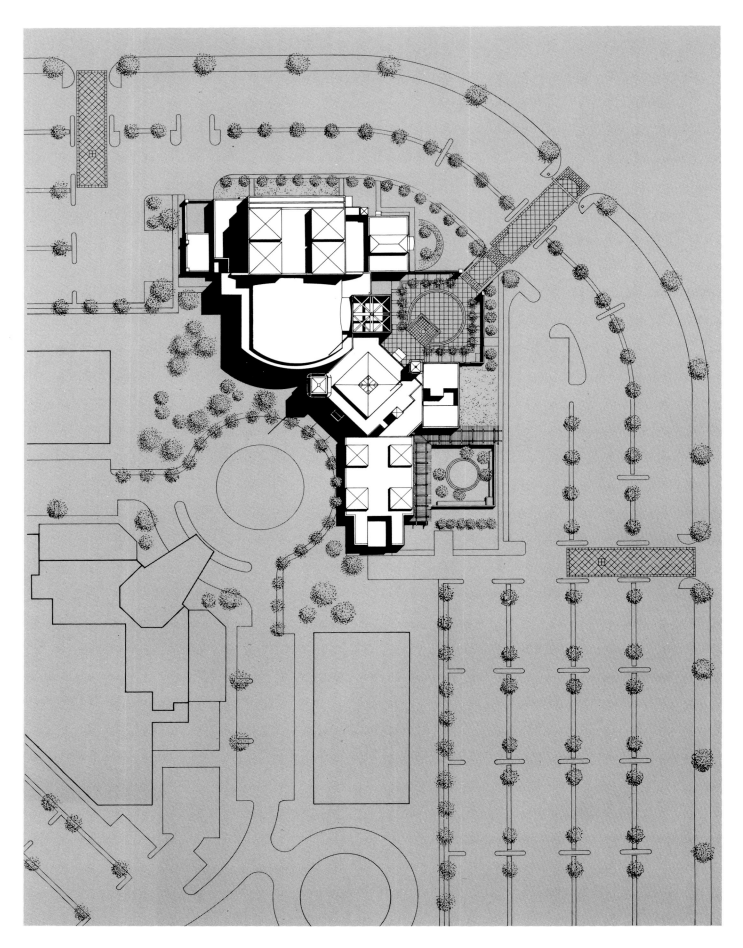

Site plan

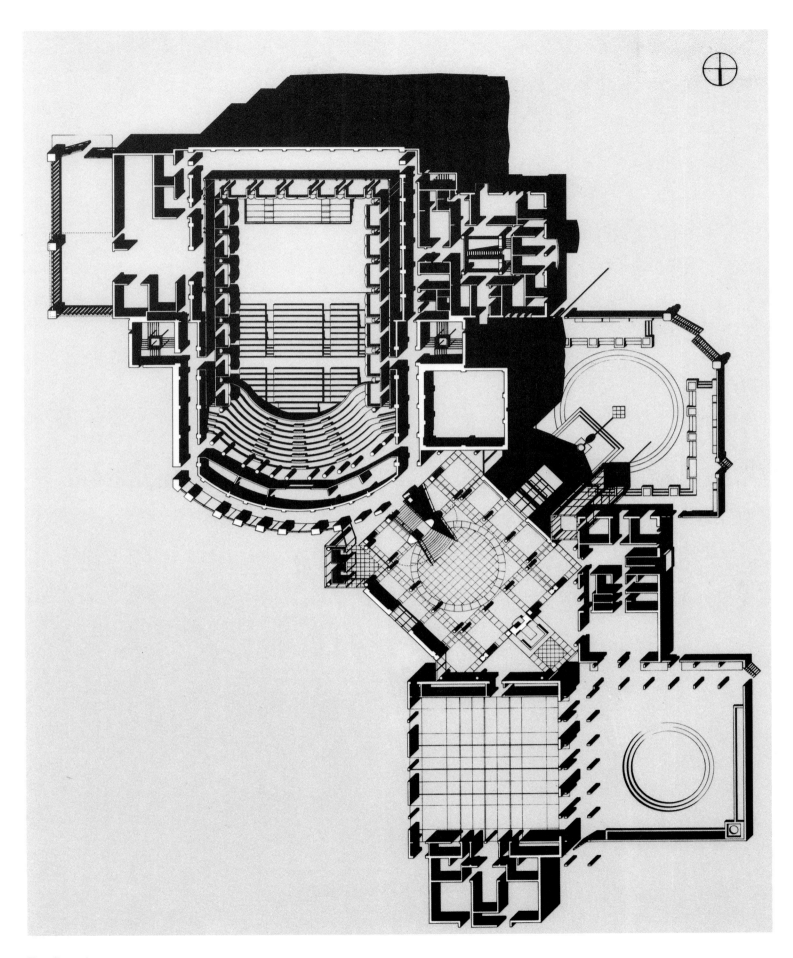

First floor plan

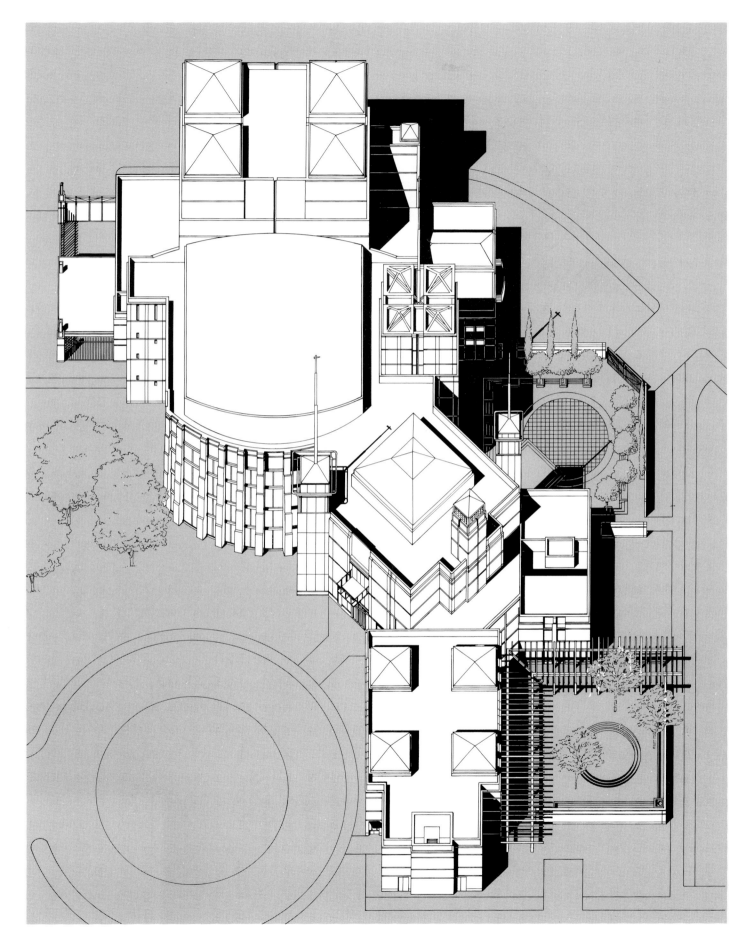

Axonometric

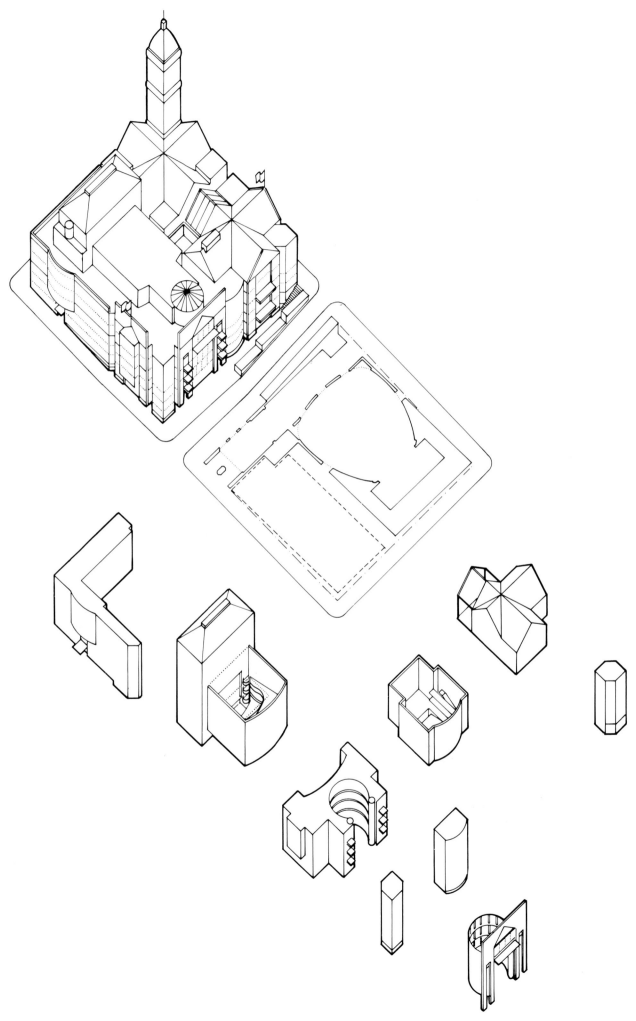

BARTON MYERS
CENTER FOR THE PERFORMING ARTS
Portland, Oregon

Portland has experienced an urban renaissance, proudly surviving the vicissitudes of the timber industry on which it is primarily dependent and the recession that has resulted in a reduced number of housing starts. Much of the credit for such civic resilience must be given to the residents, who passed a nineteen million dollar city bond issue in 1981 with the intention of building an arts centre and diversifying its business base. Myers was selected for this venture with Boor/A of Portland and the ELS Design Group from Berkeley, with each team contributing equally to the project.

The Paramount Movie Theater, built in 1929 and placed on the National Register of Historic Places in 1974, is close to the centre, and soon after registry became the Arlene Schnitzer Concert Hall, home for the Oregon Symphony Orchestra. To do so involved a major renovation, including seating to accommodate over two-thousand-five-hundred people, a 28 m by 10 m stage and a 16 m by 10 m proscenium.

Restoration was completed in 1984. This is considered the first phase of the performing arts complex which occupies two city blocks, with frontage on Broadway and Park Streets as well as to the mall on Main Street.

The second phase included the design of two new theatres across from the Schnitzer Hall. These are a nine-hundred seat intermediate theatre for touring shows, as well as repertory chamber music and dance, and a smaller three-hundred-and-sixty seat show-case theatre that provides flexible stage arrangements for drama productions. The architects took their lead not only from the old Paramount, but also from the Heathman Hotel and the First Congregational Church which has fine stone detailing, and a tall corner tower next to the site on Park Street. Main Street was closed to vehicular traffic in this phase, and paved, forming an outdoor ante-room for the theatres. The second phase buildings share a monumental, many tiered

lobby running along Main Street. The intermediate theatre has seating on the orchestra and two balcony levels, with curved fronts, side balconies and boxes that bring actors and audience closer to one another, near the proscenium. The space is illuminated by a circular lighting gallery, surmounted by a domed ceiling conceived as a metaphor for a starry sky. The smaller show-case space, called the Winningstrad Theater, has been patterned after an early English 'open-air' performance court, rendered in red to heighten the illusion. Seating is arranged on three sides in a three-tiered balcony.

In its variety, ranging from the renewed opulent splendour of the Schnitzer Concert Hall, to the restraint of the intermediate theatre which simplifies the elegance of an Edwardian hall, and the charm of the Winningstrad show-case to the baroque lobby which links them, the Portland Center reflects the various strengths of the design team and the vibrancy of the city itself.

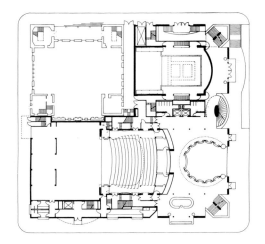

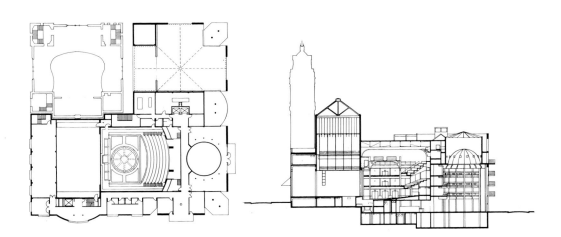

OPPOSITE, FROM ABOVE: Axonometric; exploded functional axonometric; FROM LEFT: First floor plan; fourth floor plan; longitudinal section

JEAN NOUVEL
OPERA HOUSE

Lyon, France

This renovation of an original opera house designed by Soufflot in 1754, a landmark in the establishment of theatre as a recognizable institution in the public realm, has been carried out in ways that recognize its monumental status. The interior of the building has been drastically altered, but the external image has been enhanced. The most extensive internal change has been the addition of four floors, excavated below ground, in order to provide more space without changing the external envelope and altering the delicate balance that has been established as the city evolved around the opera. This has doubled the volume of the building and also allowed the ground floor to be made more accessible from the Place Louis Pradel, by providing breathing space around the perimeter; a glazed wall has been placed within the envelope creating an external arcade. The ornate foyer, which is so integral to the historical image of the theatre, has been restored and opened up vertically to reinforce and expand the 'see and be seen' aspect that has always been a part of a night at the opera. The device of the grand staircase, such as that used by Garnier at the Paris Opera, has been retained, but in the contemporary language of the escalator, with banks of these leading up to the auditorium.

In addition to opening up the basement, the *tour de force* provided by Nouvel is a barrel vaulted roof that in one bold stroke has transformed the existing structure into a more functional and architectonic whole. The vault, rendered in parallel sheets of silk screened glass, is lit internally at night, casting off a red glow like a living membrane and giving it the appearance of a large faceted jewel. This reclaimed space has been used for additional balconies, and a ballet studio directly under the curve of the roof, the new profile recalling Palladio's Basilica at Vicenza, which Aldo Rossi, in *The Architecture of the City*, has praised as one of the most memorable and durable of urban monuments. Whether the comparison was intentional or not, Nouvel describes the structure of the vault in the following terms:

. . . being composed of dark grey lacquered semicircular arches set in the axis of the preserved façade. Its underside supports an initial bent glass skin doubled on the surface by a set of silk screened sun-blinds. The play of silk screening, in a de-materializing effect, is applied with decreasing intensity to follow the sun's course. A mechanical system allows these blades to measure the right amount of sunlight into the inner spaces. This 'smart' skin continues the precedent set at the Institut du Monde Arabe, in Paris, where steel *mushrabbiga* driven by computer to respond to heat gain and loss update a traditional environmental control.

The seating capacity of the auditorium has been increased from nine hundred to one thousand three hundred seats with vastly improved sight lines, while balcony fronts faced in perforated metal sheet, with exposed stage lighting attached to them, carry through the mechanistic feel found throughout. Nouvel has attempted to bring a venerable art form, and its equally venerated container into the twenty-first century, with stunning success.

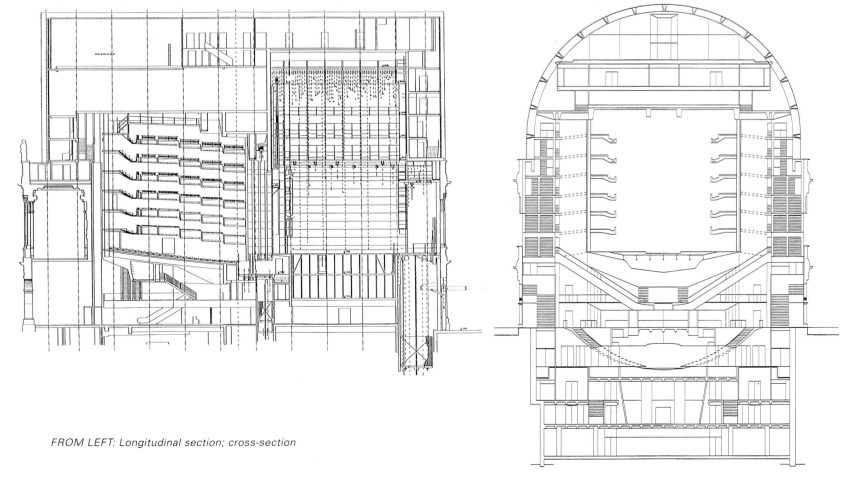

FROM LEFT: Longitudinal section; cross-section

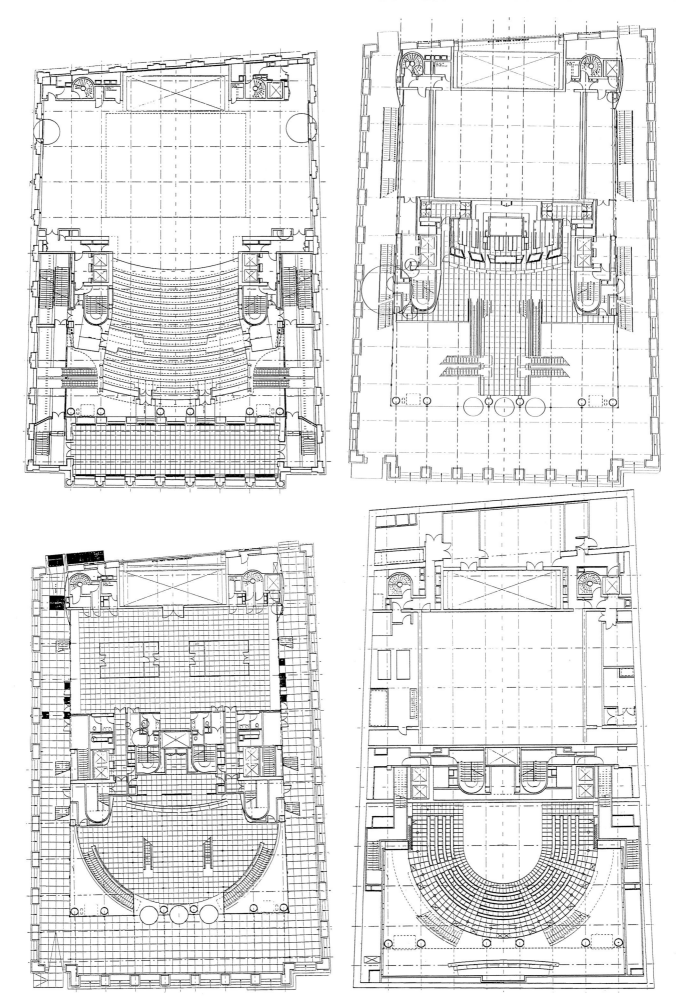

FROM ABOVE, LEFT TO RIGHT: Third floor plan; first floor plan; ground floor plan; basement plan

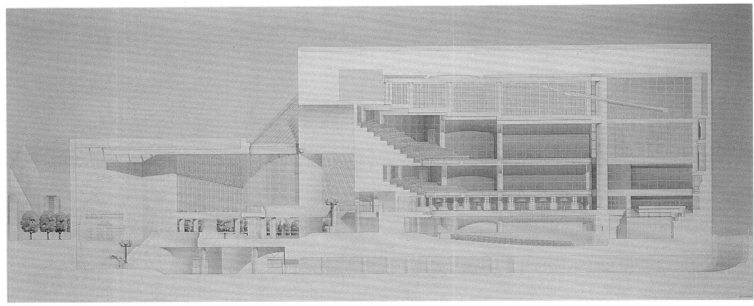

IM PEI
MORTON H MYERSON SYMPHONY CENTER

Dallas, Texas

Completed in September 1989, this two-thousand-and-seventy-four seat concert hall is the home of the Dallas Symphony Orchestra, and is one of the keystones in a citizen's backed 'cultural revolution' that has been taking place in Dallas since the mid-seventies. The client's brief to the architects requested 'acoustical and architectural qualities of worldwide distinction' which by implication would also enhance the reputation of Dallas as an internationally renowned centre of culture. The location chosen, near the new Betty B Marcus Park, is in the new Arts District which had previously not kept pace with Dallas' rapid development. This sixty-acre zone which is gradually being filled with high-rise commercial and retail developments is intended to be the cultural heart of the city with other theatres to follow.

In the best tradition of Pei's firm, the office has adopted a highly geometrical approach to the design of this hall, based on the intersection of a circle and a golden section rectangle. At the centre is the concert hall, which has been set at an angle to the street to maximize the small three-acre site. Alignment along this hypotenuse permitted the incorporation of an expensive glazed lobby on three sides of the building and along the fourth, a four-storey administration wing and a two-storey musicians wing connected by a long fenestrated corridor behind the stage. Mitigating between the building's angled siting and its radial public spaces is a sculptural armature: a 60 ft by 90 ft frame, which projects from the front of the Symphony Center to focus its main entrance and align it squarely with Flora street, the planted and colourfully paved spine of the Arts District.

The concert hall itself is a rectangle functionally divided into a performance area and a seating area; designed to ratios derived from the golden section. The square audience portion is surrounded by a series of segmented circles, evident at *loge* level through a curved bridge-like balcony that projects on columns above the main lobby to expand the public spaces. This arc is echoed by a steel and concrete ring beam forty three feet above the ground which anchors the elliptical windows that bracket the concert hall on three sides. This six to eight foot deep beam also supports a conical glass canopy which springs from another, larger arc circumscribed around the concert hall along its western edge. Another arc expands the public space to the east. This entire system of intersecting circles is characteristically reinforced by many details, such as paving patterns, light fixtures and stairs throughout the building.

For a public that has come to expect epic moves from this architect, in the best tradition of the Louvre pyramid, there is no disappointment here. Vast expanses of glass fill the 18 ft high window walls on the building's vertical façades, whilst the three ellipses have twenty foot high single panes and there are two hundred and eleven computer dimensioned sheets in the conical portion; each of them a different size because the segmented cone is skewed. Whether one accepts the architect's preferred metaphor of the wrap around lobby and its roof supported by *vierendeel* trusses like a suspension bridge, as being a 'great stringed instrument', or that of the public, who compare it to a cross between a spaceship and a warehouse, there can be little doubt that the Symphony Center lobby is a spectacular visual attraction. However, this element also successfully serves two other important functions, as both a functional buffer between the noise of the street outside and the acoustical level demanded in the hall, and as a dramatic intermediate space, grand enough, with its Garnier-inspired stair, to match the aspirations of the citizens of Dallas, and large enough to allow everyone to orient themselves without confusion or crowding.

In a surprising contrast to the modernist severity of the sweeping light filled lobby, the concert hall is dark and lush, with a red terrazzo floor, wood walls, brass and onyx fixtures, blue ceiling and adjustable acoustic canopy, suspended over the orchestra. As described by Russell Johnson of Artec Acoustical Consultants, the concert hall was designed to achieve:

... a sense of intimacy that permits each concert goer to feel close to the stage regardless of actual proximity. The perception results from the proportions of the tall narrow hall (at 85 ft, one of the tallest concrete rooms in the world) and from the treatment of its interior appointments. Detailed like a fine musical instrument in polished wood and brass, the hall uses a warm palette of more than two dozen brown hues to make its wall recede. Overhead, on the ceiling and on the scrims behind the open latticework, a lustrous night blue makes abstract reference to ancient amphitheatres where performances were presented under the open sky. The allusion is reinforced by the limestone columns that support the seating tiers and monumentally frame the proscenium ... In its varied lighting, as in all of its other details, the hall has been designed to enhance the pleasure of making and listening to music.

In spite of all this exuberance, acoustical concerns always governed the design of this building, with every possible effort taken to isolate the auditorium from potentially noisy areas. Whilst, in the concert hall the acoustical challenge was magnified by the need to create a memorable image and a geometric rationalization for a space that would otherwise appear disproportionate.

The result of all of this attention to detail has been described as 'an intense, warm sound' by the critics, in keeping with the architectural character of the space. The close correlation between architecture and sound in the hall, was not achieved easily, and rumours of disagreements between architects and consultants continued throughout the design and construction phases. These centred mostly around the form of the acoustical canopy, which Pei calls 'the tongue', as well as the monumental columns which flank the orchestra, added to provide a sense of order to the space but at the cost of some clear sight lines. Despite these conflicts, Dallas has certainly got a world-class concert hall that it can be proud of.

Longitudinal section

OPPOSITE, FROM ABOVE: Third floor plan; second floor plan; first floor plan; ground floor plan

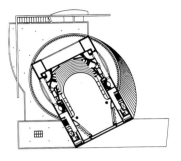

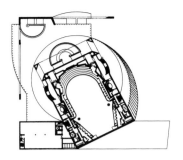

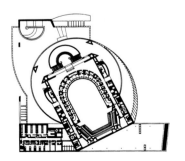

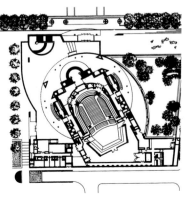

CESAR PELLI
BLUMENTHAL PERFORMING ARTS CENTER

Charlotte, Carolina

On the same commercially minded typology as Birmingham and Cerritos, the Blumenthal Performing Arts Center is part of a wider civic context in the heart of Charlotte, located near to the Square, which is the historical district at the intersection of Tryon and Trade Streets. Called the Nations Bank Complex, after the tower that dominates its northern edge, it is meant, as is typically the case in such projects, to be a source of regeneration and the focus of future growth. At sixty-storeys tall, the dark granite tower is framed by lighter piers in the best Sullivan tradition of tallness, emphasizing its height, with a cap of anodized aluminium columns as a crown.

Founders Hall, at its base, on an axis with the tower, is a continuation of the genre of urban scaled conservatories that Pelli has taken on as his own, since the Winter Park Project at Niagara Falls, built in the late seventies, and the Battery Park

Crystal Palace look-alike that followed a decade later. This complex is particularly effective as a unifying device to ease access into the diverse parts of the complex around it, as well as the shops, restaurants, health clubs and theatre ticket office that it contains. Its steep sided truss lined façade, a vain attempt to match the massiveness of the tower, has an elegant profile nonetheless, making it an effective circulation spine rendered in sparkling steel and glass.

The Blumenthal Performing Arts Center is located to the east of this spine, and consists of the two-thousand-one-hundred seat Belk Theater, which has a lobby facing Tryon Street, and the less formal Booth Playhouse which has one quarter this seating capacity, located on the mezzanine level of Founders Hall. In an attempt to disguise the fly-tower of the Belk Theater, which seems to be a major preoccupation of many architects designing theatres

today, Pelli has treated it as a distinct volume, rendered in patterned brick and articulated in a way that makes it look as if it is inserted into the block around it. This, as well as the lobby entrance, serves to enliven the street façade, providing an effective counterpoint to the internal emphasis of the rest of the complex. Unfortunately, the architect's main task was to fit a daunting list of facilities inside a fixed boundary, and he has achieved this at a cost. Hence, to accommodate these two theatres and their necessary appendages, he has stacked them, maximizing circulation and making the identity of each theatre hard to distinguish. The interior of the Belk is pure Pelli, cool to the point of detachment, smooth and sophisticated, with fibre-optic lights delivering a multicoloured show of their own and a carefully ordered pipe organ serving as a backdrop to the stage.

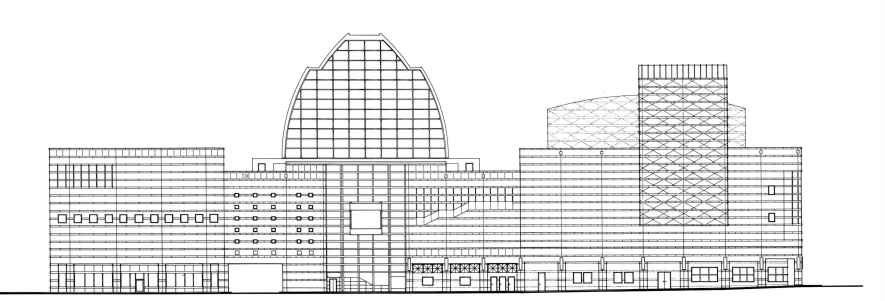

College Street elevation

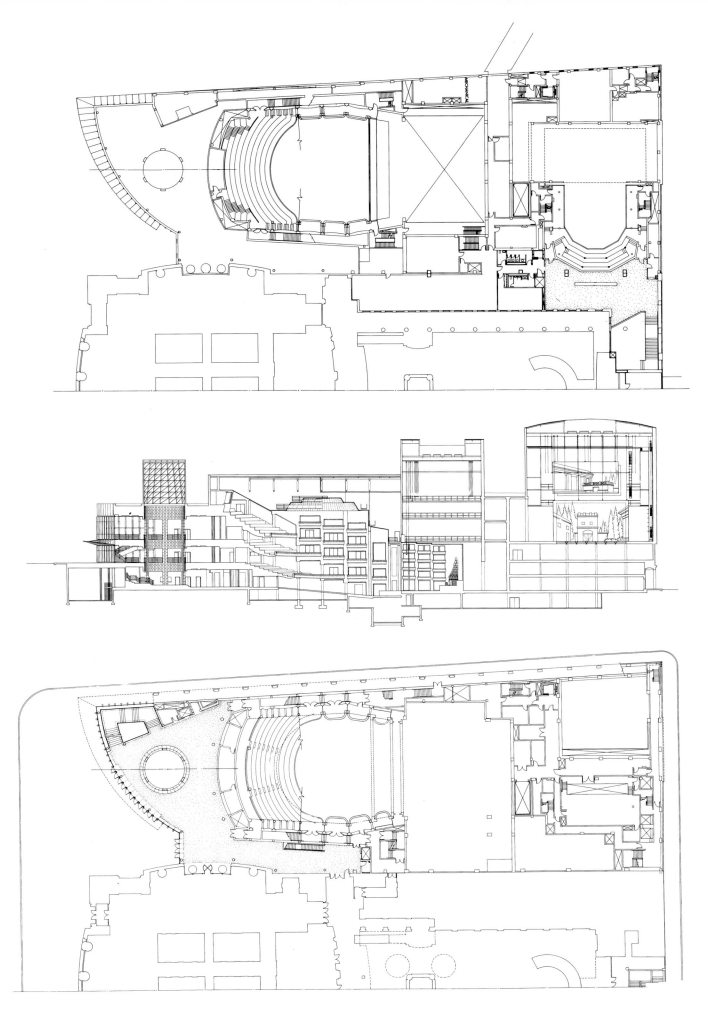

FROM ABOVE: Mezzanine plan; section through large theatre lobby, large theatre and small theatre stage; skywalk plan

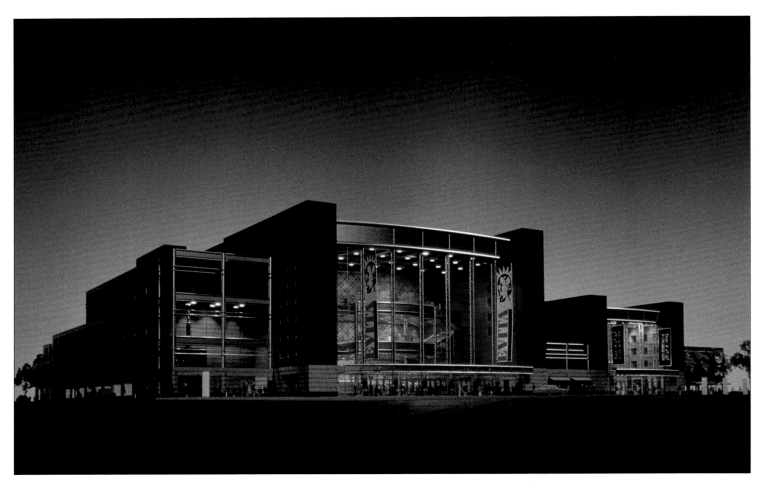

CESAR PELLI
ARONOFF CENTER FOR THE ARTS
Cincinnati, Ohio

The Aronoff Center for the Arts occupies an eighty five thousand square foot L-shaped site in the entertainment district, within two blocks of Fountain Square, the heart of downtown Cincinnati. The centre has three theatres including a two-thousand-seven-hundred seat large theatre, four-hundred-and-forty seat small theatre and a studio theatre, in addition to the rehearsal hall, exhibition space and support spaces. It will be the home of Cincinnati's *Broadway Series* and accommodate touring, regional and community dance, opera, symphony, choral and other performance groups.

The large and small theatre lobbies face Walnut Street and are connected by an interior public pathway leading from a plaza at the corner of Sixth and Walnut, through the lobbies, to a second plaza at the corner of Seventh and Walnut.

The large theatre's main lobby has two levels connected by a monumental stair. The lower lobby is part of the public pathway and the upper lobby is at the orchestra seating level. The *loge* and balcony lobbies, which are one and two levels above the orchestra respectively, are served by two open stairs at either side of the upper lobby. Additional elevators and ramps provide access to lobby and theatre levels. The studio theatre lobby, which is slightly above street level, faces and is set-back from Main Street. This lobby also serves the rehearsal hall, one level below.

The loading bays for both theatres, as well as other building services, are completely internal and are accessed off Main Street on Gano Alley. All theatre stage floors are at this level. Large freight elevators serve the rehearsal hall and catering kitchen facilities one level below.

The exterior consists of two architectural characters woven together as one composition. Performance spaces and their lobbies have a civic scale and are contained between giant masonry walls of brick and stone. Metal frame building forms, with stone and glass infill panels enclose the additional programmatic elements and have a small urban scale and character. The entire composition is tied together at the base with a 14 ft high stone base and colonnade; containing elements that enliven the urban context such as theatre lobby entrances, retail shops, stage door and support staff entrances. The use of the masonry, brick, stone and metal frame building elements with infill panels responds to the building traditions and materials of Cincinnati.

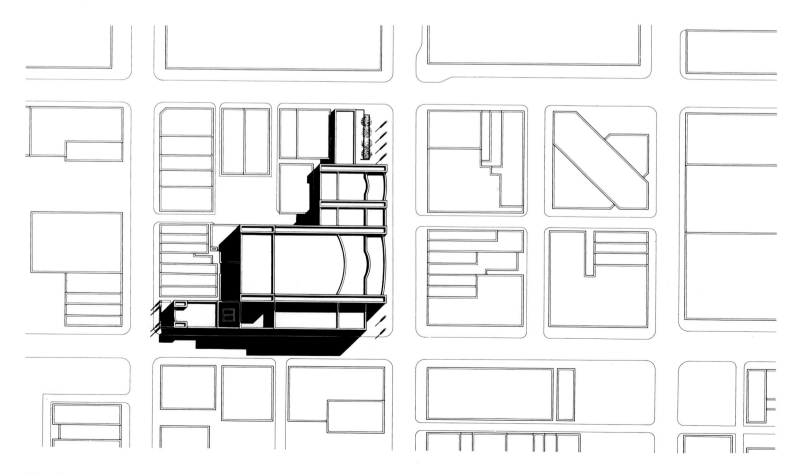

Site plan

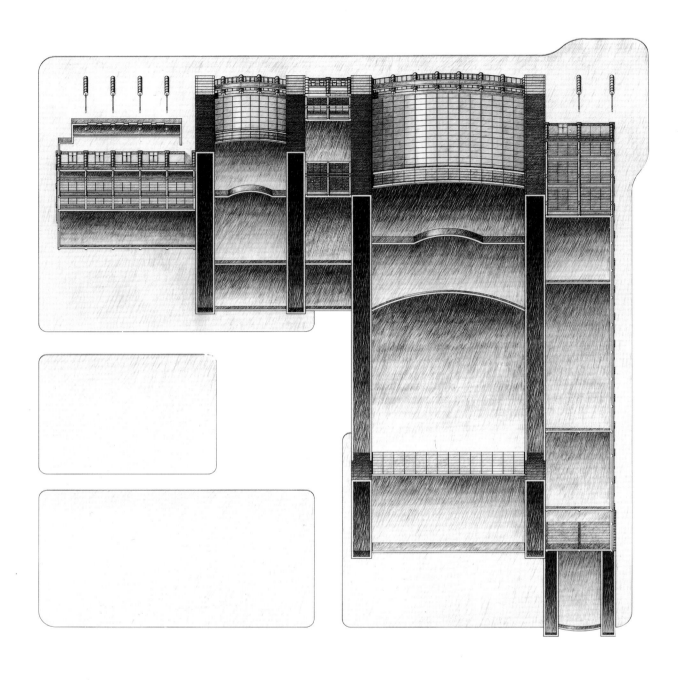

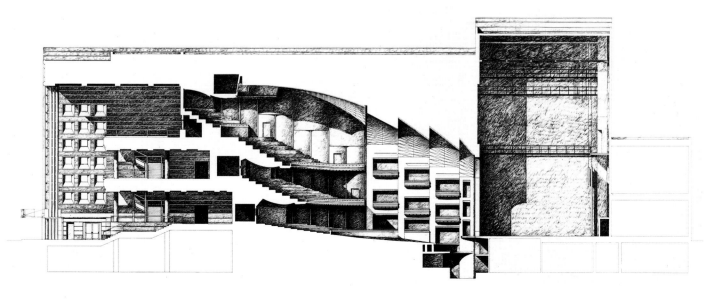

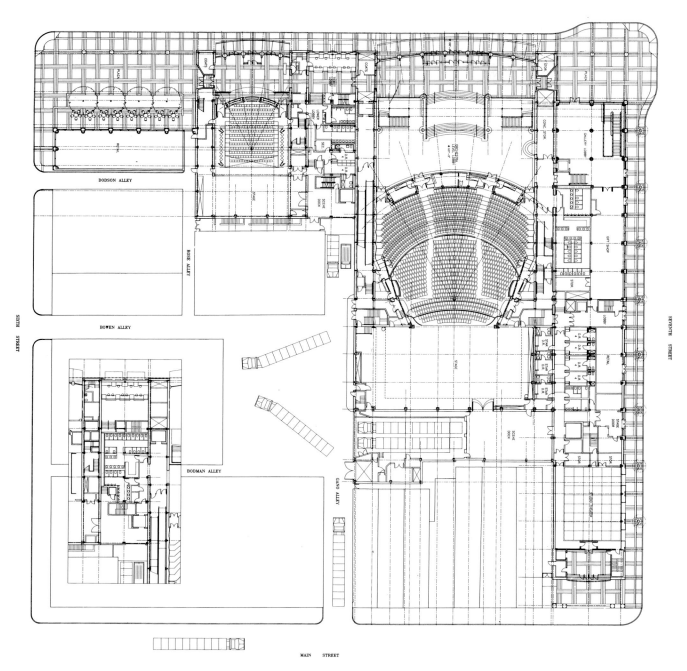

OPPOSITE, FROM ABOVE: Oblique view; section though large theatre, lobby and theatre; ABOVE: Ground floor plan

ANTOINE PREDOCK
CIVIC ARTS PLAZA

Thousand Oaks, California

Thousand Oaks is the prototypical linear city described by Kevin Lynch and this theatre – part of a one hundred and eighty two thousand square foot complex that includes offices for city administrative departments, one-thousand-eight-hundred seat auditorium, gallery exhibition space, seven acre community park and eight-hundred-and-fifty space parking structure – is meant to be its centre. The site is bounded to the north by the Thousand Oaks Boulevard strip, on the south by the Ventura Freeway, and is approached by an entrance road that rises up from the strip onto an 'autocourt' positioned on the bank of the adjacent freeway. As in the Mandell Weiss forum project, Predock has also used a processional entry sequence to orient visitors toward the Civic Auditorium, using a 'pictograph wall' – a stylized reference to the original inhabitants of the Coneys Valley – followed by a stone-clad wall inscribed with donors names and an entry tower. The plaza, with its reflecting pool, from which the public enter has been used as a datum, with the Civic Auditorium and its adjacent functions arranged above and the governmental functions set below. A centre for government is located at ground level to allow staff work spaces to connect directly to the park, whilst stacking provides a series of public terraces, contributing to the civic aspect of the centre. As Predock explains:

The site was very challenging because the Ventura Freeway passes right above. The idea was to use the mass of the building as a barrier, to visually and psychologically separate the site from the freeway, which is pretty relentless. We wanted to set the bulk of the complex; the fly-tower, large auditorium, the smaller forum and the parking structure, on the high ground and create more intimately sealed connections to the surrounding park below, where there was an existing meadow and trees. The layout exposes the day to day occupants of the building, the city employees, to the landscape. Then you get the celebratory functions of the performing arts on the high ground, with great views when you look out across the Conejo Valley to the Simihills.

The fact that the natural landscape was virtually intact, in the middle of the city, was a critical factor in Predock's design approach, down to the beige colour of the sandstone cladding, recalling the earth, and deflections of the building envelope to avoid existing trees.

The Forum Theatre, which doubles as the council chamber, has full fly riggings to transform it into a three-hundred-and-ninety-eight seat proscenium theatre, or a three-hundred-and-fifty-eight seat thrust format. A 6 m by 14 m floor lift allows air-castered seat wagons on the city council dais to be easily interchanged. The one-thousand-eight-hundred seat auditorium is less utilitarian designed as 'a road-house with the main floor and balcony sized for typical audiences', including granite lobby, zinc-clad columns, oak panels and lavender walls, echoing the night sky.

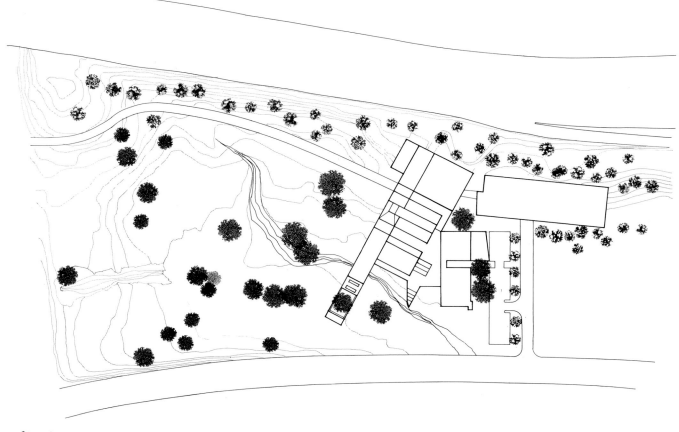

Site plan

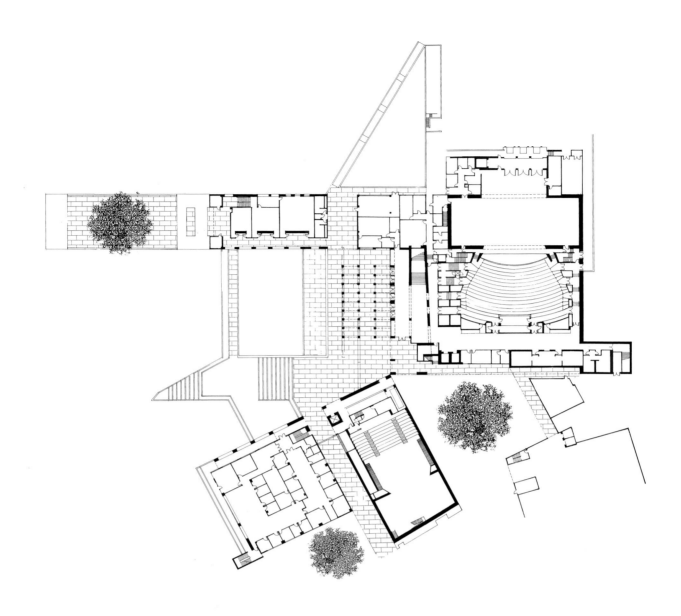

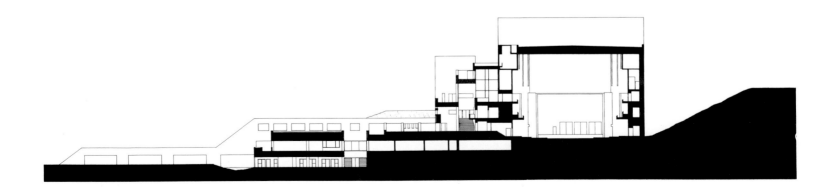

FROM ABOVE: Plaza floor plan; section

ANTOINE PREDOCK
MANDELL WEISS FORUM

San Diego, California

The Forum Theater is the second of three that will eventually serve the central campus of the University of California, San Diego (UCSD), and is used seasonally for student and La Jolla Playhouse performances in conjunction with the five-hundred seat Mandell Weiss proscenium theatre. It is located on a plateau at the south-west corner of the campus; its location specifically intended to give it a singular identity. The theatre is surrounded by groves of eucalyptus trees, planted in a clearly discernable grid, which contributes to this singularity, as well as to the ritual of arrival which the architect has used to offset the separateness of the theatrical experience by making the approach theatrical as well. Wind driven fog which is typical in this area because the ocean is so near, inspired Predock to devise a processional sequence in which theatre-goers pass through this grove, to emerge in a gravel clearing facing a 270 ft long, 13 ft high

mirrored wall, through which they then pass into the theatre. The intent was to make the approach seem random, as if discovering the building after emerging from a forest clearing reflected in the glass. The famous Salk Institute nearby, once had such an approach, before the controversial addition that replaced the trees, and Kahn's intentions were similar; an ancient city found at the edge of a forest, like Phaesilis. A ramp behind the mirror continues what Predock has called 'a procession of discovery', whilst a cantilevered steel balcony allows a last glimpse of the clearing and the ocean beyond. 'This line of demarcation', Predock has explained, 'is a threshold which makes conscious the transition into the world of dream and myth.'

After entering, the stage is directly visible on an axis with the central aisle, with access to either side or around he semicircular arrangement of four hundred seats. The auditorium is intimately scaled,

and it was intended that this configuration, surrounding a thrust stage, would generate interaction with the audience.

The theatre is separated from the rehearsal studios, which break off at a diagonal behind it, by an outdoor courtyard used for working on sets. This is Predock's bow to local tradition, and the perfect answer for carpenters and set designers averse to working indoors in such a benign climate. The rehearsal wing has an arcade extending out from this courtyard to the north, meant to mediate the scale of the theatre with the pedestrian approach to the campus; a more substantial, civil equivalent of the mirror on its public side. The mirror is especially effective at night, when most performances are held, since it can be converted into either a one-way or two-way system depending on the level of light behind it, an appropriate metaphor for the theatrical experience itself.

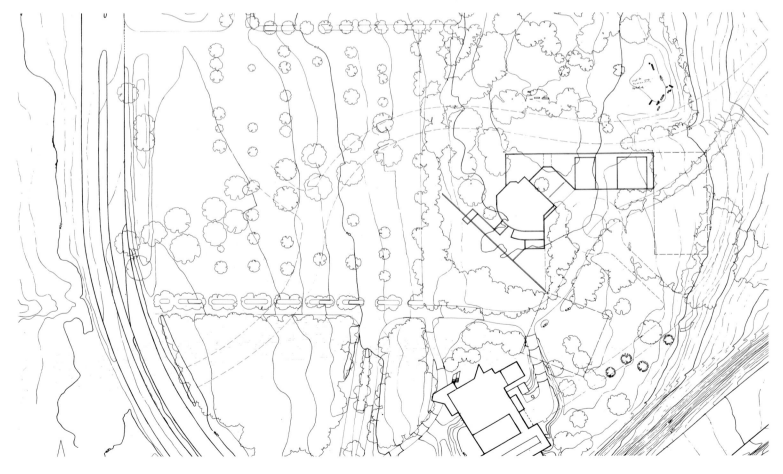

Site plan

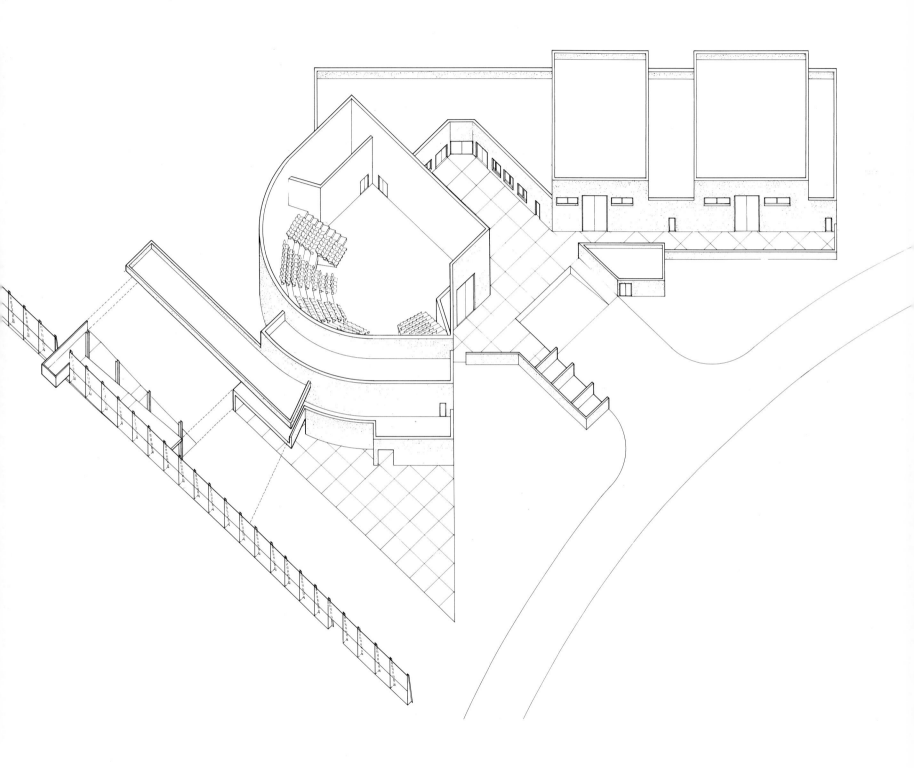

Axonometric

ALDO ROSSI
CARLO FELICE THEATRE
Genoa, Italy

Genoa is a city that is famous for looking to new horizons and always being in a state of transition, but the Carlo Felice Theatre has had a contentious history even by Genoese standards. Built on the site of the San Domenico church, which was demolished at the end of the sixteenth century, the theatre is the culmination of a long series of tragedies and false starts, finally and decisively resolved in this work.

The first opera house was designed by Andrea Tagliafichi, but it was not realized due to the fall of the Italian Republic. His second scheme, designed in 1810, was approved by the French government, essential since the city was annexed to Napoleon's empire at this time, even though local dissension prevented construction. When Carlo Felice was crowned as head of the kingdom of Sardinia, of which Genoa had recently become a part, the idea of an opera house was revived, and Carlo Francesco Barabino was commissioned to revive Tagliafichi's scheme. Again the first two schemes were fraught with conflict, but the third was completed in 1928 after only two years of construction. Included amongst its many innovations was one of the first fly-towers which allowed scenery panels to be pulled up quickly by ropes, rather than by being folded and carted off stage laboriously, and provided a prominent formal feature for the theatre.

Unfortunately, this opera house was badly damaged by bombing during the Second World War, and remained thus – with elements of the masonry shell intact but the metal structure and wooden finishes destroyed – until Paolo Chessa won the competition to redesign it in 1949. The Ministry of Public Works subsequently decided, in 1956, that the working drawings did not meet their standards and, after an acrimonious split, Carlo Scarpa was commissioned to prepare a new design. Interestingly, his first scheme involved the demolition of the remains of the theatre, even though the walls were structurally sound. This controversial decision was not resolved until 1978 when he initiated a second scheme that was terminated by his sudden death that same year.

Finally, in a new competition held in 1981, Ignazio Gardella and Aldo Rossi were chosen, from six other entrants, to design the new opera house. Rossi approached the delicate problem of interweaving the various pieces of the puzzle that remained like a surgeon, saying:

> Architectural wounds are as fascinating as human wounds: they are inwardness and outwardness at the same time, they are life mingling with death, we are sorry to close them up, leaving scars behind . . . This was how I saw the wounded body of Genoa's theatre and this was perhaps the emotion which carried me through the work.

This idea, which Rossi has elaborated so eloquently in *The Architecture of the City*, is forcefully realized here; the 'perpetuating permanence' of Barabino's original honoured rather than obliterated by the new building.

The damaged pronaos and side portico were restored, even though a new entry sequence makes the latter redundant. The prominent fly-tower not only recalls Barabino's important innovation, now considered essential in any theatre design, but is also reminiscent of the church tower of San Domenico. This structure also contains two storeys of rehearsal rooms and two of mechanical plant, which despite being added during construction actually enforce the design's original intentions rather than detracting from them as the tower was originally intentionally oversized to emphasize past connections, including what Rossi has called 'neo-classical hyperbole'. The blue-grey rusticated plaster of the tower, in contrast to the stone cladding used elsewhere, provides yet another layer of this contextual relationship. In his poem 'Litania', Giorgio Caproni described the city as 'Genova di grigie mura', Genoa of the grey walls, and this was certainly not far from Rossi's mind whilst designing this building.

The theatre is axially connected to the entrance foyer which is lit by a conical lantern that protrudes through the roof and recalls the lighthouses around the bay. However, the equation between 'inwardness and outwardness', that Rossi mentioned as a critical inspiration, is particularly evident in the two-thousand seat auditorium which is terraced to increase the capacity of the original theatre. This hall replicates a town square with a starry sky of its own, created by tiny luminaires that replace the traditional ornate crystal chandelier of the original theatre, and treads a fine line between kitsch – of the laundry painted on the walls of an Italian restaurant variety – and evocative abstraction.

These marble façades, windows, shutters and balconies that constitute the side walls of the hall also serve an acoustic function described by José Bernhart, Acoustic Consultant, in the following terms:

> The frames with glass and wood shutters on the stone walls are used to break up the extensive surface and to cut the risk of sound being reflected between the two large longitudinal walls.

Rossi's delicate balancing of historical imperatives, civic character, cultural memory and 'the subtle fusion of the damaged pieces of the past' required a lot more than basic restoration. Yet, through this process he also managed a seemingly effortless accommodation of demanding functional and acoustic considerations as well, with the result that the new Carlo Felice theatre has finally transcended acrimonious precedents and exceeded all expectations.

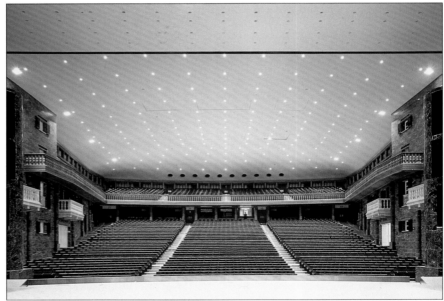

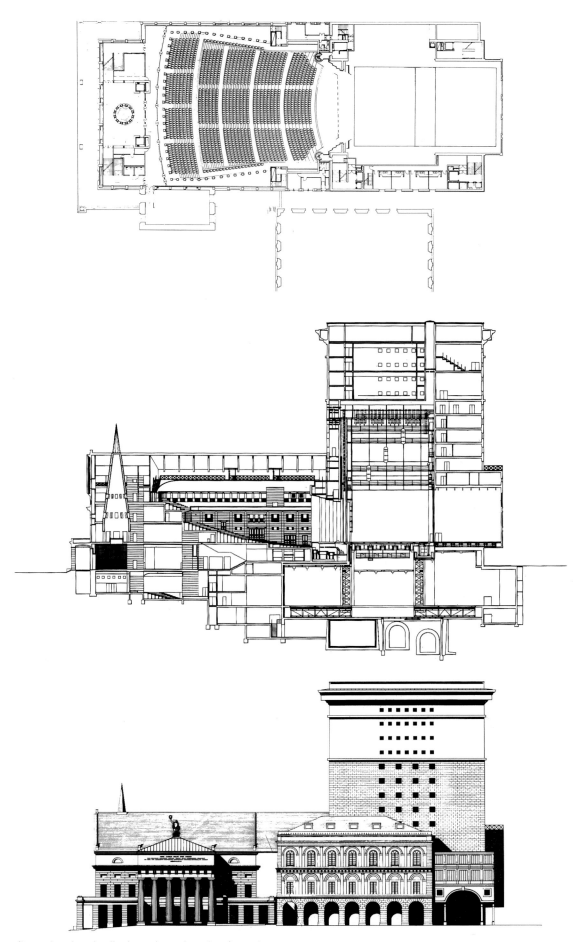

FROM ABOVE: First floor plan; longitudinal section; elevation from the square

PERCY THOMAS
INTERNATIONAL CONVENTION CENTRE
Birmingham, England

The symphony hall at Birmingham is part of an extensive complex that includes eleven halls, a mall and catering facilities located at the end of Centenary Square and connected by bridge to a new Hyatt Hotel.

The concert hall itself took five years to design; the brief from the city demanding a world class venue for orchestral music. Russell Johnson of Artec Acoustics devised the basic shape, volumetric and acoustic parameters of the room, and the strategy for the accommodation of the audience; drawing inspiration from the opera houses, theatres and concert halls built in Europe between 1600 and 1910. These provided the spatial parameters of the hall, whilst Artec utilized innovative features, to improve on performance. Johnson believes that the acoustic quality of these old halls is due largely to dimensional characteristics and heavy masonry construction. To these Artec added a reverberation chamber, a moveable acoustical canopy and the concept of flexible sound absorbent screens, using a strategy similar to that followed in IM Pei's Myerson Symphony Center in Dallas. These enable the hall to perform properly for a wide range of music, other than orchestral, and also for needs such as speech, cinema and even for product launches if the need arose.

Neil Graham led a small team of young architects through the design development phase, taking the Artec acoustical model and imposing a geometrical and structural order on it. They established a strong design framework and created two major points for all curved elements in the room. These were determined by the basic geometry of the angled walls at the front and rear of the room and were 'anchored' visually and structurally by four pairs of massive columns; based on the axes of the radix points and the key angled walls. The anchor locations act as fulcrums to turn the straight side walls into the reverse fan geometry at both the front and the rear of the hall. These points also became the locations for entrances at the rear, for the audience, and the front for the performers.

The concept of the room is a single space. The performers and the audience are together in this space and no proscenium arch is required. The space is 27 m in width and 55 m in length, with the height of the space roughly equal to the width, recreating the classic tall and narrow shape of the great old halls. The architects recognized that these dimensions had great spatial potential and worked to perfect the sculptural quality of the space, organizing the seating tiers, performance stage and ceiling geometry to spring naturally from the basic root geometry of the two major radix points. Around this framework an architectural language was evolved and refinements made, based on a classical division of plinth, entablature and roof. These were intentionally detached from the high-level volumes of the reverberation chamber in order to mould them into the ceiling soffits like a dominant 'cornice'.

At the sides of the room the audience tiers became slender shelves, which were terminated and returned to the side anchor walls, reflecting the geometry of the main axes. This was necessary because without a proscenium arch there is a danger that at the front of the room the geometry becomes indeterminate, as there is nothing to terminate the side tiers.

Whilst the architects contemplated this problem, Artec were searching for a way of establishing an enlarged reverberation chamber, increasing the access doors to this volume and introducing some additional acoustic 'shelves' at the front of the room. These were needed to help provide the early reflections necessary for the orchestra to hear itself well during a performance. The resolution of this problem was the stepping reverberation chamber, or the 'cascade' as it ultimately became known. Taking the upper volumes of the reverberation chamber as the high point in the room and the organ chamber side walls as the low-level springing point, the design team created a sculptured volume between these two locations which created a highly defined physical element at the front of the room and a proper termination for the side tiers. This also solved the acoustical shelves and reverberation chamber requirements at a single stroke. The cascade follows the curved plan geometry 'rules' and is entirely in harmony within the overall concept.

The detailed design of the cascade, with over forty heavy concrete doors required special attention. The framework of this element was formed in concrete as were all the soffits for acoustic reasons. The architects wished to visually emphasize the hanging, stepping vertical emphasis of this feature, but as sharp edges could not be tolerated for acoustic reasons they devised a partly engaged 'hanging column' detail. These columns work visually as normal columns would except that in the symphony hall they are thrusting downwards from the roof. The visual 'erosion' of the cascade, by the side tiers at the front of the room, is one of the singular architectural features of the auditorium.

After the detailed design by Ove Arup of the concrete substructure, voided piles and rubber mountings necessary to isolate the chamber from its foundations to avoid any external ground vibration from entering the hall was complete, the design team and consultants turned their attention to details and finishes. They wished to balance the strong horizontal elements with the vertical emphasis that the high building required and chose hard materials for all finishes for acoustic reasons; again following the example of the great old halls. Granite was used extensively for the plinth, or stalls, and balcony fronts at the base of the room, and was carried vertically up the anchor point side walls to strongly emphasize them and the four points to the hall.

Granite was felt to be appropriate for a hall of this importance and also performs well as a hard sound reflector. Above stalls level, walls are generally finished in thick polished plaster achieving a finish quite unlike normal plaster and reviving trade skills last used extensively in the foyers of the classic interiors of the American art deco period. Polished wood and metal, the latter both polished and matt, were chosen because of their affinity with the instruments and because of the visual richness they would contribute. Polished wood was also specified for the side screen walls, the stage, the main floors and the orchestra risers. In their material choices the architects sought to achieve the complete harmony of the audience, the hall and the performers, thus emphasizing the concept of a single space and experience.

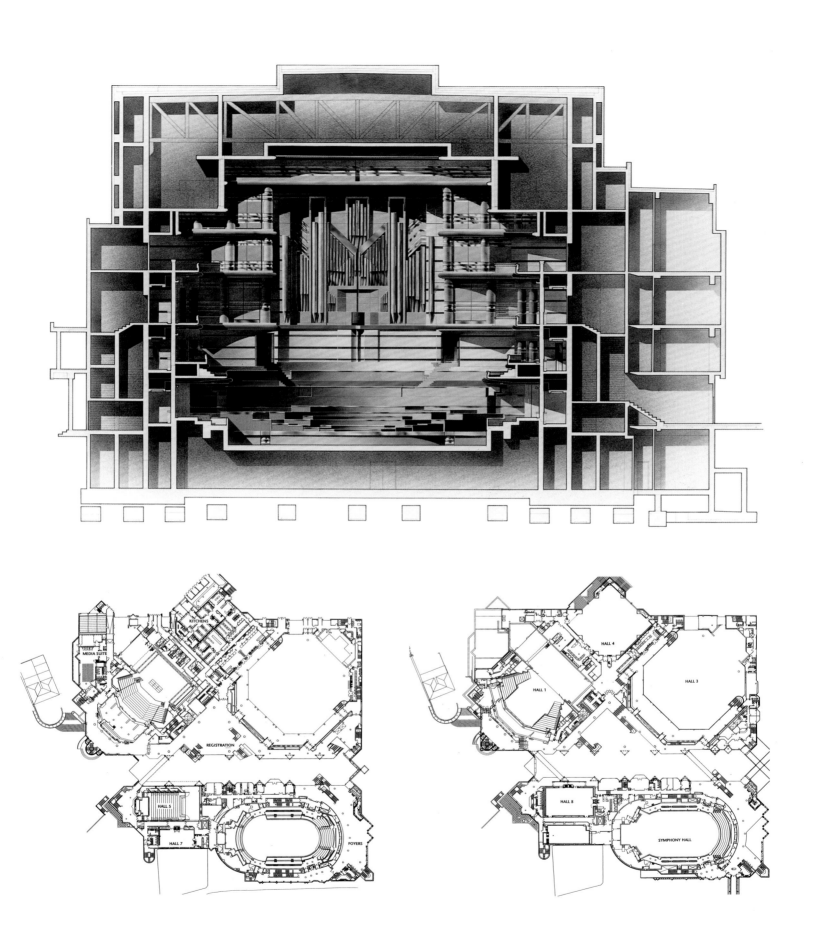

FROM ABOVE, LEFT TO RIGHT: Traverse section rendered; ground floor plan; first floor plan

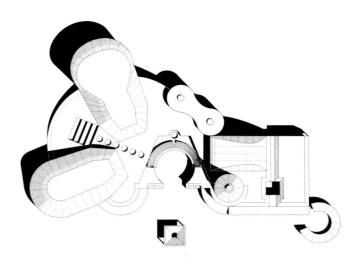

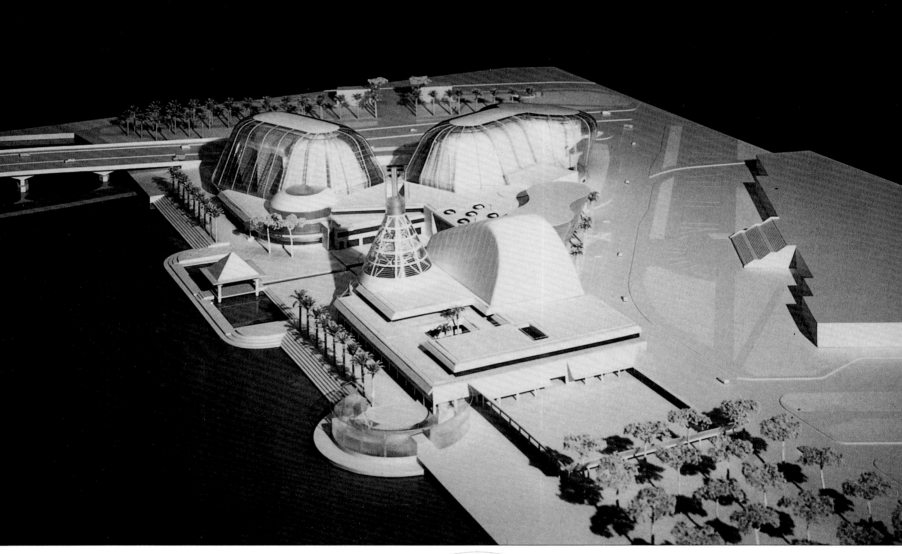

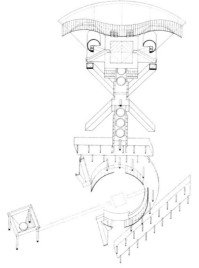

MICHAEL WILFORD
SINGAPORE ARTS CENTRE

Singapore

Recent developments in dance, drama and music in Singapore have attempted an appropriate fusion between modern techniques and local traditions; demonstrating that both exist and reinforce each other. The design of the arts centre is intended to express this fusion.

The centre will occupy a four hectare site in Marina Park, between Marina Centre and Marina Bay. Future extension of the central business district into Marina South will produce a horseshoe of downtown towers, enclosing three sides of the bay and focused towards the arts centre. The architects have taken the opportunity of using this juxtaposition to make a symbolic statement about the effect of commerce on culture, and the degree to which they should be mixed or not.

The centre contains five performance auditoria, together with an enclosed concourse and resident company rehearsal and office space. The performance spaces specifically are a concert hall (one thousand six hundred seats and two hundred choir), a lyric theatre (two thousand seats), a medium theatre (seven hundred and fifty seats), an adaptable theatre (four hundred seats) and a development studio theatre (two hundred seats).

The plan is a tripartite composition radiating from the central concourse, comprising the concert hall, lyric theatre and small theatre cluster. A clear hierarchy controls all parts of the composition with the concourse and courtyard garden forming the centre of the project. The design is open and embracing to all approaches and orientations. Transitional elements, arcades, balconies and roof terraces, surround the individual forms to ensure a human scale and smooth the distinction between inside and outside.

The three main auditoria, together with the *prasada* restaurant over the adaptable theatre, have strong architectural forms, each with its own character yet in harmony with the others, presenting a memorable roofscape. Their seating capacities, staging and acoustic requirements produce inherently large structures and their volume is reduced by rounding the enclosing envelopes of glass and solar shading. This spectacular hi-tech façade system creates changing patterns in response to different orientations and allows views out of, and into, the foyers, as well as assisting with the climatic control of the internal environment. The lyric theatre and concert hall foyers look out toward the city and Marina Bay, and protect the formal entrance forecourt; related to the Padang and civic districts. An internal street leads from the forecourt to the central concourse and promenade surrounding the courtyard.

The concourse is also connected to the more formal Raffles Avenue entrance and the esplanade, making it the major public circulation space and the heart of the project. The concourse is diverse in character, containing the foyers of the medium and adaptable theatres and two floors of retail, restaurants and bars. The esplanade expands across the arts centre frontage to form a grand promenade, containing reflecting pools and a performance pavilion situated on an axis with the courtyard garden. A circular satay club, reflecting the Singaporean love of dining, extends out into the bay and terminates the eastern end of the colonnades along the esplanade, accommodating additional commercial space and public access to the orchestra and chorus rehearsal room and studio theatre. To supplement the five auditoria and the waterside pavilion, a number of outdoor performance spaces is proposed which will add to the vibrancy of the centre. The entire esplanade and upper terraces will provide an excellent viewing platform for water-based events and festivals in the bay.

To reinforce its parkland setting, and to serve as a filter between the city and the water, the project will be landscaped to provide spaces that range from private, meditative areas to zones of intensive public interaction. The landscape design will connect the arts centre to Padang, Marina Square and Park. Extensive tree planting will provide shade for people walking around the centre, or sitting and enjoying the views and sea breezes. The actors' courtyard and upper terraces will be landscaped as places of tranquility for artists between performances.

The varied approach demonstrated by this project, of treating edges separately and creating a quasi-internal courtyard, around which the various halls cluster, continues a grand ceremonial tradition of formal, monumental architecture in Singapore, without recalling colonial prototypes. The architects have defined the design challenge as being the representation of the future aspirations of Singapore as well as its rich traditions, whilst establishing a landmark for a new cultural district, a focus for national celebrations as well. The designers have identified an important urban disjunction, noting that various stages of land reclamation have progressively detached the Bras Basah corridor and Padang district from their original seashore locations. The centre has thus lost its direct relationship with the point at which it was first established. The arts centre will reconnect the city to the bay.

This concert hall may be seen as a logical extension of technical advances made in Dallas and Birmingham. An adaptable reverberation chamber continues the flexible acoustic strategies used in each of these other halls, but in this case the scale is enormous allowing the volume to be doubled. The technological approach taken here parallels that of the double skin cladding, as both are indicative of a progressive urban vision. This is tempered, the architects feel, by a direct appeal to precedents, and they claim that the forms used have been developed from a thorough study of traditional construction in South East Asia, China and India. They note that:

> The principal spaces have roof forms which echo the soft rounded shapes found in the region. These crown a system of terraces and gardens which provide a strong platform connecting all parts of the building. Canopies and colonnades incorporated into this platform articulate the different entrances and pathways within and around the building. The scale and massing of these elements varies to acknowledge the relative importance of each frontage . . . Our research has demonstrated that platforms, vertical hierarchy and large roof forms, combined with clear constructional systems built up from aggregations of identifiable elements at a human scale, are key characteristics of the region's architecture.

(See page 223 for project credits.)

Roof plan; central concourse (worm's-eye view)

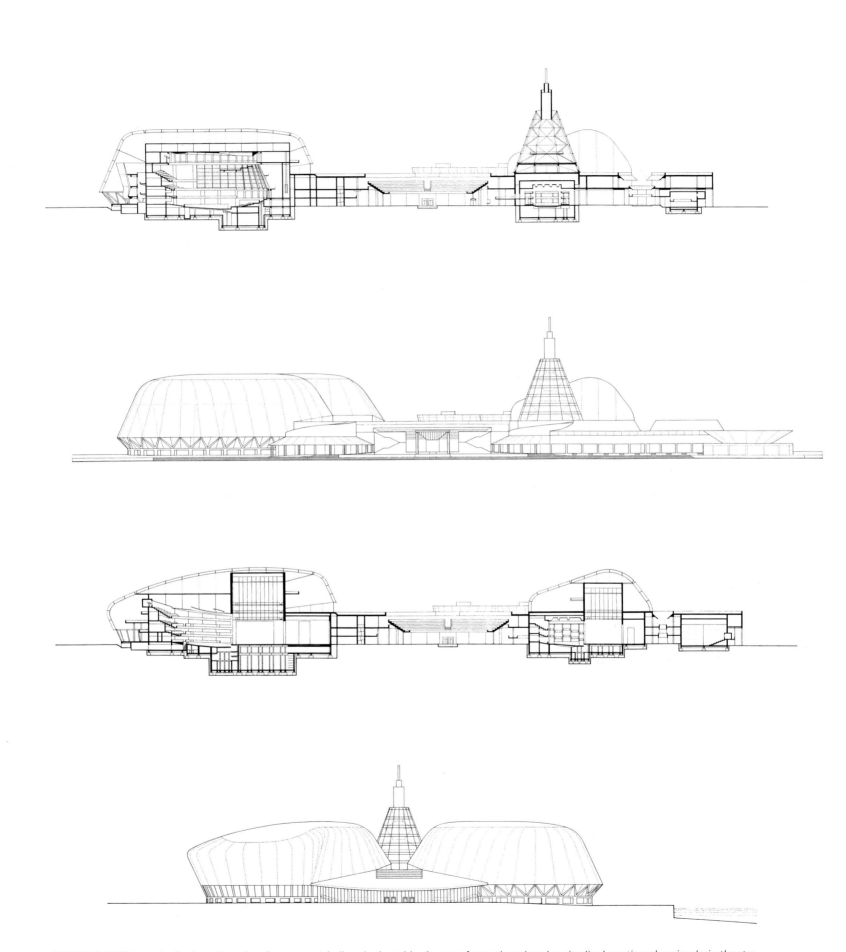

FROM ABOVE: Longitudinal section showing concert hall and adaptable theatre; front elevation; longitudinal section showing lyric theatre, medium theatre and development theatre; side elevation

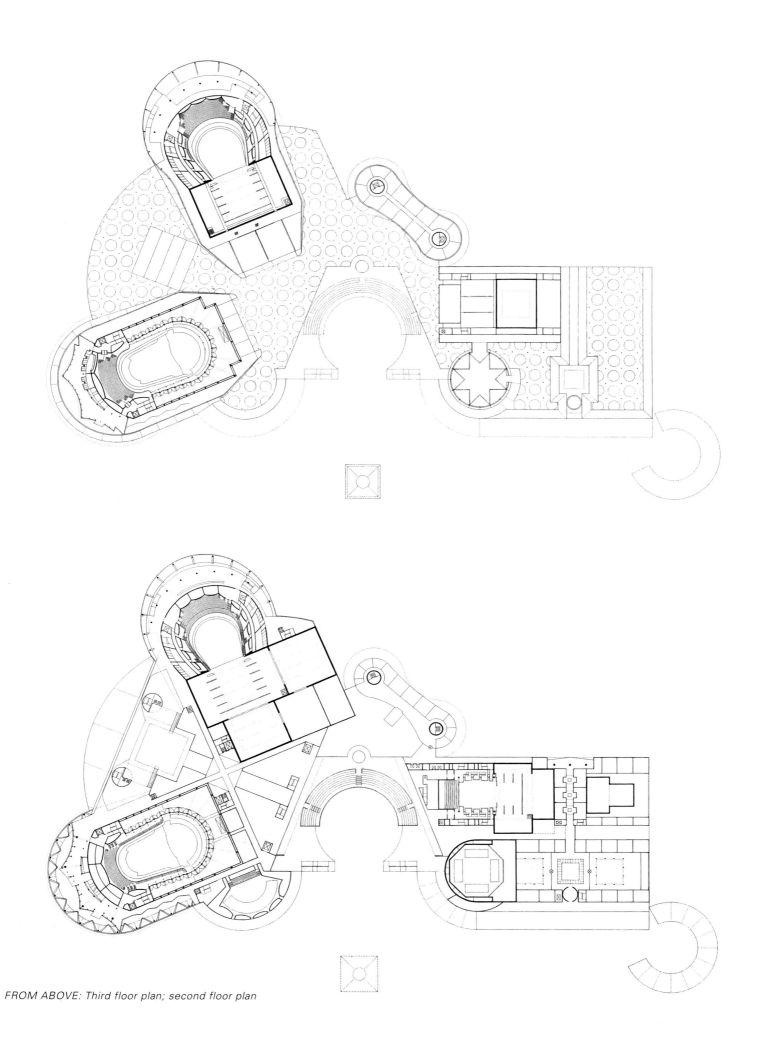

FROM ABOVE: Third floor plan; second floor plan

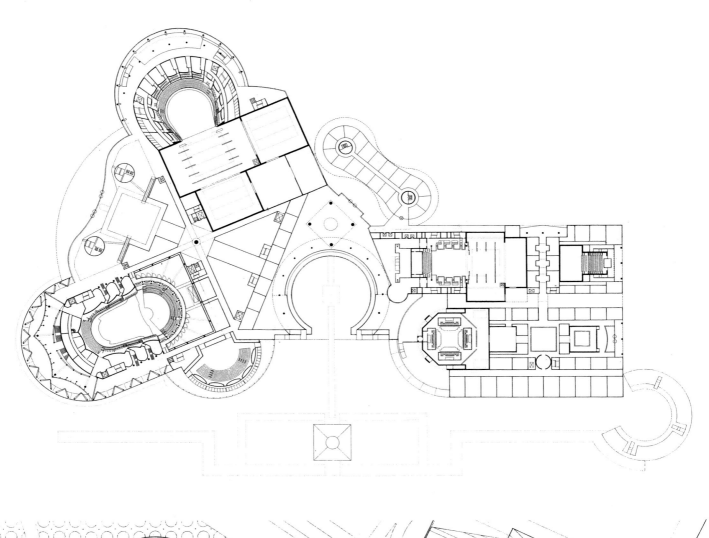

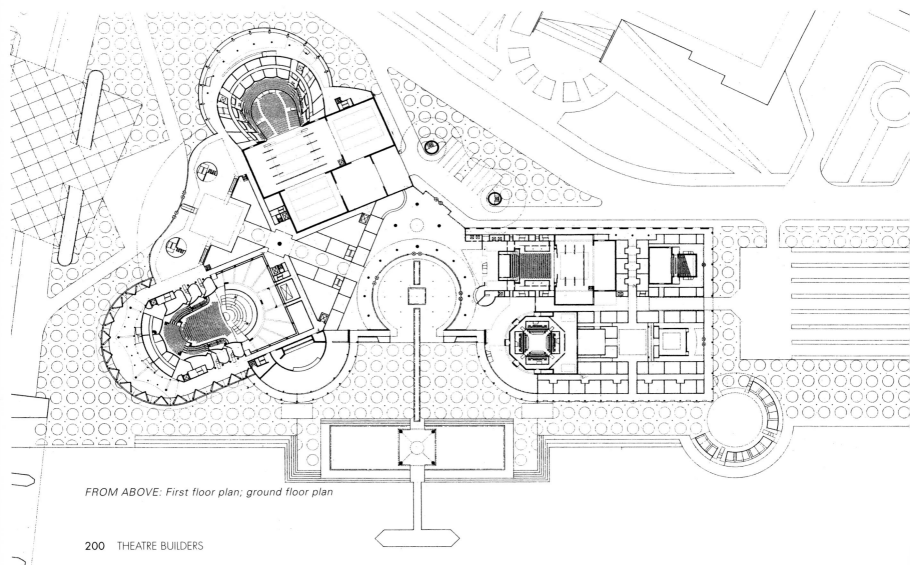

FROM ABOVE: First floor plan; ground floor plan

FROM ABOVE: Location plan; axonometric

JAMES STIRLING + MICHAEL WILFORD
PERFORMING ARTS CENTER
Ithaca, New York

Inviting critical comparison with other university centres presented here, such as the one now being designed for Maryland by Moore Ruble Yudell, this ensemble is much smaller in scale but follows many of the same design principles seen in the other examples. The Performing Arts Center is a teaching facility for theatre arts as well as a performance centre for the university. It also serves as a gateway to the campus because of its prominent location on College Avenue near the bridge over Cascadilla Gorge, and stands as a transitional element between the town and the university, to be used by both. Given its symbolic status as a gate, and its proximity to the bridge, the centre has been organized along a loggia/spine terminated by a tower near the crossing. This tower and spine set the tone for the architectural language used, the metaphor of hill town reinforced by internal plaza, campanile and church (the theatre itself).

The octagonal pavilion which signals the approach to the Performing Arts Center is a campus information centre and a shelter for the adjacent bus-stop. Its upper floor has rooms for the Theatre Arts Department and for touring companies such as the Nation Theatre of Britain. The plaza, entered from the pavement, is a place for students to meet and contains a pergola and seats. Entry to the building is from the plaza and through the loggia – a promenade approach with views across the gorge towards the campus and long views towards Lake Cayuga. Part of the loggia is enclosed as an alternative bad weather route leading to the entrance. A spiral staircase at the far end of the loggia connects to the ground level, allowing access to adjoining footpaths and the nearby multi-storey car park.

The three-storey high entrance hall is also the main foyer for the proscenium and flexible theatres. It is located in the centre of the building and connects with all the major spaces, encouraging interaction between theatre, dance and film groups and bringing guest artists and public into contact with students and faculty. The foyer opens onto the loggia enabling audiences, during the intermission, to stroll in and out and take the view. The upper balconies which overlook it are connected to the entrance level by a staircase and a large elevator – the campanile, which is floodlit at night, announcing the presence of the Performing Arts Center to downtown Ithaca. It is a new tower on a campus which already has several.

The proscenium theatre despite its spartan design – reflecting its mixed, highly pragmatic function – is the major volume in the village, and is located at the right-hand side of the plaza acting like an anchor at the opposite end of the loggia to the tower and bridge. The four-hundred-and-fifty-six seat theatre is a classic horseshoe shape with two entrances from the foyer, fixed seating in parallel aisles on the main floor and loose seating on two levels of balcony/boxes. The balconies extend completely around the room to bring the audience and performers closer, and create a more informal atmosphere.

The sound and light booths are located at the second balcony level with a technical ledge and follow-spot room above that. The forestage of the proscenium is adaptable as either a thrust stage or an orchestra pit; accomplished by an electrically operated lift. The flexible theatre is also accessible from the foyer with multiple entrances that allow arena, thrust, alley or proscenium seating. The audience is seated on adjustable platforms whose capacity varies from one-hundred-and-forty to one-hundred-and-seventy-five.

Visitors can descend from the entrance foyer to the dance performance studio located beneath the proscenium theatre. This can accommodate an audience of up to one-hundred-and-thirty-two on bleacher seating, allowing the floor to be cleared for teaching. At the same level, but beneath the flexible theatre, is the laboratory/black box studio which accommodates from fifty to one hundred people on adjustable seating platforms in a variety of configurations. Both the laboratory and dance performance studios have multiple entrances and overviewing control booths. Public audiences can also use the film forum, which is entered from a lobby below the entrance foyer, containing a raked auditorium with one hundred and three fixed seats and a small stage used for drama, with performer access from the side. Scenery/props production is at the rear of the building with truck access into the high bay area. The scenery shop opens through sound-isolating doors onto the proscenium stage and the flexible theatre allowing vehicles to be driven on stage. Costume areas are beneath the proscenium stage, and linked backstage to all performances and production spaces.

In keeping with the hill town metaphor, as well as the running commentary on the contemporary role of institutions once taken for granted, started in the Staatsgalerie, the cladding material of choice here is stone. The entrance hall and loggia are paved in marble. The pavilion, loggia and College Avenue façades are clad in open-jointed Vermont marble, whilst stucco is used on the other elevations. Originally these were to have horizontal courses of marble at four feet intervals, but this was given up on some elevations as a result of economic necessity. Pitched roofs are lead-coated copper with Vermont slate on the loggia. The steel trusses carrying the loggia roof are painted French green matching the window metal work. The soffit of the loggia is stained redwood, as are the plaza benches and the pergola, behind which are large planters containing purple and white wistaria that will grow over the free-standing structure.

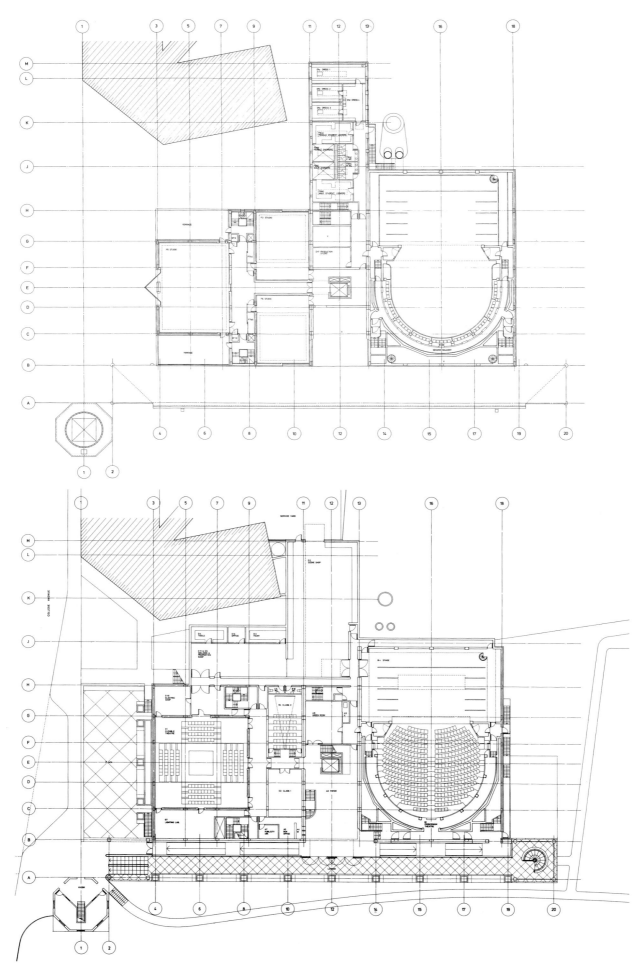

FROM ABOVE: First floor plan; ground floor plan

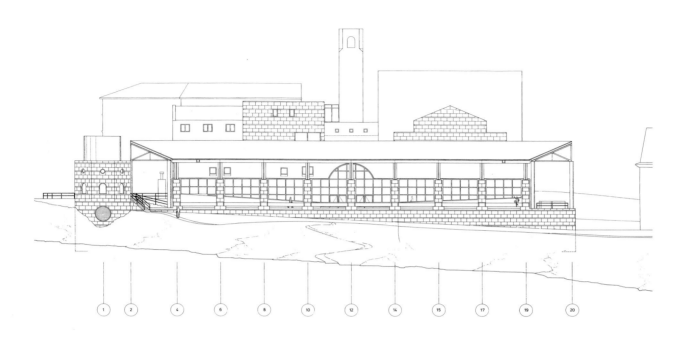

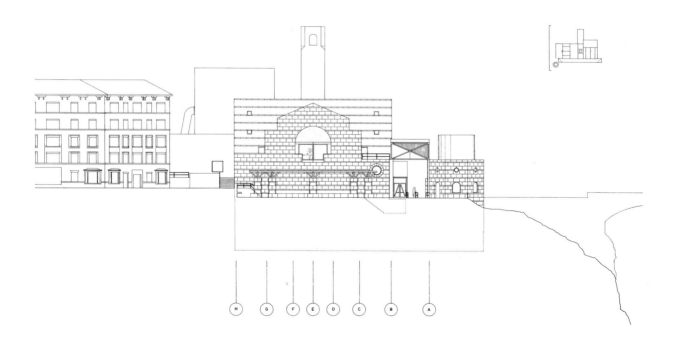

FROM ABOVE: North elevation; east elevation

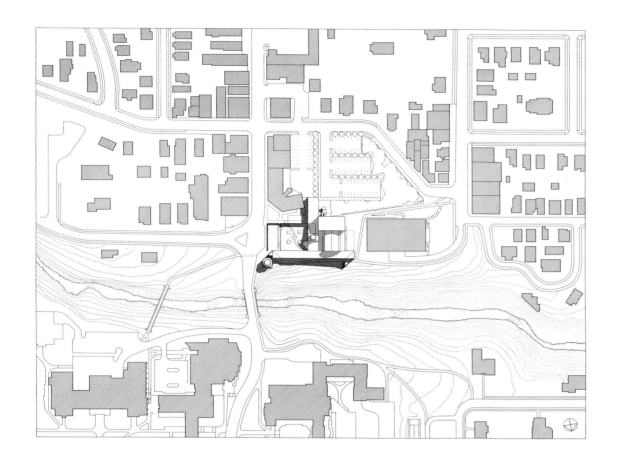

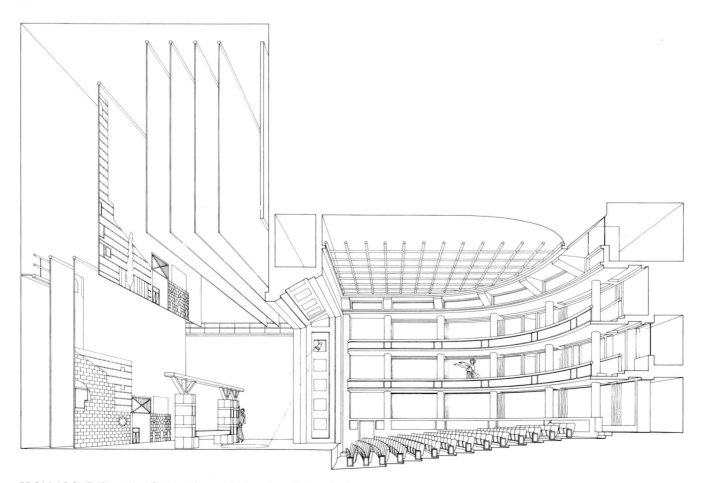

FROM ABOVE: Site plan; Sectional perspective through proscenium

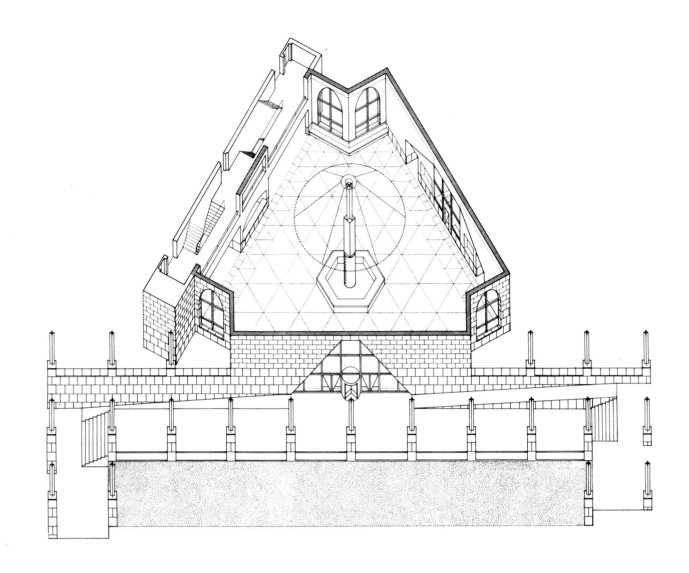

MICHAEL WILFORD
COMPTON VERNEY OPERA HOUSE
Warwickshire, England

In the same tradition as Glyndebourne in East Sussex, where the wish for an opera house to be located on a great estate has led to a surprisingly happy marriage between two seemingly incongruous building types, Compton Verney promises to provide yet another bucolic venue for cultural outings in Britain.

Gatehouses, which are traditional on English country estates, mark the entrances and set the scene for a fine approach to the opera house. To provide twenty-four hour control, these will accommodate residential staff. In fine weather, car and bus passengers will be encouraged to disembark here and walk into the grounds, enabling them to appreciate the landscape. There are alternative experiences when arriving from either the north or south; for instance, Sequoia Avenue forms a natural approach from the south, drawing visitors towards the lawn and entrance loggia, with views of the Adam bridge, lake and mansion.

In inclement weather, or if visitors are handicapped, vehicles will be directed from the gatehouse to the southern end of the loggia, adjacent to the opera house. This area is large enough for ten cars and several coaches, and its offset location avoids any conflict with other traffic. To the south, a soft parking area accommodates five-hundred cars on a gently terraced slope, which follows the natural contour of the hillside. Paved parking for two-hundred-and-fifty cars and thirty-two coaches is located north of the opera house. Coppices will be supplemented to screen these areas from view, retaining the original character of the estate.

The new opera house has been positioned to enhance the existing landscape, without compromising the mansion house and stable block. Historic plans show that the gardens have been influenced by the formal baroque tradition and the informal English picturesque. Today, the latter seems to dominate, with only vestiges of the baroque remaining. The architects have recognized the primary characteristics of the garden and reinforced them, bringing the mansion, bridge, opera house and arena into a harmonious relationship without resorting to pastiche.

The position and form of the opera house, together with the landscaping, will be disposed around the northern end of the lake in the English picturesque manner, as in Stourhead. The articulated arrangement will help to reduce the mass and scale of the assemblage, continue the rural character of Compton Verney, and allow individual facilities to be used separately, without opening the entire complex.

A fountain, between Sequoia Avenue and the bridge, marks one of the main axes of the composition. The loggia, restaurant, bridge, tea house and arena may all be seen along this spine, linking the boathouse and ice house with the mansion.

Local limestone made excavation on site difficult and expensive, and as a result the stage was placed at ground level; the height of the fly-tower was reduced by the position of the loggia, restaurant, bridge and administration pavilion in front of it. When seen from the mansion, the opera house has its own identity.

The loggia forms a pristine backdrop to the square lawn, reminiscent of the entrance to the mansion, and is open to the landscape, allowing visitors to approach from all directions and stroll out into the gardens. The ends of this arcade receive visitors arriving by car from the south and walking from the car-park to the north, and in inclement weather, which is always a consideration in such a changeable climate, provide shelter for picnickers.

The axes of the loggia, auditorium and administration pavilion converge at the centre of the spacious triangular foyer that links all the elements of this geometric composition. This area, overlooked by the auditorium entrance gallery, has been conceived as a grand room with fine views and is large enough to accommodate exhibitions and informal performances: an aperitif before the main event commences.

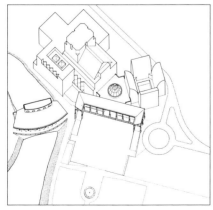 

OPPOSITE, FROM ABOVE: Axonometric entrance lobby; exterior perspective; ABOVE, LEFT TO RIGHT: Schematic down view; interior perspective of auditorium

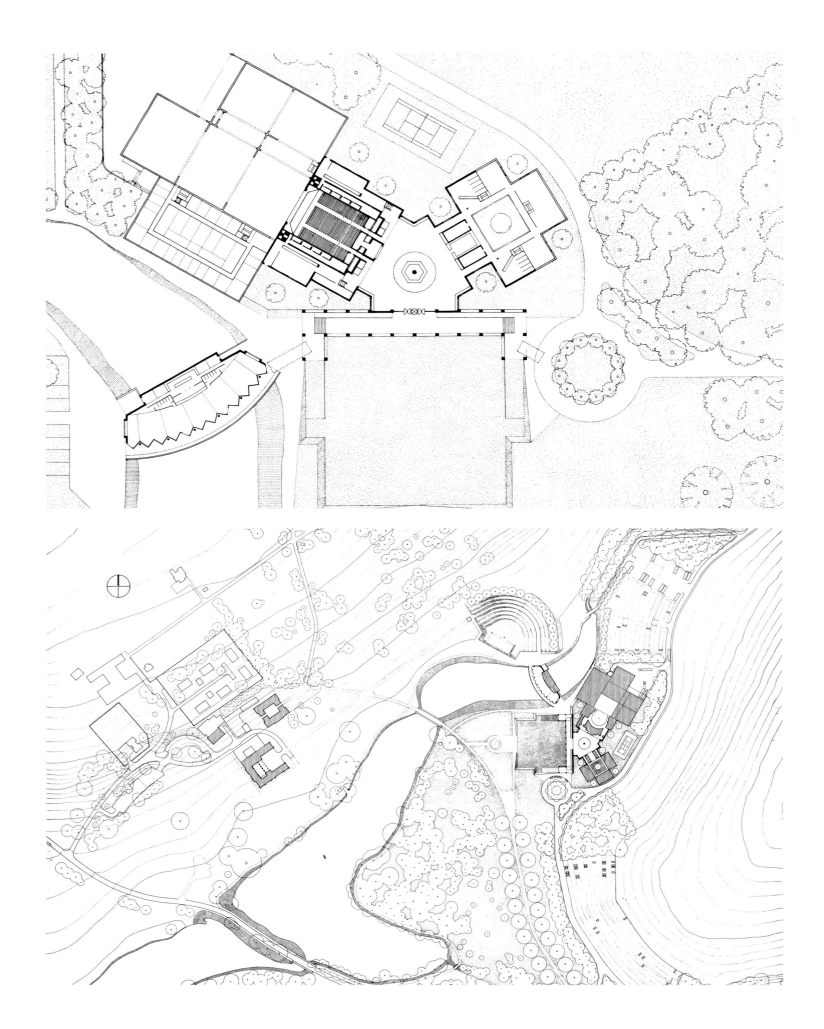

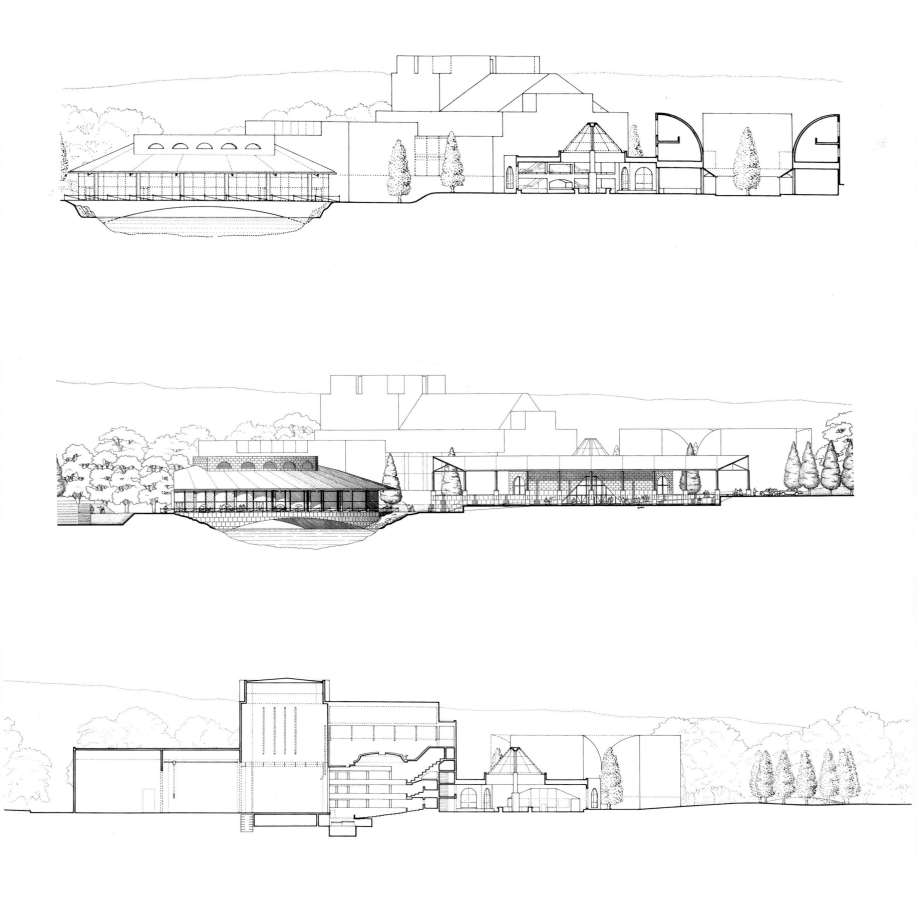

OPPOSITE, FROM ABOVE: Ground floor plan; site plan; FROM ABOVE: Longitudinal section; front elevation; section through auditorium

MICHAEL WILFORD
THE LOWRY CENTRE
Salford Quays, Manchester

The Lowry Centre will be situated at the western end of Pier 8, facing a new public plaza. The plaza is the focus of the plan and will be a sheltered and lively venue for community activity. A hotel and a retail building, both with colonnades containing restaurants, bars and arts related facilities, enclose the remaining sides of the plaza. A temporary canopy can be erected over the plaza to cover large outdoor events in inclement summer weather. The plaza will have vehicular access and a taxi rank at the northern edge of the Lowry Centre. For festivals and other special occasions, traffic can be diverted outside the plaza to allow it to be fully pedestrianized. A new public park and extended waterside promenade provide leisurely pedestrian routes to the centre. Seven, four-storey commercial/institutional buildings of varying sizes mediate between the Lowry Centre and existing housing on Pier 8. These buildings enclose a garden square and share use of the parking.

The Lowry Centre will be the first purpose built cultural centre in Britain, containing facilities for both the visual and performing arts. The building will be a landmark, and is intended to encourage public activity in an area where this is now lacking. The centre contains a one-thousand-six-hundred-and-fifty seat lyric theatre, a four-hundred seat flexible theatre with resident company facilities, art galleries to display the city's collection of Lowry paintings, a children's gallery, shops, bars and waterfront restaurant. A festive amphitheatre will be generated by movement into and through the centre. A generous two-storey foyer extends across the full width of the plaza frontage to provide convenient access to all activities.

The lyric theatre is the heart of the building. Stairs and access balconies to the three seating levels are situated within its outer enclosure. They overlook the foyer and provide dramatic opportunities for people watching before performances and during intermissions. To the left, a ramp leads into the hexagonal entrance pavilion of the children's gallery. To the right, escalators rise over a square rehearsal studio to a balcony housing a permanent exhibition called the 'Life and Work of Lowry', marking the entrance to the art galleries.

The flexible theatre has a courtyard form which can be quickly adjusted to suit proscenium, thrust or in-the-round performances. Whilst a curved foyer, with views across the ship canal, surrounds the auditorium and can be entered from the quayside. A rooflit galleria with stunning views into the children's gallery connects both theatre foyers. An upper balcony within the galleria forms part of the promenade around the centre, linking all activities. Visitors will be able to use the facilities within the building during the day, encouraging return visits to enjoy performances and exhibitions.

The children's gallery contains a sequence of interactive exhibits and audio-visual displays in the hexagonal pavilion. The three large art galleries of the Lowry Collection are arranged *enfilade*, alongside a series of smaller gallery spaces which form the northern arm of the promenade. In combination, these spaces create a flexible suite of rooms of varying scale and ambience, starting in the foyer with the 'Life and Work of Lowry' exhibit and finishing in the Lowry Study Centre.

The bar, café and restaurant arranged

along the southern side of the building at quayside level, serve both theatres and in fine weather can extend out onto terraces overlooking the canal basin. Upper level bars on either side of the lyric theatre open onto roof terraces with views across the plaza and adjacent quaysides. Corporate hospitality facilities situated on top of the hexagonal pavilion and in the dress bar, are readily accessible from the dress circle of the lyric theatre.

The layout of the building is designed to encourage a sense of artistic community. Theatre and gallery support areas are grouped along the northern flank of the building and the artists' lounge and roof-garden is centrally located above the scenery store. Truck docks are entered from the quayside. The administration tower is crowned by an illuminated sign announcing current productions and registering the presence of the centre on the Salford skyline.

The Lowry Centre has been designed to benefit from the enormous potential of this magnificent location and the special combination of facilities which the building contains. Its form expresses the building's significance as a cultural symbol and an intimate place of personal experience; a fusion between the monumental tradition of public buildings and the informal, more populist image of many cultural centres today. In this way, it echoes the intention of both the Singapore Arts Centre and Stuttgart Music School, in its decided lack of exclusivity and intentionally compromised formality. The recent trend, seen throughout this book, of making cultural centres more approachable, is reiterated again here in this project, which is firmly placed in this genre.

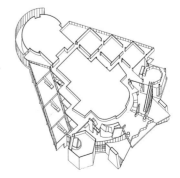 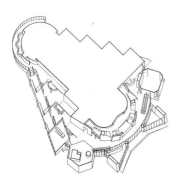 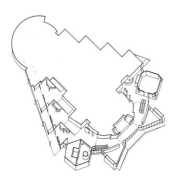

FROM LEFT: Axonometric of gallery; axonometric of upper foyer; axonometric of plaza

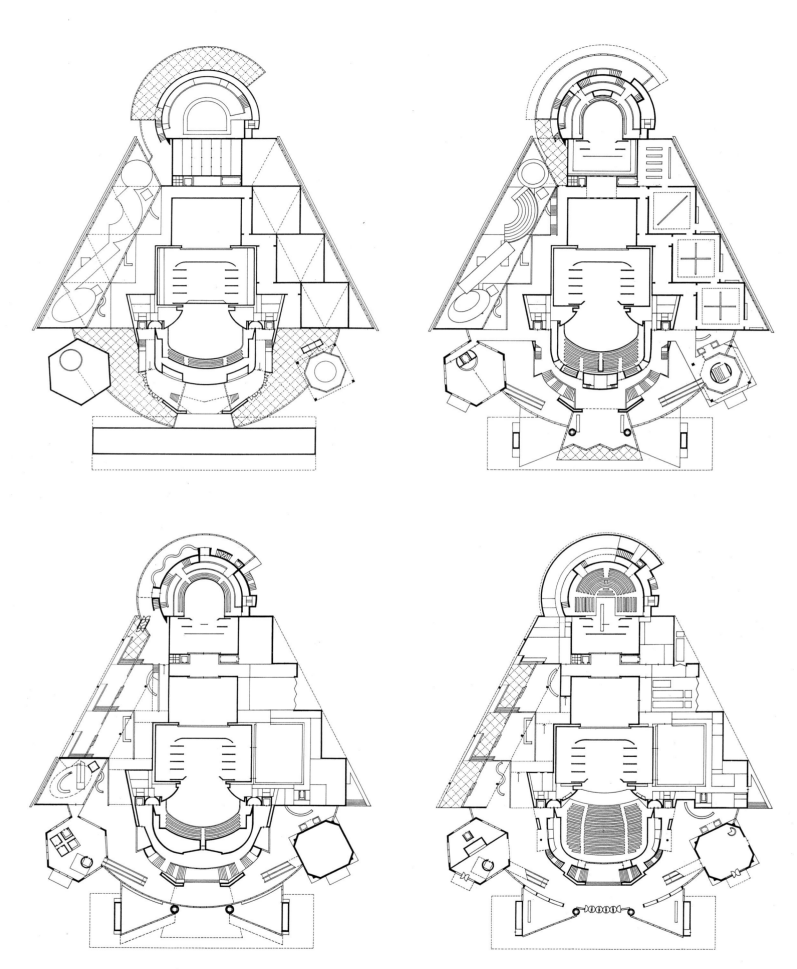

FROM ABOVE, LEFT TO RIGHT: Terrace plan; upper foyer plan; plaza plan; gallery plan

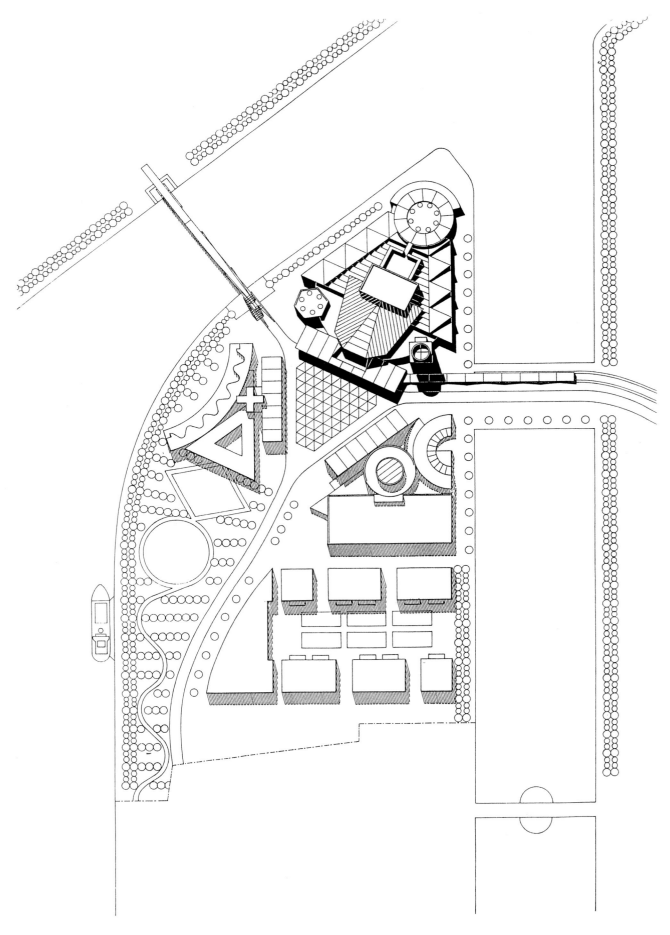

Masterplan with roof plan

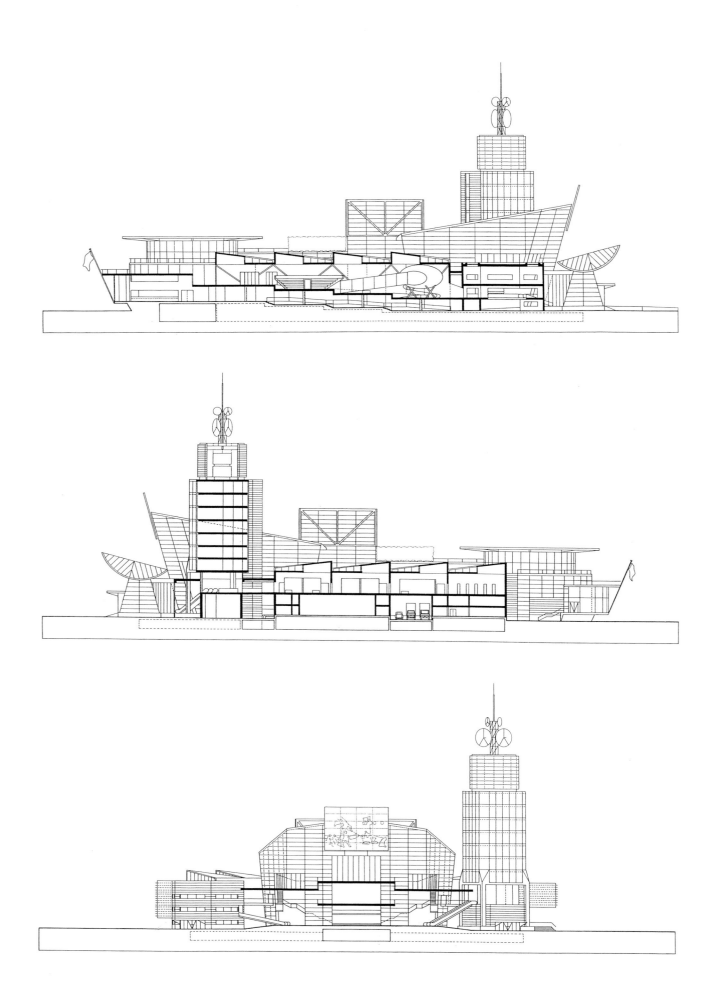

FROM ABOVE: Section through children's gallery; section through Lowry galleries; section through entrance foyer

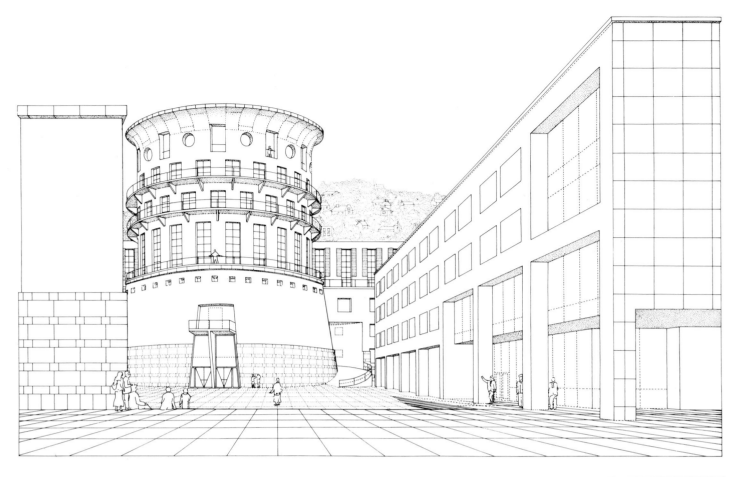

Exterior perspective

JAMES STIRLING + MICHAEL WILFORD
MUSIC SCHOOL AND THEATRE ACADEMY
Stuttgart, Germany

As a direct result of the success of the Neuestaatsgalerie, 1984, James Stirling Michael Wilford and Associates were appointed by Baden-Württemberg to prepare a town planning study in 1986. This included determining the feasibility of adding a Music School and Theatre Academy to the new museum complex. The firm was awarded the commission for the design of additional facilities in 1988, with the implied mandate being to continue the approach taken in the earlier scheme.

This new complex completes the sequence of buildings and public spaces along the 'cultural mile' flanking Konrad-Adenauer-Strasse. This urban composition continues the principle of three sided external spaces, partially enclosed by buildings, opening towards the city; initiated by the original Staatsgalerie of 1837 and continued with the Neuestaatsgalerie and theatre garden.

Passengers alight at the foot of a ramp, by which they reach the public terrace, where the entrance to the Theatre Academy is located. From the new plaza there are entrances to the Music School and the Landtag as well. A footpath, around the curved end of the academy, connects the new plaza with Eugenstrasse, corresponding to, and continuing, the footpath behind the chamber theatre and Staatsgalerie. Eugenstrasse will become a tree lined pedestrian route with service access to the kitchen, stage and existing Kammertheatre only. A curved ramp around the base of the tower allows public access to the plaza from Urbanstrasse, and this will occasionally be used by VIP vehicles making a ceremonial approach to the Landtag. Access to the underground garage is similar to that of the Staatsgalerie. The garage extends beneath the terrace and plaza on two levels and holds one hundred and forty five cars.

The L-shaped plan of the academy accommodates the extended theatre garden which will be on axis with the State Theatre, across Konrad-Adenauer-Strasse. Pergolas extend from the fountain along the width of the garden and contain alternating seats and planters. Here, and elsewhere, vines will cover the walls. An avenue of trees planted along Konrad-Adenauer-Strasse will extend this green promenade in front of the Staatsgalerie.

External surfaces of the new complex will be similar to the gallery, with veneered walls of sandstone and travertine, and natural stone paving, to continue the monumental effect. Internally materials will be different, responding to the acoustic priority here, and include timber panelling, timber floors and carpeting. The exterior of the Staatsgalerie was a statement about the dichotomy between the formality of museums in the past and the casual approach taken today, as expressed in the walls. The Music School and Theatre Academy continues this dialogue by using windows to express openness and public accessibility to what was once a private enclave. On walls where the random positioning of windows relates to the varied size of rooms, a grid of stone pilasters is superimposed to establish a visual order.

The quality of Urbanstrasse and Eugenstrasse will benefit from the façades of the new buildings which will bring existing unequal heights into unison. The long façade on Urbanstrasse is subdivided into smaller dimensions related to the scale of existing buildings along the street. The dining room, positioned to enliven the corner of Urbanstrasse and Eugenstrasse, will be a meeting place for students and contribute greatly to the urban scene.

The Music School flanks Urbanstrasse and the upper part of Eugenstrasse, and has nine floors to accommodate students and the public. The tower, intended as a landmark, particularly as seen from the Stadtgarten and city centre. It will be an addition to the historic towers characteristic of Stuttgart, such as the old château, the railway station and the town hall, whilst also relating to the circular void at the centre of the Staatsgalerie.

The main entrance to the school is from Urbanstrasse into a four-storey foyer, which links to the public entry from the plaza. The reception and dining room are at entry level, together with the concert hall and the chamber music theatre (also used for lectures), in the base of the tower. The stair and lifts rise from this foyer to the accommodation above, including the library which is entered from the exhibition gallery.

The library is a double height space that is overlooked from bay windows in a circular light shaft. The exhibition gallery is flanked by an outdoor terrace and leads to an orchestra rehearsal room which, on occasions, will have public performances. All floors have teaching rooms with room-in-room construction and acoustic splayed walls or angled corners.

The public entrance for performances is through the tower from the plaza, and is linked by a curved promenade, via a ticket office, to the lower foyer. The upper levels of the tower contain the departments of musical theory, composition and pitch training. The Senate Room on the top floor is the school's representative room, and a roof terrace above allows social functions and small open-air music events.

The entrance to the Theatre Academy, which is the first institution of its kind in Germany, is from the Konrad-Adenauer-Strasse terrace close to the theatre arch. The foyer contains the reception, ticket office and cloakrooms, as well as the stairs and lift which lead to lower and upper levels. The primary space of the academy is a fully equipped teaching theatre with large, side and rear stages. Dressing rooms, with make-up and wig making departments, form the remainder of backstage accommodation. The skylit staircase leads from the entrance foyer to teaching and rehearsal spaces above. A roof garden, with a pergola and amphitheatre, is provided for outdoor events.

In combination with the Staatsgalerie, the Music School and Theatre Academy represented a major civic investment for Stuttgart, continuing to create a definable edge along the Konrad-Adenauer-Strasse. When this wide road is placed underground in the future, the plazas created by this cultural ensemble, as well as the indoor spaces related to them, will become even more accessible to the public, adding to the richness of urban life in this city. This has been a fortuitous historical circumstance, and another example of what Edmund Bacon has identified as 'the principle of the second man', in which the power of one architectural statement in the urban fabric, literally dictates the response that follows.

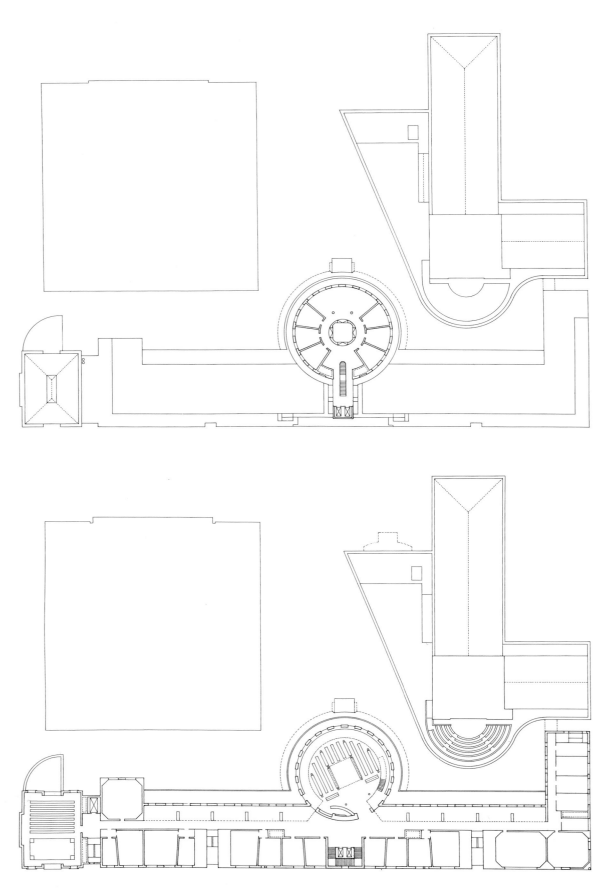

FROM ABOVE: Sixth floor plan; fifth floor plan

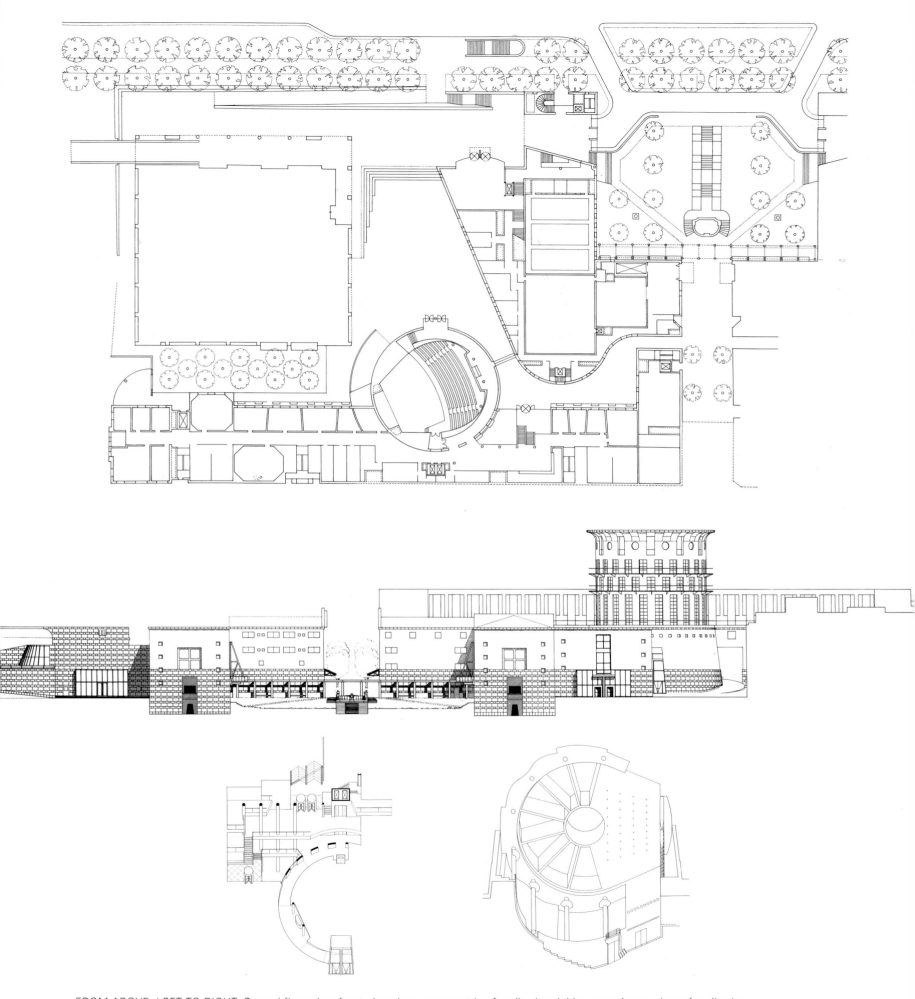

FROM ABOVE, LEFT TO RIGHT: Ground floor plan; front elevation; axonometric of auditorium lobby; worm's-eye view of auditorium

SELECT BIBLIOGRAPHY

MARIO BOTTA pp36-43

L Gazzaniga, 'Interview with Mario Botta', *Domus* (Milan, Italy), no 773, July/August 1995, pp15-18.

'Arata Isozaki', *Connaissance des Arts*, no 502, January 1994, pp82-83.

S Polano, 'Mario Botta: Under the Sign of Aries, New Directions in Mario Botta's Architectural Research', *A+U* (Tokyo, Japan), no 279, December 1993, pp4-63.

'Kyoto City Concert Hall', *The Japan Architect* (Tokyo, Japan), no 5, Winter 1992, pp238-239.

'Arata Isozaki: Convention Hall at Nara', *Domus* (Milan, Italy), no 740, July/August 1992, pp1-3.

J Darragh, 'The Iris and B Gerald Cantor Auditorium', *GA Document* (Tokyo, Japan), no 30, 1991, pp28-33.

P Slatin, 'International Affairs', *Architectural Record* (USA), vol 179, September 1991, pp88-93.

G Rondi, 'Sul Palazzo del Cinema', *Domus* (Milan, Italy), no 730, September 1991, pp57-77.

'The Latest Works of Mario Botta', *A+U* (Tokyo, Japan), no 220, January 1989, pp53-168.

M Zardini, 'First of All', *Lotus International* (Milan, Italy), no 57, 1988, pp38-69.

E Ranzani, 'Teatro a Chambery-le-Bas', *Domus* (Milan, Italy), no 690, January 1988, pp30-31.

'A Mario Botta Exhibition in Venice', *Abitare* (Milan, Italy), no 239, November 1985, p11.

KISHO KUROKAWA pp98-105

R Weston, 'Philosophy of Symbiosis', *Architects' Journal* (London, England), vol 200, 13th October 1994.

'Sazanami Hall', *The Japan Architect* (Tokyo, Japan), no 13, Spring 1994, pp148-149.

'Kisho Kurokawa', *Architectural Design* (London, England), vol 63, September/October 1993, pxxiv.

N Currimbhoy, 'New Wave Japanese Architecture', *Interiors* (New York), vol 152, July 1993, p12.

'Chinese–Japanese Youth Center', *The Japan Architect* (Tokyo, Japan), no 5, Winter 1992, pp168-169.

K Kurokawa, 'Works of Kisho Kurokawa', *The Japan Architect* (Tokyo, Japan), vol 64, August 1989, pp6-48.

'Special Feature: Kisho Kurokawa', *The Japan Architect* (Tokyo, Japan), vol 63, August 1988, pp8-43.

FUMIHIKO MAKI pp106-115

'Kirishima International Concert Hall', *The Japan Architect* (Tokyo, Japan), no 17, Spring 1995, pp74-77.

J Taylor, 'Pacific Overture', *Architecture*, vol 84, September 1995, pp118-123.

F Maki, 'Space, Image and Materiality', *The Japan Architect* (Tokyo, Japan), no 16, Winter 1994, pp4-13.

'Kirishima International Concert Hall', *The Japan Architect* (Tokyo, Japan), no 16, Winter 1994, pp20-41.

G Bosse, 'From the Youth Hostel in Kirishima to the New Kirishima Concert Hall', *The Japan Architect* (Tokyo, Japan), no 16, Winter 1994, pp42-45.

J Cohen, 'The Recent Work of Fumihiko Maki', *The Japan Architect* (Tokyo, Japan), no 16, Winter 1994, pp180-185.

F Maki, 'Notes on Collective Form', *The Japan Architect* (Tokyo, Japan), no 16, Winter 1994, pp247-297.

BARTON MYERS pp150-163

'Barton Myers: Cerritos Center for the Performing Arts', *A+U* (Tokyo, Japan), no 302, November 1995, pp90-99.

L Whiteson, 'Stage Presence', *Architecture*, vol 82, May 1993, pp74-81.

N Solomon, 'Flexible Theatres', *Architecture*, vol 81, August 1992, pp95-102.

PC Papademetriou, 'Arts Center for Newark Unveiled', *Progressive Architecture* (Cleveland, Ohio), vol 73, May 1992, pp28-29.

'Portland Center', *A+U* (Tokyo, Japan), no 235, April 1990, pp40-49.

'Part of Cerritos's Larger Picture', *Architectural Record* (USA), vol 177, May 1989, p59.

'Toronto Ballet Opera House', *The Canadian Architect* (Toronto, Canada), vol 33, August 1988, pp24–35.

MOORE RUBLE YUDELL pp116-125

L Whiteson, 'Arts Fusion', *Architecture*, vol 83, December 1994, pp48-57.

S Isozaki, 'Mover, Mixer, Maker: Charles W Moore's Life and Work', *A+U* (Tokyo, Japan), no 287, August 1994, pp2-11.

J Steele, 'Charles Moore: Place, Placelessness and the Res Publica', *Architectural Design* (London, England), vol 62, July/August 1992, profile.

A Truppin, 'With a Career Spanning 40 Years, Charles Moore's Influence', *Interiors* (New York), vol 147, September 1987, pp92-108.

RG Wilson, 'Architect; The Life and Work of Charles W Moore', *Architecture*, vol 74, March 1985, p163.

CESAR PELLI pp172-179

C Pelli, *Cesar Pelli: Selected and Current Works*, ed. V Mulgrave, Images Publishing Group, 1993.

S Peri, *Cesar Pelli*, A+U Publishers (Tokyo, Japan), 1985.

C Pelli, *Cesar Pelli: Buildings and Projects 1965-1990*, Rizzoli (New York), 1990.

A Tower for Louisville: The Humana Competition, eds. P Arnell and E Buckford, Rizzoli (New York), 1982.

Yale School of Architecture Seminar Papers, Yale University Press (New Haven, Connecticut), 1981.

C Pelli, *The Commons and Courthouse Center, Indiana, 1971-74: Pacific Design Center, Los Angeles, California, 1972-76: Rainbow Mall and Winter Garden, Niagara Falls, New York, 1975-77: Cesar Pelli/Gruen Associates*, ed. Y Futgawa, ADA Edita (Tokyo), 1981.

J Pastier, *Cesar Pelli*, Whitney Library of Design (New York), 1980.

L Doumato, *Cesar Pelli's Designs*, Vance Biographies, Monticello (Illinois), 1979.

E Saarinen, *Bell Telephone Corporation Research Laboratories, New Jersey, 1957-62: Deere & Company Headquarters Building, Illinois, 1957-63*, ed. Y Futagawa, ADA Edita (Tokyo), 1971 (1974).

JEAN NOUVEL pp164-167

'The Film-Director Architect', *Lotus International* (Milan, Italy), no 84, 1995, pp129-131.

L Baltz, 'L'Obscentité du Réel', *L'Architecture d'Aujourd'hui* (Paris, France), no 296, December 1994, pp5-7.

J Nouvel, 'Jean Nouvel: Lyon Opera House', *A+U* (Tokyo), no 280, January 1994, pp118-43.

B Carter, 'Ancien Nouvel', *The Architectural Review* (London, England), vol 193, October 1993, pp44-49.

B Shortt, 'Jean Nouvel', *Architecture*, vol 82, September 1993, pp74-75.

'Teatro dell'Opera a Lione', *Domus* (Milan, Italy), no 752, September 1993, pp25-45.

J Lucan, 'Elogio del Chiaroscuro', *Domus* (Milan), no 752, September 1993, pp33-34.

'Opera Buff et', *RIBA Journal* (London, England), vol 100, August 1993, pp44-45.

D Picard, 'Nouvel au Coeur de Lyon', *Connaissance des Arts*, no 497, July/August 1993, pp28-35.

J Nouvel, 'On Designing', *Domus* (Milan, Italy), no 742, October 1992, pp17-28.

'Project pour le Nouvel Opera de Tokyo', *Connaissance des Arts*, no 485-486, July/August 1992, p84.

ALDO ROSSI pp188-191

K Stein, 'Portrait: Aldo Rossi', *Architectural Digest*, vol 51, January 1994, profile.
P Dickens, 'Aldo Rossi', *The British Journal of Aesthetics* (Oxford, England), vol 33, April 1993, pp193-194.
J Garcias, 'Deux Etoiles Italiennes dans l'est Parisien', *L'Architecture d'Aujourd'hui* (Paris, France), no 283, October 1992, pp92-97.
S Gutterman, 'Aldo Rossi, Architecture, 1981-1991', *Architectural Record* (USA), vol 180, May 1992, p50.
G Canella, 'Essence and Appearance of a Theatre', *A+U* (Tokyo, Japan), no 260, May 1992, pp42-73.
G Rondi, 'Sul Palazzo del Cinema', *Domus* (Milan, Italy), no 730, September 1991, pp223-227.
G Pigafetta, 'A Project that is still Cause for Discussion: The Carlo Felice Opera House', *Abitare* (Milan, Italy), no 296, May 1991, pp223-227.
Z Freiman, 'The Architect of the City', *Progressive Architecture* (Cleveland, Ohio), vol 72, February 1991, pp49-63.
A Ferlenga, 'The Theaters of the Architect', *Perspecta* (USA), no 26, 1990, pp191-202.
V Savi, 'Das Neue Teatro Carlo Felice in Genua', *Werk, Bauen + Wohnen* (Zurich, Switzerland), vol 77; no 44, December 1990, pp2-9.
M Grassi and V Savi, 'Nuovo Teatro Carlo Felice, Genova', *Domus* (Milan, Italy), no 719, September 1990, pp33-49.
'Completata la Riconstruzione del Teatro Carlo Felice a Genova', *Casabella* (Milan, Italy), vol 54, July/August 1990, p33.
J Bernhart and E Doutriaux, 'Aldo Rossi a Genes', *L'Architecture d'Aujourd'hui* (Paris, France), no 268, April 1990, pp152-157.
P Fumagalli, '*Autobiographie Scientifique*', *Werk, Bauen + Wohnen* (Zurich, Switzerland), vol 76; no 43, September 1989, p21.
'Projeckte', *Werk, Bauen + Wohnen* (Zurich, Switzerland), vol 75; no 42, September 1988, pp56-64.

PROJECT CREDITS

The Esplanade – Theatres on the Bay, Singapore Arts Centre, Singapore pp196-201

Client: Public Works Department and the Singapore Arts Company Ltd
Architects: Michael Wilford and Partners, London, in association with DP Architects, Singapore
Mechanical/Electrical and Structural Engineers: Public Works Department, Singapore
Quantity Surveyors: Public Works Department, Singapore
Acoustic Consultant: Artec Consultants Inc, USA
Theatre Planning Consultants: Theatre Projects Consultants, London
Cladding Design: Atelier One and Atelier Ten, London